Will the Church Lose the City?

**Edited by Kendig Brubaker Cully
and F. Nile Harper**

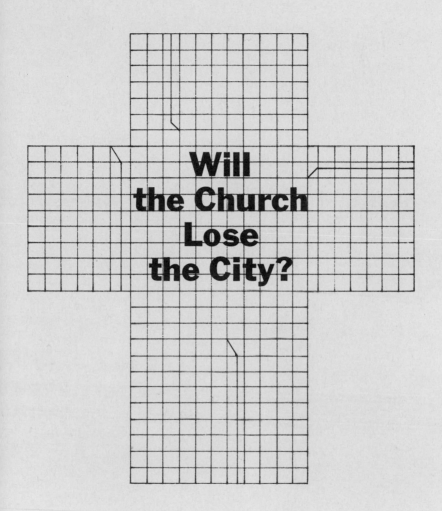

Will
the Church
Lose
the City?

The
World Publishing Company
New York and Cleveland

Published by The World Publishing Company
2231 West 110th Street, Cleveland, Ohio 44102

Published simultaneously in Canada by
Nelson, Foster & Scott Ltd.

First Printing—1969

Library of Congress Catalog Card Number: 73–86449
Printed in the United States of America

The material from "Life in the Cities of Tomorrow" by
C. A. Doxiadis copyright 1968 Christian Century Foundation.
Reprinted by permission from the November 6, 1968 issue of *The Christian Century*.

WORLD PUBLISHING
TIMES MIRROR

Contents

6   Contents

Preface

Since the chapters of this book speak for themselves, only a brief prefatory note seems necessary. It may be of interest to readers to know how the book had its genesis. The editors, serving together in a theological faculty in the heart of Manhattan, frequently found themselves asking the question: What implications for theological education are to be found in the city? Such conversation led naturally into the bigger question: What is the relation between the church itself and the urban milieu in which it is destined to operate more and more—if it survives—in the years to come?

An attempt has been made to bring together a variety of materials representing the several disciplines as well as different visions of the future of the church in the city. The editors wish to encourage a serious questioning as to whether or not the church has accomplished very much of significance in the cities during the last several decades. There has been much attention given to "city church work" by the denominations. Where do we stand as the result of this effort? Where does the church stand in relation to the intense economic, political, and social problems of the city? What is the meaning of declining numbers of white Protestants and increasing numbers of black and Spanish-speaking Protestants in the cities? Is there an overriding continuity that moves through-

out all of the off-again, on-again commitment of the church to
the city? It is to these matters of urgent concern that we invite
your attention.

KENDIG BRUBAKER CULLY
F. NILE HARPER

Contributors

DAVID W. BARRY, Executive Director, New York City Mission Society.

KENDIG BRUBAKER CULLY, Dean and Professor of Christian Education, New York Theological Seminary.

DAN W. DODSON, Professor, Center for Human Relations and Community Studies, New York University.

ROBERT W. FRIEDRICHS, Professor of Sociology, Drew University, Madison, N.J.

WILLIAM HAMILTON, Professor of Religion, New College, Sarasota, Fla.

ROBERT T. HANDY, Professor of Church History, Union Theological Seminary, New York City.

F. NILE HARPER, Professor of Church and Community, New York Theological Seminary.

ROBERT S. JACKSON, Associate Professor of English, Rockford College, Rockford, Ill.

RALPH KAMINSKY, Associate Professor of Public Finance, New York University.

JOHN P. KILDAHL, Associate Professor of Pastoral Theology, New York Theological Seminary.

WILLIAM KLASSEN, Professor of Religion, University of Manitoba.

MARTIN E. MARTY, Professor of Modern Church History, University of Chicago.

HOWARD MOODY, Minister, Judson Memorial Church, New York City.

LYLE E. SCHALLER, Director, Center for Parish Development, Evangelical Theological Seminary, Naperville, Ill.

GEORGE W. WEBBER, President, New York Theological Seminary.

GAYRAUD S. WILMORE, JR., Chairman, The Division of Church and Race, The Board of National Missions, The United Presbyterian Church in the U.S.A.

G. H. JACK WOODARD, Associate Director, Services to Dioceses, Executive Council of the Episcopal Church.

Part I
Viewpoints on the City

Chapter 1

A
Historical View

BY ROBERT W. FRIEDRICHS

The reticence of historians to address themselves to the city per se is understandable: its origins predate "history" (man's written record), while its fate is yet to be sealed. The present discussion shares in that modesty—indeed, is forced to do so by its brevity. It represents, then, not a brief history of the city, but rather *a historical view*. The article "a" is used quite self-consciously, for there will be as many historical views as there are historians. This is not to admit any lack of historicity. It is simply an acknowledgment that the tapestry of history—urban as well as any other—provides one with a wide array of patterns and threads. The particular thread and the particular pattern claiming the attention of one student of history need not be identical with those forcing themselves upon the attention of others to be good history. This is particularly true when we confront the self-evident fact that not only is the tapestry still on the loom, but the earliest design is still but dimly perceived.

A "Transaction-Maximizing System"

The particular "view" of urban history to be developed in these few pages anchors itself firmly at both ends of the historical continuum—in the earliest and in the most recent forms by which man has come to conceive of the city symbolically. Taking the latter first, a "student" of the students of the contemporary metropolis would find the following functional definition of the city today not atypical: The city, to the contemporary urban specialist, may be viewed as a "transaction-maximizing system." A student of the protoliterate and earliest historical period discovers, of course, a much simpler symbolic representation: the first ideogram representing the city yet to be disclosed—in Egyptian hieroglyphics—is a cross surrounded by a circle. Separated by five millennia, the two paradigms challenge the inquiring mind. For if common strands are discovered running through each, the historian may be in a position to identify the warp and woof that binds present-day megalopolis and the earthen structures of Bronze Age man in one continuous tapestry.

I would argue that we are in a position to do just that—that what is striking is not the contrast between the two, but their essential identification. The cross in the ideogram represents quite clearly the manner in which the early city stood as the site and center of divergent paths—actual "streets" within the city perhaps, a figurative representation of the fact that the city sat astride (or guarded from nearby) the crossroads of man's earliest human traffic. In its role both as defender of that "crossroad" (not to exclude a watercourse) and as a site of exchange in services and goods, it acted to "maximize transaction." It was the magnet—the center of the social field of force—which served as the site of man's cultural exchange and growth.

The circle is easily deciphered by anyone who has strayed far enough from the relative security and integration of the twentieth-century West to have approached a city before dawn—as the author did but two decades ago in China—and had to wait patiently for the city gates to open. It is, of course, the city wall (moat, or both). For the city's roots lay not simply in "exchange." It stood for *containment* as well—for man's vividly felt need to join others of his kind in huddled security from the threats of nature and of others *not* "his kind."

But how can the open city of today—the "transaction-maximizing" creature of the urban sociologist—be construed as "walled"? Is not the modern metropolis physically identifiable by the very breaches it has made in that "wall," by the tentacles that reach out by rail, pavement, and air to the hinterland? If history is to add but a single insight to our current grasp of the city, it should be this—that the mentality that created the wall was in turn formed by it, that only as one adds the image of *enclosure* to the more self-evident one of "exchange" may the metropolis of today be grasped in its full splendor and misery.

The reader should note that the "transaction-maximizing" function of the city is used by the urban specialist of today as but a phrase that would condition a more fundamental part of speech. The noun so conditioned was "system." It is perhaps a mark of our intellectual urbanization that we find the term so neutral in import. "System" presumes interrelatedness, "transactions" between each segment and all others. But it also assumes *closure*, the "wall" of Bronze Age man. Both "wall" and "system" are equally fabrications: Neither is granted by nature. Each was constructed out of man's interminable search for security in an existence whose only natural "closure" is death. Urban man, who has only just learned to live without walls, remains huddled within his self-generated "systems," and the city remains, with Turgot, ". . . a mausoleum, a monument to the arrogance of the great and the wretchedness of man. . . ."

If indeed the city was and still is to be characterized by the paradox of crossroad and wall, transaction and system, then the dialectical paradigm so constituted should serve to shed light on both the city's origins and her development, perhaps even upon the larger world that has come to define itself in the city's terms. Certainly our case cannot remain satisfied with the criterion afforded by semantic analogy. The historian would remind us that man's record is no less ambiguous than man himself. Let us see to what extent, then, the paradigm serves to clarify the urban path we have chosen to tread.

Wall before Crossroad

The first thing we discover is that the wall came *before* the crossroad, enclosure *prior to* transaction. Indeed, the archaeologist has of recent times demonstrated the somewhat startling fact that the wall (to say nothing of the stockade) would appear to have preceded even the argicultural revolution by thousands of years. Social transaction—and the resultant cultural innovation—may have come to dominate the urban scene, but is there no instruction in the discovery that such transaction demands as context the sense of collective security and corporate identification symbolized by the wall? The modern metropolis, though hindered periodically by disproportionate growth in one technical sector as over against another, is at its best when viewed in terms of its transactive function. But is not even the crossroad threatened when the security upon which it was predicated is no longer in evidence? History reminds us that walls were not simply built for physical defense, even in the Bronze Age. The seventy-five-foot thickness of those unearthed at Khorsabad are not to be explained in terms of military utility. Having in fact lived for six months in a spacious home *atop* a dirty wall in Szechwan—with breadth left over for full-scale picnicking—I find it difficult not to assume, with Robert Frost, that walls may serve at least as much as *symbols* of security. Indeed, it is impossible to reject—with the evidence presently available to the archaeologist—the possibility that the wall may have in fact served a symbolic purpose in the first instance and only later proved itself a military boon. One should be reminded that the wall, with attendant gates that opened and closed to reflect the daily cycle of morn and night, far outlasted their defensive role in Europe—in German cities, well into the nineteenth century.

If social transaction rests dependent upon a sense of corporate security, as the crossroad demanded the wall, then the plight of the contemporary city may be seen in a new light. The wall is clearly gone—except as it has been rebuilt through law and practice by those who ring the city in their own symbolic and physical defense. In the latter case, even the crossroads metaphor is denied, and the metropolis is transformed into prison. Neither—the city as prison or as crossroad without a wall—provides the physical or psychological basis for lasting security or productive identification. In the former, urban man may be expected—with prisoners everywhere—to create a life style which evidences as its single bond with his fellows an intractable opposition to the larger system that has imprisoned him. The product of the crossroad without a wall, on the other hand, may move freely—by grace of education or inheritance—from crossroad to crossroad, one human transaction to the next. But, with no corporate identity, no collectively derived circumference, he is guided but by a calculus of personal gratification.

The efforts of today's environmental engineers have "transaction maximization" as their primary goal. That they have been relatively successful is attested to by the plethora of mammoth cloverleafs, airports, tunnels, bridges, helicopter pads, and expressways that have lifted a burden once carried almost single-handedly by the railroad. They have been considerably less successful in goading suburbia to raze the walls the latter erected as the city's own were breached. No thought whatsoever seems to have gone into the need to create a functional substitute for the city's original ramparts—the provision for an alternative focus of collective identity, a symbol of corporate security and mutual aid. The historian, then, is the least surprised to find that the city, once man's bastion against those forces—natural and human—which would threaten his social unity, is presently their primary locus.

There are those who would argue that, whereas the wall was a physical and symbolic product of the protoliterate and Bronze ages, history proper may be seen as a single linear movement toward the erosion of barriers, urban and otherwise. The historian would tell us otherwise. The city's ramparts have been continually breached, but also—till the onset of the industrial revolution— continually rebuilt. If the last one hundred and fifty years have seen our urban walls razed and not rebuilt, we are reminded that the European living toward the end of the Middle Ages could point to a considerably longer period in which the wall overwhelmed the crossroad both as symbol and in fact. That the period is known today as the "Dark Ages" need not imply that its polar opposite—the crossroads without the wall—should in contrast be dignified with a term suggesting "enlightenment." The historian's "Enlightenment" has been used instead to designate a period in which the wall was still very much in use. He would remind us furthermore that the period dominated by the ramparts of the castle and the walled cloister was also a period of remarkable stability in Western Europe—a moment in Western history, as yet unsurpassed, in which man encapsulated himself within a religio-philosophic universe that afforded him a remarkable sense of unity with his social, psychic, and physical environment. The segmentation of wall from crossroad may have delayed his technological growth, but it granted him a sense of ultimate security which he was to lose with his reclamation of the classic tradition built on the dialectical interaction of wall with crossroad.

Illustration of the Dialectical Mix

That the genius of the city lies in the dialectical mix of transaction
with system, cultural marketplace with rampart, may perhaps best
be illustrated by the footprints left in history by that most remarkable urban people of the West, the Jews. There was little in either
the record or the tradition of the larger Semitic stock from which
they stemmed to suggest the catalytic role they were to play in
the fundamental cultural revolutions of the past thirty-five hundred
years. Initially but a cluster of nomadic tribes identified only by
their loyalty to a common cultic tradition, their history in fact
began with their captivity and forced "urbanization" at the hands
of a Bronze Age Egypt. The latter setting differed from that provided by the city-states of the Tigris-Euphrates delta—the Hebrew
tribes' original point of cultural reference—in that, after an early
period of development, the cities that had sprung to life along
the Nile discarded their initial dependence upon separate massive
city walls. The latter occurred in conjunction with the unification
of the urban settlements within a single "state." This precipitation
of the concept of "nationhood" for the first time in history is to be
explained in several ways: (1) by the manner in which the valley's
walls, together with the deserts beyond, provided natural barriers
against easy access on the part of marauders; (2) the fashion in
which cooperative endeavor in primitive hydraulic engineering
along the river's alluvial banks rewarded efforts in the direction of
intercity cooperation; and (3) the way her achievements in the
construction of a tomb architecture of heroic proportions—functioning as surrogate for city rampart—stood as symbol of the
strength and unity of her originally diverse peoples.

It also suggests the reason that Egypt—rather than the Hebrew
tribes in their earlier nomadic life—appears to have provided the
context for man's earliest experiment in monotheism. For the process of unification that occurred in the name of a series of dynasties
and kingdoms in social fact represented the "urbanization" of the
entire Nile basin. In this sense the valley took on the character of
a single "city"—a heterogeneous population brought together
within a single cultural network of interaction, with the river and
its accompanying network of canals serving as common "crossroad" and her natural ramparts and monumental tombs providing

a wall's physical and psychic security. The gradual development of competitive foci of power (upper versus lower Nile; the priesthood versus the military) that accompanied the maturation of the social fabric might then be expected to elicit further effort at symbolic—and politico-religious—unification. The revolutionary effort by Amenhotep IV to initiate a monotheism focused upon worship of the sun (and upon himself as god-king) thus might be interpreted, *from the standpoint of the history of the larger process that is "urbanization,"* as a functionally inevitable stage in the dialectical interaction of "crossroad" and "wall."

Though the time was apparently far from ripe within the rigid structures of the Egyptian society of the time to sustain the egalitarianism implicit in a monotheism, there is no reason to assume that the Semitic clans tracing their common lineage to a quasi-mythic Abraham would have been unmoved by the conception. Indeed, being members at or near the bottom of the Egyptian caste structure, their attention might have been drawn to the radical notion of a single universal deity, as adherents of the ruthlessly suppressed religion sought the relative anonymity of a comparable "underclass" position, in an attempt to survive. What the Hebrews as a group could have been expected to bring to such an encounter would have been the self-conscious bond of kinship symbolized by common cultic allegiance that had sustained their separate identity during the generations they had been buffeted by Egyptian norms and Egyptian deities—a kind of "wall-within-the-wall" mentality that apparently made it possible for them to enhance their corporate experience by means of the "transactive" function of the urbanized setting without succumbing to a one-to-one identification with the latter's symbolic "wall."

Whatever direct or indirect impact the Egyptian experiment with monotheism may have had upon the Hebrews, it is difficult for the historian to ignore the startlingly close temporal sequence involved, for the exodus would appear to have taken place but two to three generations after the reign of Amenhotep IV. But even if we were to set such evidence aside, one conclusion seems unassailable. It is that *the shift in self-understanding on the part of the Hebrews—from a cluster of clans wed by a common cultic tradition, to a people defined by a covenantal relationship, to the single universal deity—took place in an "urban" context.* The monotheism that the Western world was ultimately to inherit, then, may be seen historically as a function of the dialectical interaction of "crossroad" and "wall." Indeed, if the geographic congruence and historical sequence we have noted were indeed to be sustained, then the monotheism of the biblical faiths may be viewed as a product of the impact of a specified stage in the urbanization of the world's first nation-state upon the self-identity of a constituent people, who, though open to the "transactive" feature of the urban scene, could draw upon a collective identity and tradition which granted it stability and security in the very midst of symbolic change.

If this were the only instance in which history was to demonstrate, through the Hebrew peoples, the creative impact of crossroad upon wall, the episode would remain instructive. As it has turned out, however, her appropriation of monotheism was but the first in a long series of points at which she served as catalytic agent in the development of Western culture.

Indeed, even her settlement in the Palestinian plains failed to diminish her essentially "urban" role, for the walled cities built there in response to the new Mosaic vision sat astride the crossroads of empire. Serving the caravans that linked Egypt with Mesopotamia and buffeted by the periodic military inroads of one upon the other, she remained at the center of cultural transaction between Asia and North Africa. The Babylonian captivity served but to reinforce the "wall" she drew about herself, preparing her people for the Diaspora that was to thrust her deep into the heartland of the forthcoming center of creative transaction, Europe.

With the fall of the Roman Empire, her scattered peoples found themselves serving the relentless demands of urbanization in a fashion novel to man's historical experience until that date. In a time of political fragmentation, the transnational Jewish community was unique in its capacity to provide a consistent means of trustworthy communication and interchange between the newly isolated urban fragments that remained, assuring at least a measure of continuity to the urbanization process throughout the Western world. It was a role denied the Christian church by its division between Constantinople and Rome and, later, through the manner in which the Muslim faith shattered the last Augustinian hope for a single City of Man. The natural history of the city thus was able for the first time to transcend the political and religious barriers that had till that time defined the city's symbolic "walls." Even the restraints that came shortly into play on the life options of the Jew in a Christian Europe acted to fortify the Jewish contribution to the urban integrity of the otherwise "Dark Ages." Prohibited from owning land, their skills were funneled instead into urban pursuits. Held outside the Christian covenant, only they were provided with the final justification for the accumulation of capital—the privilege of lending money at interest. The Jew, having formed his very identity in the crucible of crossroad and wall, thus not only enabled the process of urbanization to transcend the disintegration of the Roman Empire but also was thrust into a specialized urban role that was to spark the Western world's next great outburst of cultural activity.

For, although it has been habit of late to assign responsibility for the rise of capitalism—which was in turn to underwrite the Industrial Revolution and the urban explosion it fathered—to the inner-worldly asceticism of the Calvinist, it is well to note that the Puritans were in fact spoken of colloquially as "the English Hebrews." Werner Sombart's massive rebuttal of Max Weber's Calvinist thesis, a rebuttal that placed primary responsibility for the origins of modern capitalism upon the shoulders of European Jewry, would certainly have received a wider hearing if the intellectual community had been less afraid of the fuel it might grant the professional bigot. Though the small size of the Jewish communities relative to the Calvinist populations of northwestern Europe suggest that the latter would have played much the greater role numerically, it would be difficult to deny the paradigmatic role played by the Jew, schooled as he had been in the discipline that underwrote capital accumulation. Again the peculiar dialect of crossroad and wall served, through the mediation of a people bred to its use, to extend the sway of the city.

But of even greater significance to our brief account of the trail through history left by that epitome of urban man, the Jew, is the manner in which the extension of that urban mentality to the West as a whole led to the reintegration of the Hebrew peoples into the larger City of Man. Though a harrowing tale—both of that City and of the People who sought reentrance—it speaks to the fundamental character of urban man's present plight.

The uniqueness of the tribes of Israel resided, as we have suggested, in the manner in which their covenantal "wall-within-a-wall" mentality enabled them to sustain and respond creatively to a wider range of cultural "transactions" for a longer period than any other Western people. Nurtured in an urbanized Nile valley more than three millennia ago in a physical setting that put a premium on symbolic surrogates for an actual city wall, it was possible for them, with the appropriation of monotheism, to extend the range within which their covenant secured them to encompass the farthest crossroad. With the development of modern capitalism and the urban explosion of the nineteenth century which was its ultimate product, the mental set of Western Europe and the Americas finally began to approximate the transcultural sophistication of the Jews. At the same time, the correlative movement of the Jewish psyche beyond its inner wall and into the larger urbanity of the nineteenth and early twentieth centuries resulted in a massive extension of Jewish creativity. Indeed, with the exception of Darwinian evolution, all the latter-day paradigms by which modern man has sought to grasp his world had their point of critical mass at the intersection of a Jewish consciousness and the larger intellectual tradition of the West—in the dialectical materialism of Karl Marx, the psychoanalytic insights of Sigmund Freud, and the mathematical models of Einsteinian relativism that destroyed our commonsense world.

The Riddling of Walls: Dangers

But the riddling of "walls"—both mind-set and city—are fraught with danger. If done too rapidly, with insufficient attention to the provision for functional alternatives, the community laid bare stands shorn of the security and corporate identification that we have found to be as crucial to the city as it is to the psyche. In no section of Europe did the Jew forsake his "inner wall" as rapidly as he did in the German-speaking areas. Congruently, Germany, weaned last among the nations of Europe from the symbolic security of her city walls, outpaced both England and America in the rapidity of her urbanization. Only Japan exceeded her rate among major world powers—a fateful pairing. The holocaust that consumed European Jewry in the 1930's and 1940's, then, should remind us of the risk that confronts the urban *Zeitgeist* when the walls of the city are razed with little or no provision for symbolic surrogate. Six million Jewish and tens of millions of non-Jewish European and Asian lives were forfeited as the German and Japanese peoples sought to reclaim the collective identity and corporate security they had lost so precipitously in the abandonment of their "walls."

The tragic lesson was far from lost upon the Jewish remnant: The wall they had begun to forsake would have to be rebuilt. Indeed, the demand was for more than the spiritual and ethnic wall that had sustained her for millennia in the Diaspora. She would demand nothing less that the physical and territorial walls of ancient Israel. And there she has come at least momentarily to rest, a physical symbol of strength and unity to those of her peoples who continue to risk the intimate transactions of the larger world.

History would remain to caution the heady in-gathering that once again would worship at the Wall. Though Israel stands as urban oasis strategically located to nourish an essentially preurban Muslim world, the reacquisition of a physical boundary was in fact a historic *reaction* rather than a historic affirmation grounded in the nature of worldwide urbanization. The leveling of physical barriers to cultural transaction represents a crucial stage in the transformation of cities of man to the City of Man. New mobile walls of steel and a heightened sense of territoriality are no less fraught with danger than the dissolution, with no replacement, of the city's symbolic ramparts.

This modest inquiry into the city in history took as its key the common strand running through man's earliest and man's most recent representation of the city—the cross within a circle of Egyptian hieroglyphics and the "transaction-maximizing system" of the contemporary urban specialist. It found in each a symbolic characterization of the crossroad enclosed in a wall. After noting the manner in which the urban explosion of the past hundred years had come to deny further functionality to the "wall"—in contrast to the Dark Ages' denigration of the "crossroad"—it turned for insight to tracing the path through history of that epitome of urban man, the Jew. There it fortified its original impression that the genius of the urban scene lay not in the crossroad or the wall taken alone but in their dialectical action one upon the other. If the

larger history of urban man, together with the special history of
the Hebrew peoples, has anything to offer the student of the contemporary metropolis, it would lie with precisely this realization.
The urban conglomerates of today, their walls shattered by their
transactive calling, are in desperate need of the symbolic integration and corporate security once supplied by the wall. The only
proximation available today is the wall raised by the city's suburbs
for their own defense, an edifice that transforms the city into
prison and provides urban man with but the cement of mutual
frustration. Denied the coherence and sense of community represented by a wall generated from within, we may expect the frag-
mented consciousness of the city to respond with ethnic and class
isolation punctuated by outbreaks of aggression against all who
stand outside.

The Role of the Church

That the church has a stake in the outcome is self-evident. What
might not have been clear but for the perspective of the historian
is the *identity* of their interests. The church is not to be understood
as but one of a number of relevant institutionalized forces that may
refortify urban man. Rather the prehistorian makes clear that *the
city was in fact the creature of man's religious consciousness*. The
purpose of the city, an Egyptian scribe wrote, was "to put the gods
in their shrines." It was neither agriculture nor the marketplace,
the archaeologist tells us, that led men to raise the first city wall
and mark out the first crossroad. It was rather their consummate
need to gather in worship. The city's first masters were her priests;
her first permanent edifice, her temple. The crossroad and wall
that stand as paradigm for the city stand also as paradigm for
man's religious consciousness. Only later did religion become in
turn a creature of that city, as our brief account of the foundations
of the faith of Western man would testify.

Thus, only as the church comes to recognize that she is both
creator and creature of the city—and beholds thereby that the
crisis confronting urban man is identical with the crisis confronting
the City of God—will she be in position to begin rebuilding the
City of Man.

Chapter 2

A
Sociological View

BY DAN W. DODSON

From a sociological point of view, one would have to say that social institutions have a singular capacity for adaptation and adjustment. Hence it is clear that churches and religious organizations will survive in the inner cities of America. What their form and function will be is another matter. In this latter regard one can anticipate trends and suggest possibilities as to the types of adaptations which will come about. A case can be made for the following possible directions for the church of the future.

The Church Will Lose Its Drive as a Social Movement

When churches were in their highly sectarian stages, they were vital instruments of social change. The ideological content of their movement determined what they were trying to accomplish. As time went on, they sacralized these memories of their beginnings, and tried to socialize the young into the mythologies they created about themselves. At times people were disciplined if they did not believe in the dogmas of the group.

As the movement goes along, it must make the decision to remain narrowly sectarian and stay small, or else temporize with its beliefs and become popular.[1] Most choose this latter course. The community-church movement, the ecumenical movement, and other types of latitude within belief systems suggest the extent to which this erosion of ideological content has taken place among the church groups. Within most congregations today there is probably a greater difference of belief than is there difference of beliefs between faith groups.

The city has a way of secularizing these sacred aspects of religious heritage. Harvey Cox[2] has suggested that a major function of the city is this secularizing role. It catches those who are committed to the narrowly sectarian, those whose perspectives are lesser worlds in the great encounters, and transforms them into urbane, sophisticated people. Its impact on religious sectarianism is suggested by the overheard encounter between the religious fanatic and the hardened old immigrant in their interchange in New York City's Washington Square Park.

As the tract distributor handed the old man the pamphlet, the old man said:

"Vot ist?"
"It's about Jesus," said the tractster.
"Vot about him?" asked the immigrant.
"He is coming," responded the religious one.
"Ven is he comin'?" asked the old man.
"No man knows the hour or the day," replied the distributor.
"Vell, he's no good man or he vould let us know ven he is comin'," said the old man, shrugging as he walked away.

In other words, that to which one is committed has to be validated against those whose experiences and heritages are sharply different, and for any such communication to be meaningful, the religious experience has to be relevant to the encounter in which others are engaged.

In the past the great motivation was to bring to other people "The Word." Those outside the religious orb were encouraged to join the fellowship. This fellowship included worship, teaching, social contact, and service. Primarily, however, the dynamic of religion was to help people find a set of values which gave life meaning and structure and purpose. It was felt that this set of values, usually referred to as one's "faith," had redemptive and regenerative qualities. If one "believed," he was saved.

Nowhere was this better illustrated than in the ministry. The one who devoted his life to the ministry was looked upon as a sacred person. The symbolic "laying on of hands" to indicate the succession of priesthood had real meaning. As a consequence, the minister had an authority which commanded loyalty and support. No minister could preach if he did not himself have the authority of being the "Lord's mouthpiece." He could not approach his leadership as a search into a fuller life, with his own doubts and misgivings exposed. Today the role conflict in the ministry is tremendous. These mythologies are no longer believed as they once were. A large segment of the ministry does not believe in the creeds and dogma of their denominations and persuasions. A large segment of the ministry does not believe in the divinity of Christ in the sense of the miracles of the immaculate conception or the physical resurrection. Religious leadership of all faiths has a considerable segment which literally joins in the idea that "God is dead"—at least in the senses in which religion produced such complete dependence upon transcendent power.

Many more such evidences could be suggested to substantiate the position presented here. Suffice it to say that if the church is looked at as a social movement, it has lost much of its dynamic or force. There is great experimentation by some church groups within the inner cities of America today to find ways of better engaging and serving the masses of the ghettos and others who live lives of alienation, social disorganization, and impersonal mass-culture anonymity. Most of this effort has failed, except to the extent that it relied upon techniques and methods borrowed from the secular world.

The reason they have failed, or at least succeeded so little, is that in this secular, materialistic society, they had nothing to offer except service. There was little they had to offer that had the "redemptive and regenerative features" of a new and fresh ideological orientation that would give lives of urbanites who are caught in the throes of social disorganization meaning and structure and purpose.

In other words, the modern religions of Christendom and Judaism have met the encounter within the large city, and they seem to have "run out of steam." The organizations, the myths, the rituals, and the structures have been made sacred, and people still use them as vestigial remains of their heritage, but the substance which made them meaningful and dynamic has been lost through the secularization process produced in the great urban encounter.

The Church as a Source of Identity

A major function which the church is continuing to provide in the city is a means of identity. Glazer and Moynihan[3] point out that in New York City ethnicity—now three and four generations removed—is still a source of one's identity. People still perceive themselves first as Italians, Jews, or Irish and secondarily as Americans. In this great encounter within the city, identity becomes very important. The Negro group is now on what has been referred to by one of the black leaders as an "emotional binge" trying to perceive "who they are." Increasingly as the WASP (White Anglo-Saxon Protestant) groups become a minority and a peer among other minorities, they too turn to the search for identity.

Herberg indicates how this basis of identity is shifting from hyphenated Americans, i.e., Italo-American or Polish-American, to a communal basis.[4] In other words, rapidly there is intermarriage and association within the Roman Catholic group, and increasingly these subgroups are shifting to faith as the major source of identity. He contends that this is a secular religion whose main tenet is a "faith in faith" rather than a "faith in God." He sees America moving to a tri-faith basis of identity and as a result rapidly developing a tri-faith approach to communal problems. He points out that if one asks a person what his background is, he now tends to say Protestant, Catholic, or Jew, whereas he formerly said English, Irish, or Jewish. Of course, this frame of reference leaves out the Negro population.

If one conceives religion as an effort to become identified with and establish identity with power, it would not be hard to make a case that modern man's religion is rapidly becoming an effort to become attuned to large social structures, of which church organizations are only one. Galbraith points out that at many meetings of representatives of corporate society, it is not unusual for one to be asked "Whom are you with?" before he is asked his name.[5] Presthus also indicated that we are rapidly becoming a corporate society and that one's conscience is more often the reflection of the interests of his organization than it is the "wee still voice" of conscience.[6] Be this as it may, it indicates some of the ways in which government and corporate society are now used as a reference by many who formerly depended upon the church as a guide to conscience.

It also, however, indicates the tendency for people to use the organization of the church as a power base with which to identify in communal life. In this sense the church performs a sort of tribal function. In a mass culture, where people tend to be a nameless face in the crowd, there is a need to belong and have identity. In many respects the church provides this.

In this context one asks himself what the church perpetuates through its numerous programs and activities which presumably socialize the membership into the group. In January of 1967 the Roper Poll told a church gathering at Buck Hill Falls, Pennsylvania, that in all the poll taking they have done since they started, they found no significant differences between the answers of church people and non-church people to questions of social concern which they have posed to them.[7] One becomes nonplussed: What with all the preaching, admonishing, praying, worshiping together, and graded Sunday-school lessons, why has there been no difference?

Perhaps the answer resides in the position taken by Emile Durkheim[8] many years ago in his study *The Division of Labor*. He contended that morality stems from the relationships created through the division of labor. If each person were completely sufficient to himself, there would be no need for morality. Morality emerges out of the quality of relationships which exist between groups. One should refer to a situation as being more or less moral rather than expecting that people can be taught what the structure does not reinforce. If this position is correct, then the reason the church members respond no differently is that the church has not led them in restructuring the society to the end that relationships between groups are more moral. If people "learn what they live," in John Dewey's terminology, then if they are to learn differently, they must live differently. Hence, instead of religious education being built around the traditions of the group, with emphasis on the heritage of the "tribe," the curriculum should be the arrangement of significant encounters which restructure "life space" to the end that people live differently, i.e., more morally.

If one examines the "life space" in which the socialization occurs, it is not difficult to understand why church membership makes little if any difference. In the modern city the church has been the last bastion to be overcome in the campaign to eliminate segregation within the society. Instead of the church being a place where committed people meet to deepen commitment to move out to change life, the church became a sanctuary where people hid from the encounters. In this context they learned to hide from involvement and participation and soon became isolated from and irrelevant to the great encounters of their life and times. As this withdrawal from the encounters took place, congregations became idolators of tradition, heritage, and creeds which were no longer relevant. It was a concentration on identity with a group heritage without a devotion to the group's innermost commitments. In community life the church became a power bastion behind which groups hid to fight secular battles. The church will not likely lose this role in the city.

The Church Will Be Uniracial

In spite of the many protestations of world brotherhood proclaimed from pulpits and propounded in literature, there seems to be little in the modern responses to "the gospel" which binds men together in a common fellowship across the lines of racial difference. In the great transformations within the cities of America occasioned by the white population moving out and their replacement by the Negroes, there is little to indicate that men of the same denomination but different in color could be brought to a common altar in a common fellowship.

As this separation occurred between the races, other things began to happen. The white became ensconced in the suburbs of the cities, while the Negro was constricted to the inner city. In the suburb the church tended to become a country club with a steeple on it, where people belonged for social reasons first, and spiritual reasons only secondly. There were endless rounds of food-serving and social fellowship, but little encounter with the great moral issues of the times. Shielded from the "raw-meat" encounters which the city provided, and without windows through which to view this unfolding human estate in the inner city—views which, by the way, have ever pricked the consciences of righteous men— these escapees from the great urban encounter lost their capacity to inculcate in the young the great spiritual heritages which were theirs.

When the church became identified with the power arrangement of the society, it lost its spiritual passion. One cannot be on top of the power arrangement of the society, preoccupied with developing the rationalizations as to why the power arrangement is justified, and not experience moral dry rot. The moral thrust of any era is to be found in the push of the little man from the bottom, demanding more fulfillment for more people. As the church became filled with these refugees from the encounter, and the power arrangement built into the present religious structure, those who wished to make serious witness to their commitments practically had to find secular channels through which to do it. The church had lost its moral imperative. As Henry Lloyd once said:

> Seldom does the new conscience, when it seeks a teacher to declare to men what is wrong, find him in the dignitaries of the church, the state, the order that is. The higher the rank, the closer the tie that binds these to what is, but ought not to be.[9]

If this great exodus and its moral dilemmas characterize the white church, what about the indigenous church of the inner-city minority? Traditionally the church was the major institution through which Negroes could mobilize to exert any influence whatsoever. As alternate channels of power leverage have developed, the church has waned in influence. In some measure the militant group has written it off, for it has been identified with gradualism, patience, fortitude, and forbearance. Malcolm X often said the Christian religion provided the perfect rationalization for the continued servitude of the black man—i.e., it taught people to "turn the other cheek," "return good for evil," and "love those who despitefully use you." These are virtues of "resentment," to use Nietzsche's phrase,[10] for use by people who are powerless, who must turn the symbols of their humiliation into symbols of virtue. When people achieve power, these are no longer relevant.

The black church, so long as it serves the powerless, will be a pressure for morality; it will be a social movement. As it becomes a part of the power arrangement, it will go the way of the churches of the whites. It will tend to look back with pride on what the group has accomplished, sacralize the accomplishment, and teach the mythologies which it is now generating to the young. It will, like the white, have a strong tribal quality, but lose its relevance to the human estate. In all likelihood, for the foreseeable future it will remain a uniracial church.

The Prospect of a New Dynamic

In spite of all which has been said concerning the static position of organized religion in the city, there are also other variables which cannot now be assessed. The human spirit cannot be "bottled up" permanently. While the city has been looked upon as the place of "godlessness" and sometimes defined as "the place where sin is," the great religious movements have tended to come out of the cities also. In this era of social unrest, when normlessness and anomie pervade the human condition, there is still a considerable yeastiness in the religious sphere. Heretofore the church has looked to revivals of spirituality as groups within it have developed new ideologies or newer methods of interpreting the old truths in modern contexts. One keeps looking for signs of these new departures in the modern urban community. At present several suggestions offer promise of the restructuring of the establishment of religion. In the Roman Catholic group the Ecumenical Council offers some hope. Here a ferment was recognized and legitimated which had long lain dormant within the church. Persons who become disenchanted with the authoritarian structure and unexamined dogma are now being heard. Dialogue has opened up between the Catholic and other religious groups. In this persuasion a renaissance seems to be in the making.

A new sort of commitment is developing. It might be described as "profane," out in front of the altar where the action is. It is replacing rituals designed to shield people from encounters in the world. In all denominations there is growing concern with the inner city. Types of ministry which seem more relevant to this situation are being tried. The inner-city ministry is being experimented with on many levels by many groups. Except for the more sectarian Puerto Rican church, the trend is to "get out in the street where the action is" and test commitments against the unfolding life of the city. In the ministry there is a growing number of young men who refuse to take traditional pastorates. They identify these with "the Establishment."

Strange as it may seem, there is a good likelihood that the new dynamic of religion will come from the so-called "hippie" group of youths who are now alienated from the values and norms of American culture. It is singular that they are turning to Zen

Buddhism and other religions of the East in their search for ideological or spiritual meaning. The militant Negro group, singularly enough, has found a considerable attraction to Islam. Both suggest the possibility of a new social movement becoming generated in the cities which could conceivably become considerably competitive with the Judeo-Christian ideologies now so strongly identified with "the Establishment." If this should happen, it would be the first time in the history of Christianity, perhaps, in which the new spirit, the new morality, was not channeled through some accommodation within the broad stream of the existing framework of religious faiths. This is to say that within the past the new thrust was either through a new denomination, a schism within an existing organization, or else through some new order being constituted within the faith to channel the new departures.

Another possibility is that the churches will lose their moral dynamic but that the edifices themselves will become sacred and will become cultural temples such as those that characterize many of the older civilizations. In this instance there will be an air of sanctity about them which stems from an awe of the architecture and culture of the past. Ancient rituals may still be performed as a matter of curiosity for those who have an aesthetic interest in them. Under these circumstances, these temples would perhaps still have an associational value for those whose roots of identity are involved in its history. For instance, an observer pointing out one of these architectural and aesthetic, status-oriented churches remarked, "There, sir, is one of the highest-powered ecclesiastical clubs of America." If such transformation of religious institutions should come about, they would perhaps still be presided over by high priests, who would be specialists in the historical traditions of the people. He would, perhaps, still perform sacerdotal functions, not because people really still believed in them, but rather as "good-luck" rituals.

Will the Church Lose the City?

In some respects this has already happened. In many respects the church is utterly irrelevant to the modern city. The discussions to this point have outlined some of the factors involved. Others could be added. However, this is not the complete story. This has been an era of science, objectivity, rationality, and secularization. The vast organizational structures have reduced man to a nameless face in a mass. Individuality and personality have suffered as man has sacrificed these affective aspects of life to the materialistic and automated developments which have allowed him freedom from want and economic security. There are some indications that these trends are running their course. Students at colleges and universities are in revolt. They contend that these pressures for rationality and objectivity have all but destroyed the affective side of human existence. Many are "opting out" on the system which makes such sacrifices of selfhood necessary. They are flaunting the mores and manners of the Establishment. They are in a serious quest for one of man's oldest desires, the quest for community. They find the old myths untenable, and the old rituals stifling—since they stifle the creativeness of the human spirit and keep it from producing a mythology and ritual more related to the present human estate.

One does not expect these small rents in the cloak of culture to indicate great change. They do indicate, however, that "Man does not live by bread alone." These deviations may just be the harbingers of a new trend, a new ethos, a new religious revival. If they are, it obviously will not be in the old forms; it will be a spiritual renaissance throughout the body politic. The issue is whether the present religious establishment can become relevant to this new need. James Baldwin,[11] in *The Fire Next Time*, warns Negroes not to identify with this culture and its values. This, he claims, will destroy itself, and Negroes will be destroyed if they identify with it. Few students of the present scene can deny that there is a serious increase in the amount of alienation, anomie, and social disorganization within the present society. Few can deny that the old ideologies have waned in their capacity to hold the nation to common goals, common values, and consensus on vital matters. Mills[12] and others who provide the ideological base of many of these deviants contend that in the United States the military, the corporate industrial complex, and the politicians constitute a power structure against which the average citizen is impotent. These ideological deviants of the so-called "New Left" contend that the "complex" is on its way to destroying us. In this they would find support from such statesmen as Senator William

Fulbright.[13] In this interpretation of our moral stance as a people, they would share the concern of Baldwin.

To a large extent the church has already lost the city in the sense of its being relevant or dynamic as an instrument of moral reform in the lives of modern urbanites. If it is rescued from its present malaise, it will likely come from the pressures of these deviants from outside. It is very hard for a status institution to reform itself.

Chapter 3

An
Economic View

BY RALPH KAMINSKY

There is a basic difference between an economic view of the city and the kind of interest economists have usually shown in urban problems. Until recently this interest was mainly displayed by specialists in particular fields of economics who, for one reason or another, had had their attention diverted to urban issues. More often than not this concern was stimulated by requests for help originating outside the economics profession—for example, by governments, public administrators, planners, business organizations and associations, labor unions, and civic agencies. As a result of their efforts in the urban area, these economists have deepened expertise in their fields of specialization. Some public-finance economists have gained unique expertise in the area of urban and metropolitan finance and in such related problems as fiscal relations among governments in the American federal system. Others have developed particular insights into transportation problems as these manifest themselves at the urban, metropolitan, and regional scales. Still others, in labor economics, have applied analytic techniques to the city seen as a labor market.

However important such work has been—and it has been important—"zeroing in" on the city from the vantage point of a particular specialization within economics does not normally lead (though it might) to an economic view of the city. Rather it is the frontier of the specialized field which is pushed farther out. There is an analogy to be drawn between the notion being expressed here and the other chapters in this part of the book. In precisely the same way that by itself neither a historical view, nor a sociological view, nor an economic, psychological, or aesthetic view will necessarily lead (though it might) to a total view of the city, so will a public-finance, transportation, or labor-market perspective on the city be too constrained to pass for an overview of the city as an economic environment.

The very notion of an economic view of the city implies a marriage of the traditional broad-gauge concerns of economics to the city seen as a unit of classification and analysis. As for the traditional concerns, these have had to do with certain performance characteristics of economic systems—their efficiency, their levels of activity, their growth and stability, and their equity. As for the city seen as a unit of classification and analysis, this notion is less easily formulated. Accordingly, in this review we shall adopt the simplest possible definition of the city. For our purposes the city will be seen as an agglomeration or concentration of people and activities, the basic advantage of the city being the relatively easy and multifarious contacts among its people and activities which concentration facilitates.

The economic view of the city presented here will be made under four headings. First, the relation between the economist's notion of efficiency and man's propensity to agglomerate into cities will be examined. Second, the economist's approach to urban problems will be illustrated by an examination of the so-called urban transportation problem. Third, another urban problem, that of urban governmental expenditure and taxation, will be surveyed. In this context we shall consider some aspects of the urban poverty question as well as the relation between the city as an economic system and the city as a political system. Finally, we shall briefly consider the performance and growth of urban economies.

Efficiency, Concentration, and Urban Structure

The concern with efficiency is fundamental to economics. Man has wants. He also has the means to satisfy them. Historically, and especially in the Western world, man has greatly increased his capacity to satisfy his wants; but wants have also expanded enormously. Western man may today be nearer to satisfying certain minimum needs than he has ever been at any other time in recorded history, but it is doubtful that he is any nearer to satisfying his wants than he was, say, two centuries ago. Accordingly, as long as there is a discipline of economics, the efficient use of resources will be central to its subject matter. We begin, therefore, by relating the notion of economic efficiency to the conception of the city as an agglomeration of interacting people and activities.

Up to a point, the very process of agglomerating people and activities increases the range of wants man can satisfy with his limited resources. The more widely activities are dispersed in space, the greater will be the time and resources needed to transport people and goods and to facilitate all forms of communication. Space commands that a price shall be paid to overcome it. Agglomeration, on the other hand, obliterates space. In so doing, concentration reduces space costs and frees resources that can be turned to the satisfaction of additional human wants.

There is in all of this a *reductio ad absurdum* with interesting implications for an economic view of the city. If agglomeration reduces space's costs, then absolute agglomeration would eliminate space costs altogether. If all activities were agglomerated at the same place and at the same time, no resources would have to be devoted to transportation and communication. Total agglomeration is, of course, a physical impossibility, but long before the physical limits are achieved, economic considerations dictate that agglomeration shall cease. At some point, as urban concentration intensifies, the economies of this concentration begin to be offset by the diseconomies of congestion. And if, indeed, the processes of agglomeration have anywhere gone too far, congestion costs will more than offset some of the advantages of concentration, and a process of urban dispersion will then take over.

As a practical matter, the form and structure of cities are not dictated by individuals, or groups of planners, or governments who have weighed the advantages of agglomeration against the disadvantages of congestion and decreed that a particular city shall be laid out in a particular way. Cities evolve. They are results of hundreds of thousands of separate and unique location decisions taken by the households, business enterprises, governments, and other institutions which comprise them. The form and organization of the city are then the result of a vast sorting-out process. In this process each decision-making unit works out a reconciliation among three influences which shape its final choice of where to locate in the urban agglomeration: (1) its judgment as to its space and location needs; (2) the options at different prices offered by the urban economy; and (3) the funds available for purchasing one of the options. From among all of the possible reconciliations possible, it has to be presumed that each household, business enterprise, and/or governmental unit seeks to make its best buy. In this way each member of the city finds his place in it, and the city as a whole is formed and achieves organization. The entire sorting-out process can be readily illustrated either by looking at the location decisions of particular households, business enterprises, and governments or by considering particular locations in the city and asking, "What goes there?" We adopt the second alternative and apply the question to a specific part of the city, its central business district.

The central business district is clearly the most preferred location in any given city. Notice, this is not to say that all activities would prefer to be there. Rather it says that there are no other general areas outside this district which are as attractive to as wide an array of activities and enterprises as is the central business district. Two obvious pieces of evidence confirm this. First, the center of the city is the busiest, that is, the most congested, part of the city. And, second, central locations are the most expensive; that is, the highest rents and land values are found downtown. In the competition to be downtown, not everyone succeeds. Those who can use the center most effectively, so that they can overcome the money and congestion costs of being there, win out. Those whose activities are somewhat less productive lose out. Depending on their particular circumstances, these activities settle for their second or third most preferred locations, as the case might be.

At the present time central business districts in American cities are experiencing important transformations. On balance they are becoming relatively more attractive to office-type activities than they are to manufacturing. Modern industrial processes require large sites on which highly automated single-story plants can be laid out. Such sites are extremely difficult to assemble, and land costs downtown are also prohibitive. In addition, manufacturing implies goods handling and movement and the problem of coping with downtown congestion. Thus space and congestion costs have reduced the attractiveness of downtown for manufacturing, while developments in highway transportation have made outlying sites more accessible. While manufacturing has responded to the push from the center and the pull of the suburbs, office activities have remained downtown. Unlike manufacturing processes, office functions can be carried out in high-rise buildings. Accordingly, great land costs downtown are overcome by piling up such activities in multistoried office buildings. This is not to say that all office activity remains downtown or that all manufacturing leaves the center. Clearly a wide array of office activities is also being located in outlying areas; and some specialized manufacturing in printing, clothing, toymaking, and jewelry production, to cite a few, still have a strong affinity for sites in or near central business districts. This is not the place to review, industry by industry, its affinity or aversion to the center of the city. The essential point is that, as seen by the productive enterprise, the location decision is part of the process of achieving efficiency. As production and transportation technologies change, past decisions may be revised. The economist looking at these decisions in the aggregate sees them as major influences on the organization and physical form of cities.

Far more space is devoted to residential use than to any other urban purpose. And again this space comes into use as the result of countless separate location decisions. Each household wants spacious shelter and a location with access to jobs, shopping, and important public amenities, including schools and recreation facilities. Depending on such factors as the occupations in the household, the age and size of the family, and its life-style preference for urban or suburban living, these factors of access and spacious shelter weigh differently in its preference. Simultaneously the urban environment offers each household an array of options, each with a different price tag on it. Each household in turn has an income constraint. Ultimately the household effects a three-sided reconciliation among its preferences, available options, and the funds which can be allocated to the purchase of shelter and a place in the city.

Governments which must also find their place in the city behave in more or less analogous fashion. Many sites are required to provide many kinds of public services, and all sites are costly in terms of both tax revenues expended on them and revenues lost as they are taken out of taxable (property-tax) uses. But since they occupy relatively little urban space, we shall, in the interest of brevity, pass over further analysis. Suffice it to say here that considerations of economy loom large.

All of this is not to argue that cities are shaped and formed only by the economic motivations of households, business enterprises, and governments. Physical land features, for example, are important. Cities along seacoasts are shaped differently from those along rivers, and these in turn are different from those which are entirely landlocked. Cities vary by virtue of their age and the transportation technologies available at the time of their early formation. Railroad and mass-transit cities, for example, are much more compact than the newer truck-transportation and automobile-based cities. Some cities still bear the marks, often of beauty, of historic planning and zoning decisions—for example, Central Park in New York City and the commons of the older New England towns. But in the final analysis it is not the national or man-made constraints on location decisions which give them their final form. It is instead the decisions themselves. And in this first portion of this chapter it has been our effort to show that when the economist looks at the city as a whole he observes two important things. First, there is a basic tendency of activities to agglomerate, because agglomeration economizes resources needed to overcome space; second, agglomerations or cities are remarkably similar and orderly in their structures, because economizing location decisions dictate that it shall be so.

The Urban Transportation Dilemma

In the introductory section of this chapter it was promised that the urban transportation problem would be discussed, partly because of its inherent importance and partly as a way of illustrating the economist's approach to major issues of widespread popular concern. Now that the description of how cities are formed has laid the basis for such an undertaking, it is called to the reader's attention that in the above heading the word "dilemma" has been

substituted for "problem." Problems imply solutions; dilemmas
imply resolutions. To the layman starting with the suggestion that
in urban transportation we have only a choice among alternatives
which are at best only partially satisfying may seem self-defeating.
To the economist it is commonplace, for it is in the nature of economic problems that solving them is apt to require choices among
goals which are basically incompatible.

The typical urbanite states his version of the urban transportation problem in terms of a complaint. Traffic is congested, the ride
is slow, service is inadequate, the costs (subway and bus fares,
tolls, parking fees, gasoline taxes, etc.) are too great. In registering
these complaints, urbanites are articulating their goals. When it
comes to moving about our cities, all of us want to move quickly,
comfortably, and cheaply. Furthermore, and by virtue of the way
in which our cities and workdays are structured, we want to move
mainly to and from the same places, and at more or less the same
time. Given these five goals, we are caught on the horns of the
considerable dilemma that urban transportation can be improved
with respect to any of these five goals only at the cost of sacrificing
one or more of the remaining four.

One example will illustrate this paradox. Assume the goal of
increasing average automobile speeds. This implies some combination of (1) higher costs for more road and related facilities;
(2) fewer cars on the road, implying more mass-transit riders
and/or car-pooling, both of which reduce privacy and comfort;
(3) a reduced propensity to travel at the same time, which can be
achieved by staggering work hours; and (4) a reduction in the
propensity of trips to converge on the center of the city, suggesting
that activities in the city should be further decentralized. The
reader is invited to play the game. Select any other goal and try
to improve on it. Unavoidably, one or more of the other four goals
will be diminished. Conversely, select any one goal and sacrifice
it, and gains will accrue which can be distributed in various ways
among the remaining four.

The economist's way of resolving such dilemmas is to allow the
consumer to express his preference. At the same time, the economist insists that certain conditions prevail before such a system is
allowed to operate. Among these is the condition that each option
have a price attached to it, such that the price reflects the costs of

providing that option. Once this is done and the consumer expresses his preference, the economist is loath to argue that the consumer should have acted differently. Thus economists as a rule do not argue that people should eat more butter and less margarine, see more movies and buy fewer books, spend a little more on shelter and a little less on clothing, or anything of this general sort.

In the transportation area we also allow consumers to express their preferences. There are costs in driving automobiles, and there are prices to be paid for riding mass-transit facilities. But something seems to have gone amiss. Our streets and highways are generally congested, while ridership on mass-transit facilities is declining. Thus, given the urban transportation systems available, there appears substantial evidence that we are not using these systems most efficiently overall.

While we must admit there is some controversy within the profession on this point, those who share this view argue that this overuse of automobiles and underuse of mass transit reflects distorted pricing. By subsidizing highways we have made it too easy for automobile owners to take to the highways, and we have read congestion on our highways as a signal that more investments should be made in them, to the neglect of mass-transportation facilities. It is as if in a competition between butter and margarine, subsidies had been given to butter to keep its price down, and we then built more butter factories in response to its increasing consumption. Thus it is argued that if auto users paid a more appropriate price (in gasoline taxes, tolls, parking fees, and the like) for using roadways and parking facilities, and if mass-transit riders were offered better facilities even at somewhat higher prices, there might well be a marginal but voluntary shift from automobile to mass-transit use. Intuitively it is clear that such a shift would yield a superior reconciliation among transportation goals.

There is still one enormously difficult question to be answered. Suppose urban transportation prices were not distorted and that under these conditions urban residents continued to show a strong preference for automobiles: Should the urban community follow the consumer signal and emphasize highway construction to the detriment of mass transit? We can no longer argue a shortage of funds, for we have implied charges on automobile users sufficient unto the need. The argument against such a procedure is that cities based on automobile use will sprawl out and that many important noneconomic urban values will be lost. Economists are not indifferent to the issue at hand, but they are at a loss for a means to resolve it. What is at issue is the question of what kind of cities we actually want—cities with strong and intensively developed cores, or cities diffused and spread over larger areas. Philosophers, sociologists, planners, and aesthetes may one day be certain of just what constitutes the "good city." Economists will have to content themselves with suggesting the design and financing of a transportation system to serve it.

Urban Fiscal and Poverty Problems

No economic view of the cities would be complete without some reference to urban fiscal and poverty problems. Broadly stated, the urban fiscal problem is simply that urban governments, especially in our larger and older metropolitan cities, are experiencing increasing difficulty in financing the services which urbanites expect them to provide. Since the federal and state governments are also experiencing similar problems, it may be that urban governments experience these difficulties mainly because they are governments, and not because they are urban. At the same time, there is evidence to suggest that the fiscal pinch is greater at the city level than it is at the state or federal level. The influences which account for this can be summarized and discussed under four headings, as follows: (1) poverty problems are disproportionately concentrated in cities, especially in older cities in larger metropolitan areas; (2) fiscal responsibility for solving problems still rests far too heavily on urban governments; (3) the political fragmentation of urban areas makes it difficult for urban governments to raise revenues; and (4) the principal tax instrument available to cities, namely, the property tax, is inadequate to carry the revenue burdens which have been placed upon it. We consider these influences in turn.

In the first part of this chapter a somewhat abstract picture of the processes of urban growth and formation was presented. What emerged was a pattern in which an ever-increasing share of the nation's people were becoming agglomerated into large urban areas, with the distribution of people inside these areas undergoing a trend to suburbanization. The causes of this suburbanization are to be found in the shift of job opportunities, new transportation and other industrial technologies, and new life styles made possible by increasing income and increasing leisure. Not all people have, however, been equally absorbed by this trend. The aged, the relatively unskilled workers, the culturally deprived, and the black and Puerto Rican minorities have remained behind, bottled up, so to speak, in enclaves of urban poverty. Space does not permit us to analyze this process in detail, nor is it particularly relevant to do so here. What is significant is the stark reality that poverty is unequally distributed in urban areas and that its concentration in older central cities is not the result of particular urban choices but is instead the consequence of national and metropolitan growth trends beyond the control of these central cities.

While the present hot debate over strategies to overcome poverty demonstrates that we do not yet know the most effective way to cope with the problem, it does establish that programs to overcome poverty are going to cost vast sums of money. These sums are going to have to be spent over and above the large amounts needed to satisfy public demands, not related to poverty issues, for better schools, recreation facilities, police and fire protection, sanitation services, and so on. Suburban communities with growing tax bases and relatively minor poverty problems are already finding it difficult to keep up with rising public expectations. Poverty apart, these same demands for better services in general also exist in the older central cities. Given this, the fact that these older cities also still have disproportionate shares of the responsibility for financing poverty-related outlays in the fields of health, welfare, and education almost certainly ensures that neither the expanding demands for traditional services nor the added new programs in the poverty area are likely to be met out of tax sources available to local governments.

The problem is exacerbated by the political fragmentation of urban areas. Some communities do not provide public services—as in the cultural and recreational fields, to cite one area—partly on the grounds that their residents can use the facilities in neighboring communities, and partly out of the fear that outsiders will use the local services "for free." To the extent that contiguous cities in metropolitan areas often respond to such motives, public services tend to be underprovided in general. There is, however, an even more serious problem on the revenue side. Neighboring cities may be seen as locked in a competition for affluent residents and taxable enterprise. In this competition the fear of migrations resulting from tax increases also tends to diminish the revenues which urban communities are willing to raise to meet legitimate needs.

Finally, cities are in fiscal trouble because their principal tax instrument, the property tax, is particularly deficient. Among its weaknesses, several stand out. Unlike the income tax, it does not automatically yield more revenue as urban incomes increase. Discretionary increases aimed at increasing its revenue productivity tend to be self-defeating, as increases in property-tax rates may slow growth in the tax base and in some circumstances may be offset by migrations to avoid it. This occurs at a time when there is an urgent need to overcome great obsolescence in old cities. Ultimately, the property tax falls indirectly but in a disproportionately burdensome way on the poor. Since the poor allocate larger proportions of their income to securing shelter than do more affluent people, the poor contribute heavily to the property-tax revenues of government. As a result, the effort of older cities to overcome poverty may involve these cities, more than new suburbs, in self-defeating programs of taxing the poor to help the poor.

All of this points to a combination of reforms which could solve urban finance on a viable basis. First, urban governments should be relieved of all fiscal responsibility for poverty programs. Because the distribution of poverty reflects national trends, it is preferable that the federal government use its more powerful and equitable income tax as an instrument to deal with it. Second, certain functions which are most efficiently provided on the metropolitan scale and which have important effects on the urban regions as a whole, notably the transportation system, should be financed out of area-wide sources of revenue. This, of course, would be achieved if users paid their way. Experts in urban fiscal policy have also suggested a family of lesser adjustments which would contribute to an overall solution. Space does not permit us to catalog them here. It should, however, be abundantly clear that if only the poverty and transportation problems were solved along the lines suggested, all cities and especially our older cities would have a reasonable chance of coping with their remaining fiscal problems.

Urban Economic Growth

No economic view of the city would in any sense be complete if it did not include some considerable focus on the issue of growth. Statistically, this is the concern with increases in urban output and incomes per person over periods of time. Because cities do not increase their output and income at identical rates, the concern with growth points to the question, "What determines how particular cities fare in interurban competition for a share of the national growth?" The growth issue is also important because growth is the lubricant which permits us to achieve other important social ends. For example, it is difficult to envisage greater degrees of economic equity in a national or urban economy which was not expanding in the aggregate as well.

In their efforts to understand urban economic growth, economists have developed two sets of ideas which have sometimes appeared to be in rather fundamental conflict. On the one hand, some economists have seen the stimulus to growth in any given urban area as originating outside the urban area itself. Theories of this kind are related to the so-called urban-economic-base concept, which holds that all activity in a city can be viewed as taking place either for export or to support the local economy, with increases in export activity providing the basis for second round increases in the local economy. Others have argued that such an approach fails to support the more fundamental bases for growth. These growth bases include the local endowment of natural resources, the quality of the local labor force, the entrepreneurship of the local business community, and the actual location of the city vis-à-vis all other urban centers in the national economy. While on first sight this debate may seem highly theoretical, it does have some important practical implication. Advocates of the export-base theory tend to support policies aimed at encouraging selected industry in the exporting group as strategy for promoting local growth. Exponents of the alternative view are more concerned with improving the local environment for growth. Thus they are concerned that the local area's labor force be upgraded, that local entrepreneurship be stimulated, that public services be at a high level, and so on.

Whether or not we as yet have a firm theoretical understanding of the processes of urban growth, we can make some significant observations about the effects of growth. The fact that cities do not grow at equal rates gives rise to national systems of cities, with cities of different size serving different functions in the national economy. At one extreme are cities which include, and provide for the nation, certain selected services of a highly sophisticated and esoteric kind in business, industry, the arts, etc., such as New York City. At the other are the embryos of future local and regional centers which in their embryonic state may still be based on the production and export of a small range of industrial products.

Second, individual cities cannot maintain a monopoly on growth, because growth spills over from area to area. If, for example, growth in any one region is disproportionately rapid and wage rates in the local area are disproportionately high, people will migrate in from lower wage areas. Over the long pull this tends to equalize earnings area by area, as wage rates in the fast-growing areas are prevented from running too far ahead of wages in more slowly growing areas. Conversely, areas with good resources but relatively low wages may attract capital from more affluent areas, with a resulting increase in their rates of expansion. Tendencies of this kind are evident in the United States, as labor migrates to the North and far East, and capital migrates into the South.

Finally, the basic tendency for the nation's population to urbanize is destined to continue. Notwithstanding its already enormous size of some twenty million people, the New York region, for example, is projected to have some thirty million people by the year 2000. It is fashionable these days to speak of cities as being in crisis. It is, however, important to observe that today more people live in more cities at higher levels of living than has ever been the case in human history. This trend will continue. The so-called urban crisis is mainly a crisis of rising expectations focusing on equal participation in the benefits of urban life. Urban economies have had and will continue to display great capacity for growth. The real issue is whether or not there will be a commitment to deploy this growth wisely.

Chapter 4

A
Psychological View

BY JOHN P. KILDAHL

A reporter, on his first day of work for a New York City news-paper, was given the following assignment by his editor: he was told to ride the subway all day and all night to observe the people who rode the subway.

The new reporter put his token in the turnstile, entered the sub-way at seven A.M., and observed. He watched the morning rush hour, packed in, hanging on, one amidst millions. He saw the midday crowd of women shoppers and the schoolchildren coming home after three o'clock. He watched the construction men coming home shortly after three-thirty and four o'clock. He watched the office workers coming out about five. He watched the people going out for an evening about eight. He watched the many thousands of young adults coming home from night educational courses at ten. Later he observed the night people, with all the idiosyncrasies, occupations, and interests that made them night people.

After eighteen hours on the subway, the reporter returned to his editor. He was asked, "Did you look at the people?" The reporter said that he had looked at them all day, and into the night, and the wee hours of the morning. And the editor replied, "Those are the people that you are writing for, and never forget it."

The reporter had observed the people of the city. What kind of people are they? They are the people to whom the church hopes to minister. As this chapter progresses, let it be remembered that those faces on the New York subway and on the buses, five million of them each day, form the group about which the central question of this book is being asked. A second large group constitutes those who never venture so far from home as to take a subway ride. Those are the terribly impoverished who scarcely leave their own blocks, who do not venture from their neighborhood. A third segment would be those people who have put themselves above riding the subway, who more often would be found in taxis or private transportation. They literally do not rub shoulders with the other two groups in our city population. This latter group is relatively small. This chapter is concerned with the subway riders and with those who are so isolated that even a subway ride is outside the limits of their turf.

The psychology of the city is the subject of this chapter. But the psychology of the city is many things. Therefore the topic will be limited more specifically to some descriptions of the *life style* of the majority of city residents. Next, there will be a description of the life style of the church, the typical way in which the church goes about its business. And third, we shall explore how the life style of the city and the life style of the church can be compared and contrasted. It is hoped that they should better be able to speak and communicate with each other, so that the church will be prepared to help the city and not to lose it.

The main thesis of this chapter will be that the city man lives in a world of *deed*, whereas the church man traditionally has lived in a world of *words*. City man lives on the behavioral level; church man has typically lived on the verbal level. City man lives in the realm of doing, whereas church man has lived in the world of thinking.

These are contrasting life styles, and they pose a problem somewhat akin to a Frenchman and a German trying to communicate with each other, each in his own language. While there may be some commonalty, it is undeniable that they speak a different language.

In addition to the language differences, there is a basic difference in the way life is experienced, a difference in the understanding of what constitutes the good life, and a basically different way of understanding and dealing with the problems that confront one in daily living. These contrasts between city man and church man will be the concern during the discussion which follows.

If the city and the church cannot accommodate themselves to each other, if they cannot develop a common perspective or begin to appreciate more fully the framework from which each views life, there will be a widening breach, possibly culminating in the extinction of the church as we now know it. Analogously, the dinosaur became extinct when the environment in which it lived was no longer able to provide those nurturing experiences which a dinosaur needed in order to survive. The environment and the dinosaur became alien to each other, and it was the dinosaur which had to go. In somewhat similar fashion, the city will not go. Rather, the expectation is that the population of the urban areas in the United States will increase by about one hundred million people during the next twenty-five years.[1] What will be required of the church if it is to adapt to this new environment? What can make it a force for constructive growth, rather than only a vestige of an earlier cultural era?

The Life Style of the City: Doing Things

The life style of the mass of city residents is one in which *doing things* predominates. It is not a style of life oriented to the academic milieu or to the rational, intellectual, and verbal world of most of the persons who become officials in the church.[2] For example, picture the reticence of a foreign-born person in engaging in free, intellectual dialogue. Consider the intellectually impoverished world of some ghetto resident who does not have the interest, the academic background, or the money to devote himself to printed materials.

The world of the factory worker and the laborer has as its raw material the manipulation of things and objects. This is the raw material to which he devotes himself during his working day. It is these things with which he is comfortable in the evenings and weekends when he is not working. On the end of a hammer or at a sewing machine such a person feels at home. Here he feels no inferiority or inadequacy. But of what use are those skills, and of what use is that kind of a sense of personal identity in a discussion group where the most valued skill is the manipulation of words and ideas?

The typical inner-city resident does not feel that he has the finesse to write a letter to a congressman. But it is becoming in-

creasingly obvious that he is taking over in those fields where physical activity is crucial. It is the ghetto child who is becoming the best
basketball player, because basketball can be played on the street,
dribbling can be practiced on the sidewalk, and intellectual subtle-
ties have little place in the actions of the basketball floor.

The preferred life style of a man can often be seen in what he
chooses to do in his free time. The inner-city resident will not
devote himself, usually, to anything that is not action-oriented. If
he watches TV, it will be those events which are lively, whether
they be sports, comedy, or a dramatic show involving action.

In both work and leisure activities, the life style is experiential
and behavioral. This is the time when a protest march is understood, but not a letter to the editor. It is a style where action
speaks loudly, but not words. It is the style of strategy and tactics,
but not of pronouncements. This is a style where one deed speaks
louder than a thousand words about deeds.

In summary, among those persons where the church has had
little impact, the *behavioral* style of life predominates. That is particularly true among the impoverished, the foreign-born, and the
less well-educated. Let us consider now how the church compares
with these people who live their lives predominantly on the
behavioral level.

The Life Style of the Church:
An Obsessive-Compulsive Captivity

The church man lives in a different world. His character structure,
(i.e., the typical way in which he handles his problems)[3] is vastly
different from the character structure of the inner-city man. The
first difference to be noted is that the church man thrives on the
academic model. The typical clergyman has had about twenty years
of formal classroom education, and those years have been influential in helping him to develop a style of life, a way to think about
things, and a way in which he addresses himself to problems.

Many clergymen tend to treasure every jot and tittle of intellectual subtlety, and this is the game they like to play. For the
classroom teacher and the preacher from the pulpit, the production
from the mimeograph machine and the book are sources of great
satisfaction. The raw materials for the experiences provided in

church are essentially *verbal*: the worship service, prayer, Bible study, and discussion groups.

There is an obsessive-compulsive captivity of the church, in which certain religious forms of generations or centuries ago are regarded as nearly sacred. These are thought by some persons to be *the way* in which one is to be religious. By "obsessive-compulsive" is meant a preoccupation with thoughts, ideas, and acts which are repetitive and which often exist only for their own sake, rather than leading on to some new action. It is this obsessive-compulsive captivity of the church which is often fostered by the kind of church men who derive a major life satisfaction from cherishing and nurturing words, thoughts, and ideas, and who derive considerable satisfaction from their personal ability to manipulate these aspects of their environment.

Many church men have had a life experience from early childhood in which a sense of personal identity has focused around their intellectual and verbal facility. Naturally, deriving personal satisfaction from this character structure, it is this style which they promote in their vocational pursuits. Seminary education, further, is based on this academic mode. Intellectual and doctrinal precision has become an enjoyable game to play. Church meetings are often felt to be failures if they have not produced a *statement* about something. In almost monolithic fashion the church has been held captive by this peculiar life style in recent generations. However, the city dweller has been seeing life from a different perspective and has been seeking his life satisfactions and the solutions of his problems through different mechanisms. The church and the city dweller have gotten out of step.

The obsessive-compulsive character style[4] has a number of specific qualities, and it is well to observe how the style of church life has taken on many of these qualities. Some of these characteristics have come to be virtually equated with spirituality and godliness. In this life style there is a special *sense of duty* or oughtness which is particularly attached to moral obligations of an overt nature. This sense of duty becomes almost the highest good in life, and it often leaves a person unable to face even an objective query about what he is doing. The matter is not open to discussion. It is simply the way things must be. There is a right way to do things, and it brooks of no argument. This tyrannical, if shortsighted, sense of duty leads to a highly controlled and *controlling style of life*.[5] One feels that he has to take charge of things because of his inner sense of conviction, and that no one else can quite be depended upon to complete a task properly. Therefore, delegation or *sharing of responsibilities becomes extremely difficult*, because the obsessive-compulsive character believes that he must personally attend to every last detail of a project. This leads to extreme *sensitivity to interference* on the part of others. Such a person's attitude may border on being actually defiant and rebellious, if one's rights to control a project are impinged upon.

Inasmuch as such a person feels that he has to do the full job himself, he will often have a *perfectionistic attitude* toward his own work. His standards of perfection, of course, will be his own, but he will often be able to perform inordinate amounts of work in great detail because of his highly developed sense that things have to be done his own way. The perfectionism will often take the form of an outward, observable neatness, and there develops a *priority on the appearance of things*. This outer appearance of things being neat, orderly, and under control is extremely important in this obsessive-compulsive mode. Often there is an inordinate delight in dialectic nuances and a pedantry that takes the form of fondness for definition and exactness, which, of course, may often be only a *verbal exactness*. Consequently, there is often an *inability to feel pleasure and joy* unless the circumstances are precisely quite right. When the appearance of things and this penchant for verbal exactitude are not satisfied, there is often an *irritability and gloom* which interfere with the on-going process of living. The direct, immediate experience of pleasure and joy is often given less importance, as opposed to the need for postponing gratification in favor of getting a job done neatly and thoroughly.

In the eyes of others, such persons often give the appearance of being rather boring and somewhat slow-minded. Because the emphasis is on detail and precision, very often the activities of such a person become tedious and cumbersome. Overly concerned with precision, a person will find it difficult to come down solidly on a single point of view and stand by it. Rather it will be his preference to weigh the arguments from every angle, seeing the good and the bad, searching for more and more data, and viewing with alarm from all sides. This habit can actually cripple a person against taking any definite action out of fear of not being exactly right. Such need for perfection has the eventual outcome of stopping all action. The perfectionist retreats behind his rationalizations, excusing himself for not taking a stand on the difficult issues of the day because utter certainty is impossible.

Another characteristic is *the inability to let go.* It takes the form of a kind of stinginess, or a proclivity for gathering, collecting, and hoarding. Accompanying the need to control everything is the tendency to keep everything within his own grasp. This clinging to everything serves to make one cherish the past unduly, partly out of honest reverence for it, but also partly out of fear of losing contact with any aspect of one's past.

These traits combine to form a unified whole in which there is enormous persistence, diligence, and just plain hard work. There is a great sense of determination, a love of order and reliability, and a capacity for unusual thoroughness. On the other hand, there is a great propensity for unhappiness, irritability and bad temper, pettiness, and a tendency to tyrannize in such an obstinate fashion that others become bored and annoyed.

This has been a caricature, and like all caricatures the picture has been exaggerated for the sake of clarity. This picture of the obsessive-compulsive style has been exaggerated so that various aspects of it can be seen, and no one person or church would fit the description exactly.

We claim that the church has been taken captive by the obsessive-compulsive style, and that this obsessive-compulsive captivity makes the church in many ways ill-suited to minister to the needs of the city dweller. While the world has changed, and especially those who live in the inner city, the style of ministry has changed *less* than has the city. The character structure of the academically oriented clergyman is not in keeping with the climate of the city.

Some Psychological Signs of the Times

Consider how many speeches the average person now listens to in the course of a year. Will the average adult perhaps listen to a half-dozen speeches in the course of a presidential election? And perhaps to the President of the United States a few times a year on the occasion of a special crisis? The history of the last twenty-five years is one in which there has been a lessening of the impact of words. Words are cheap; their proliferation in every form of communication has partly deadened the population to the impact of those words. In contrast, consider the magnetic quality of the fireside chats of Franklin D. Roosevelt a generation ago. The nation drew close to its radios, intent on the rapport and the feeling and the impact that the speaker could make with his words. Consider the magnificent words of Winston Churchill during World War II. He brought the English language to new heights, mobilizing a people with his words when little else was able to reach them.

While words always have had and surely always will have an impact, it should be remembered that obsessive religious rituals are only one way among many in which to go about one's sacred tasks. While the verbal prayers of the church may reach some people, it is more likely that sensitivity training and group encounter will reach more deeply into the inner lives of persons who have not had the experiences which could make prayers meaningful to them.

The shallowness of purely verbal experiences can be illustrated also in the field of psychotherapy. Psychotherapy began with middle- and upper-class people who were intelligent, well educated, and accustomed to expressing themselves in words. As a verbal form of treatment, psychoanalysis worked quite well for the people in that culture for whom it was intended. Psychotherapy has been found to work less well with people who are not oriented to a verbal style of life. In therapy other ways of reaching people had to be devised. Group therapy was instituted, and then behavior therapy. Now even nonverbal behavioral forms of interaction are being adopted because of the need to cut through the layers of insulation which a person has built up against letting words have any impact upon his feelings or his actions.

The life style of Jesus had a large element of the behavioral mode in it. It rather seems as if Jesus thought it just as virtuous to give someone a cup of water as to state in a propositionally proper way some doctrinal truth. This is an age when it is easier for most city people to understand the latter of Christ's two commands—to preach the gospel and to heal the sick. We need not deplore the fact that he had two commands rather than simply the first command. The first command tends to be more verbal, and the second command tends to be more behavioral. It is on this second level that life is lived more meaningfully by city residents.

Healing now captures the attention of a young person more than does preaching. Healing means not simply working with a physical disease, but healing all the places in society that are less than healthy, including the spheres of life where poverty, racism, and war have rent asunder man's relationship to his fellow man. Two thousand years ago, as well as today, people were reached by something that is concrete, experiential, and personal. Many times Jesus would heal first, and it was in response to his healing that people would ask him what had happened, and then he would proclaim the gospel. The *deed* of love came before the *word* of love in many cases. However, the obsessive-compulsive style tends to begin and end with the verbal experience. In the city today, very clearly the prayer for "all sorts and conditions of men" will include primarily those persons whose most meaningful experiences are behavioral rather than verbal.

The Example of the Seminary

The danger is that the highly educated, among whom are the clergy, will be called upon to minister to a world that could not care less about the intellectual games that the academically oriented like to play.[6] The seminary of today, for example, is often based on an academic model, whereas the parish should be, and often is, based on a therapeutic model. The seminary community has in these past decades been based on a book-learning, intellectual model. In contrast, the medical-school student is a physician from the first day he walks into medical school, and after his first two years of academic orientation, his experience is almost entirely clinical, and bedside. He lives in the midst of the atmosphere which will later be his milieu; namely, sick people and the hospital. In contrast, the seminarian is largely divorced in seminary from the life that he shall later live.

The danger is that seminary education can be based on a model that does not experientially prepare one for the healing, helping model that is the parish pattern. In the seminary the raw material is the books, whereas in the parish the focus is on people. It is not too much to ask that seminaries keep before them the model of a healing community, in addition to the model of a community of scholars. While the highly educated may enjoy their intellectual games, to transmit the gospel only in verbal, intellectual terms to a generation that does not know that style of life is to ask for failure.

Some Emerging Solutions

Fortunately, there are many signs that field education is increasingly being combined with classroom education.[7] This is the day of action research. Clinical training, that is, on-the-job experience, is becoming a part of all education. The case-history approach in business has brought the Harvard Business School to first rank among business schools because it more quickly prepares a man to take his place in the business world.

The first task of a psychotherapist is to establish rapport with his patient. The first task of the church must also always be to establish rapport with its community. That means speaking the language which the community speaks. The language of the city today is a different language from the language which the church has traditionally used. It is not unusual for a traditional cultural institution to fall behind the community in which it lives. The youth change first, while adults are the carriers of the cultural tradition. But the church must now gear into a behavior-oriented model and throw off its obsessive-compulsive captivity. The day of being preoccupied primarily with ideas is over.

There is not a chance that the current generation of young people growing up in the city will turn out the way their parents did, and perhaps not the way their parents wish they would. Young people, who must become the focus of the church's ministry, are now giving their lives to a kind of behavior that is alien to that of their grandfathers. Their values are not puritan, not necessarily the values of the middle class, not necessarily those of the capitalist who believes in saving his money so that he may obtain some later gratification. The church must understand this new mode of expression, become a part of it, and equip its members even in the midst of training to relate to the person for whom actions speak loudly and words matter little. All churches must become community-oriented, person-oriented, healing-oriented, and not primarily book-oriented. The task of establishing rapport with this generation means that the healing forces of the church must be action-focused.

Columbia University, after its recent difficulties, is becoming community-minded. Part of its mission will be that of a healer in Morningside Heights, New York City. Such a demand on that university would have been unheard of one hundred years ago. But not anymore. If it is to survive in this society, it must take into account the immediate needs of its environment, as well as long-range needs that students will face after they graduate. Education as an isolated period in which one prepares for the future is an antiquated model. The danger of that old model is that the ideas come to be an end in themselves, and the fun will consist in playing with the ideas rather than in using the ideas to heal the hurts of mankind.

In similar fashion monasteries are moving to the city. Mental hospitals are being closed and the patients are being brought into the community, the therapy consisting in doing what they will be called upon to do once they are well again. Schools must be in the world. Churches are moving to shopping centers and store-fronts, becoming Monday through Saturday operations. The idea that faith can be separated from life is being discarded as religious institutions make their way into the marketplace.

Jesus did not talk about the gospel; he demonstrated it. His was not the obsessive-compulsive trait of talking about how superb it is that religion believes in healing the whole person. Rather, he forgave sins and healed the body, and said, "Take up your bed and walk." He did not abstractly speak of the definition of what love is. He said, "Neither do I condemn thee." The danger is that church men who love academia will be one step removed from experiencing and demonstrating the gospel. And in so doing, the church could divorce itself from the mood of the masses of this generation.

Where the people are is where the church must be. The church can use its college brains, but must talk high-school language, and relate directly, humanly, without the intervening barrier of abstract intellectualizations. In the dichotomy between doing the gospel and talking about the gospel, it should be remembered that one deed of love is worth a thousand words about deeds of love.

One experience of the gospel at the hands of a fellow Christian is worth more than a thousand words about how wonderful the gospel is.

The church may lose the city if it does not establish rapport with it. Rapport between a thinker and a doer has never been easy to accomplish. But it is the task of the church to come off its intellectual detachment and get its hands dirty in the marketplace—doing those deeds which the people in the city know and understand best.

Chapter 5

An
Aesthetic View

BY ROBERT S. JACKSON

What does the city look like from an aesthetic point of view? I cannot enter into that question without entering another one simultaneously, a much more profound and difficult question, and one which I cannot hope to answer here in anything like the fullness which it deserves: What is man?

Even if I had the space and time, I could not of course fully verbalize that nature which I share with the reader—too much mystery and uncertainty is in us as it is in the rest of the basic stuff of the universe. Nevertheless, one part of us can and must try to verbalize it, and how else can I approach meaningfully the various aspects of the subject I am undertaking here? What, after all, is a city? And what can we meaningfully say about an aesthetic view of it, if we do not also talk about man?

A city is a dense aggregation of men, in the ordinary way of speaking, and the arts are the product of certain peculiarities in man, in which he differs apparently from the rest of the universe. But that is only to state the connection most bluntly, and it must be said more subtly also. Since the city is such a concentration of man's life and activity, it is also a center out of which his aesthetic life flows most potently and luxuriously. I am simply saying that the arts flourish more in cities, and less outside of them. But consider also that the city does not only produce art; it is itself a work of art: Chicago, Cleveland, New York, London, Paris, Rome—

these are not the names of mushrooms that grow up because of the effect of spring mists on dungheaps; they are made by man and by the arts of man. They are the result of man's peculiar aesthetic powers expressing themselves upon the face of the universe. We do this. We reshape the universe. We do it in order to make the universe suit us better and to give us a feeling of being at home here. Our cities are certainly one of the grand shapes of this effort.

And consider further that the city is also a more or less pure aesthetic image. I am thinking of the great cities (or city-states) of the Western world, pictured in Plato's *Republic*, St. Augustine's *City of God*, and Vergil's *Aeneid*. I cannot speak of the large number of inheritors of these visions, such as More's *Utopia*, Campanella's *City of the Sun*, Swift's *Gulliver's Travels*, or such recent variants as Huxley's *Brave New World*, Orwell's *1984*, Cox's *The Secular City*, or Skinner's *Walden Two*, save to mention their names. These aesthetic shapes are the very models out of which the actual cities are made; seldom acting literally, but acting very powerfully nonetheless, these forms which are the spelled-out paradigms of man's own heart are the fundamental blueprints by which he guides his hands and his machines in the making of the cities in which he also lives his bodily life.

Man's Bodily Life

I must bring up the subject of our bodily life, and not talk only of art and aesthetics, if only to place this "higher" aspect of our nature into proper perspective—though physical existence is also much more important than that. We simply must acknowledge, no matter what else we may say about ourselves, that we are beasts. No doubt we do not need the present eruption of violence in our cities to show us this truth. We have, wrapped up with all the rest of ourselves, our primitive animal nature, and we always have had it. But the present violence helps, because we have a vast tendency to idealize our nature and to dream that we actually are that ideal thing, instead of a very material animal nature mixed up with that ideal. We must dwell upon this animal nature for a moment. We live by sucking within ourselves the material environment around us, drawing in oxygen, ingesting soil in the form of minerals like salt as well as in the form of vegetable and animal products. We also surrender back into that environment part of our own material existence; we urinate and defecate regularly, and we vomit, spit, suppurate, snivel, and bleed under certain conditions. We respond directly to the material environment; when it is cold our blood vessels shrink, when hot they expand. We sweat. We pant. We blink. We reproduce ourselves sexually. We hate and envy as well as admire and love one another. And all of these things, in one way or another, we share with cows, dogs, lions, rats, ants, or other "lower" animals.

But although we cannot do anything else without also doing the animal things, we do something the rest of the beasts cannot: We can symbolize ourselves and our experience. Not only can we do so, we must. We can symbolize our beast side, as I have been doing in the preceding paragraph, as well as other aspects of ourselves. And I must do this, like all other men, at the risk of failing to become a man. Of course, all men do not have to symbolize themselves in precisely this same way. Each man must do it in his own way. But do it he must. It is not enough, for example, for man to "have sex." He must also symbolize it. He must satisfy his perceptual, reflective, imaginative, and emotional (to mention a few) relationships to sex. Most men do so instinctively, as it were, mostly through talk with one's beloved, his friends, parents, counselors, etc., and he does so in a large variety of moods or tones, sober, allusive, joking, and so on. But one may also write as well as speak, in letters, poems, stories, essays, even books. The symbolizing can be nonverbal, in the form of winks, looks, hand motions, grunts, shouts, or actions of many types, among others the making of bridges, roads, cars, airplanes, rockets, computing machines, banks, shopping centers, and a great deal of the rest which goes to make up our cities.

I know of no evidence that man may circumvent his need to fulfill the beast level of his sexual character. But neither do I know of any evidence that he may circumvent his need to symbolize it. The most precise form of the fulfillment of these two needs in relation to each other is, of course, marriage. In marriage the sexual union is surrounded with a more or less dense forest of verbal and other symbolic forms. Where the so-called "marriage ceremony" is not performed, either it is not missing in fact or the so-called marriage does not represent the human fulfillment of the partners.

I suppose that what is called "rape" is a primary form of the result when the symbolic fulfillment is omitted. Man's capacity to be sexual both biologically and symbolically is basic but not unique. He has both sides to his nature in all of his functions. The symbolizing capacity is man's aesthetic side, and it is this side of his nature which makes him a *peculiar* beast.

Ambivalent Wholeness

We can state this more abstractly by speaking of man as both natural and artificial. It is related to the ancient concept that man is the union of a god and a beast, a union represented in classical art in the figure of the satyr (or faun), the creature with the lower body of a goat and the upper of a man. The chief exemplar among the satyrs was Pan, whose name signifies "all" or "everything," which I take to allude to the joining of the two sides of man into his wholeness. I take him to mean that for my context here; in fact, Pan seems to have represented the joining of larger opposites also, such as heaven and earth. In the Judeo-Christian tradition, much the same kind of ambivalent wholeness is discovered in man. It is he who is made part of the creation in an orderly sequence with the rest, but into whom only does God breathe his own spirit, so that the Psalmist asks: Who is man that he is made "little less than God"? And while God makes a prohibition against representing himself in the form of anything that is in the heavens above or in the earth beneath, he does not hesitate to image himself in the form of the speech of men. In that man is a created being he does not have any special status; he shares this with the rest of the universe. But that he is aware of this fact and that he expresses it symbolically: in this he is unique (as far as we know). Man only of all the creatures of the cosmos says, "O Lord our Lord, how excellent is thy name in all the earth."

If this is an accurate account of the nature of man, or accurate enough to remind the reader of his own method of defining the ambivalence we share, we certainly are going to expect to create structures which develop out of such a duality when we aggregate together into dense social groups. And of course this is precisely the way the city does develop—on the one hand to satisfy the needs for shelter, food, the nurturing of marriage, family, and social groups, that is, the instinctual or beast needs; and on the other hand to accompany all this with symbolic expression. Homes are not only for shelter but are decorated with symbols, structures expressive of individual or class identities; beans are packaged in stores with pictures of beans on the outside of the carton; various national cultures—Italian, French, Chinese, German, Swedish, as well as those of other, more exotic countries—create methods of cooking and presenting foods which relate symbolically to the country of their origin; marriages and families are defined by a vast array of symbolic structures of clothing, neighborhoods, buildings, memorized or half-memorized verbal formulas, certain kinds of taste, and mutual understandings; and broader social groups include much the same kind of thing. At the level of satisfying instinctual needs, the city sounds fairly simple, but at the symbolic level I have only begun to describe the complexities. The communal function made possible by man's potential for complex psychic life and organization has led to the great network of communications systems—telephones, radios, televisions—extensions of his nervous system, as Marshall McLuhan perceives them. It is hard to say which creates which, the city's creating the communications network, or the communications network's creating the city. Similar complexities arise as a result of the extension of man's walking or carrying capacity: persons and food are carried from point to point in vehicles and on foot according to routes carefully designated by symbolic systems of markings on roads, door handles, one-way signs, and the like. How the growth of the city has literally artificialized the surface of this earthen globe! Does one not perceive it with distinctness and clarity when from several thousand feet in the air at about ten o'clock at night from an airplane beginning the slow circles for landing at O'Hare Airport he peers down from his window at the patterned lights below terminating in the broad arc defined by Lake Michigan on the one side and fading off into more sparsely lit areas on the other? The city is not merely a convenience for food, shelter, and society; it is a grand artifact, perhaps the grandest design resulting from the necessity we have to stamp our own image upon the face of the universe.

Art as a Function of Man

I have been speaking of art as a function of man, not of art for art's sake, and that is because I must say what I think is true. As some persons maintain of God, so I maintain of art (for art's sake): It is a concept once alive but alive no longer. It belonged to the nineteenth century. During its own period the *beaux arts* flourished. By placing the *beaux arts* in this light, I do not denigrate them. Oscar Wilde was one of its adherents, and his comedy *The Importance of Being Earnest* illustrates its artistic product. I have enjoyed its performances and would be delighted to see something of its spirit imported into the overearnest climate of American life; I need this kind of comedy personally for the fulfillment of my own artificial needs. But in saying these things, of course, I reassert that I do not believe in the aesthetic theory which produced it; I want it for my own sake, I consider it needed for man's sake, and I may cry out for it for God's sake, but if it is there for art's sake, that is only because these other concerns are prior.

The arts are functional in man's existence and therefore a genuine part of his mission as man. They are not merely possible to us, something permitted, and they are certainly not frivolous, as certain large portions of American society at all levels of wealth and status still maintain. They are something we need, and the *beaux arts* are simply a more specialized, more subtle, more sophisticated expression of that need, and as such they are more likely to emerge within the more concentrated communities of our common life, the cities. To be sure, during certain periods of history the arts have been produced by persons living away from city locations. This was true during the Romantic period—by Wordsworth in England, for example, or Thoreau in this country. But in the broad sweep of culture, the story of the cities tells also the story of the arts. Athens, Alexandria, Rome, Florence, Moscow, Paris, London, Boston, New York, Chicago, and San Francisco tell the origins of the larger part of the history of Western painting, sculpture, dance, drama, poetry, and fiction. Even those artists who did not live in one of those cities had once done so, or had visited frequently, or had close personal connections in one or more. The same thing is true when one considers not the origin, but the place where the finished products are now located. The products of man's aesthetic vitality are found at the Louvre, for example, or in the British Museum. Yet something is happening to the experience of men in the traditional urban centers which is changing both the character of the fine arts and the "city" in which they are produced.

The growth of cities is the expected outcome of a concentration of men, but this concentrated expression of our nature is accompanied by a concentration of the great problem of our nature. The unique duality of man presents him with a problem he does not share with the rest of nature, the necessity to reconcile himself to both sides of the ambivalence which is he. This need to fulfill both sides of our nature and to articulate the two in relation to each other so that the one does not destroy the other—this has always been man's hardest task. The city is invented to make it easier to fulfill each side and is itself the fulfillment of each. For many, many persons at certain stages in their lives, or in the history of their communal development, one city or another has functioned admirably, not only to fulfill each side but to assist in the articulation of one side with the other. But at other stages of their lives or of their communal history it has exacerbated the difficulties of such fulfillment, even immensely. Perhaps one reason for the great difficulty is that since the model of achievement is so grand, failure, when it results, is heightened by comparison. The character of the present failure is not merely the special problem of the ghetto, where the development of symbolic achievement is miserably stunted in favor of the search for mere jungle survival; it is also found in the "upper" side of society, where the silent and unbrutal despair of the oversophisticated has been generated—their very cultural achievement has isolated them from their animal nature and led them into hypocrisy, arrogance, and coldness of life. In the healthy city, groups such as these help to fulfill one another's needs, but in the sick city the groups are alienated from one another. The need is for reconciliation, and the failure of it is the failure of man to become himself. The aesthetic side of man's nature obviously has a role in the reconciliation.

My uneasiness with the old concept of the *beaux arts* is not my own alone, but it is declining, as it were, by itself, and it is partly the cry for reconciliation that has produced the shift in their character. The arts are becoming reinvolved in the lives of people. Drama, for example, is moving away from the aesthetic of the proscenium arch and the unseen "glass wall" separating artists and audience, and more and more toward audience participation in the action. This is evident in movements toward small intimate theater, theater-in-the-round, psychodrama. These are movements back toward the concept of the theater as liturgy, in the traditional sense of a communal action whose end is spiritual cleansing or purgation, the same effect described of drama in Aristotle's *Poetics*. The new theater is not "pure theater" in the recent modern sense; it is impure.

Something similar has occurred in the graphic arts: Pop art, op art, and kinetic art, for example, are not "fine arts" in the traditional sense, not even "art objects." They require something else to be mixed in, particularly something from the "impure" world of man himself. They tend to require the viewer's participation in order to fulfill whatever it is they are. Pop art, with its special attention to the debris of modern civilization—"Coke" bottles, junk tires, etc.—is an attempt to assimilate the near-beast level of cultural awareness to the more symbolic level and is a more or less direct effort at reconciliation of man's dual nature. Op art achieves its effects because of the characteristics of man's visual apparatus and nervous system. And kinetic art attempts to join the aspects of time and motion to the traditional space which the art form shares with man's own life. The new tendency seems to me less evident in the literary arts; however, some signs of it may be seen in mixed-media poetry such as "concrete poetry," where the poem is printed out in such a way as also to paint a visual picture such as the face of a man or the Eiffel Tower, both of which could be seen in the library exhibit at Northwestern University in the fall of 1968, or in those paintings or sculptures which also have audible or printed words as part of their effect. Such effects are at least efforts to reintegrate aspects of man's experience which previously have been analyzed into their (presumably) purer separate forms.

Each of the movements I have been discussing here has some right to be considered post-modern, and some of the signs of the significance of the period we are living through can be seen in the fact that the affinities of several of them should be found in the pre-modern period, rather than anything later than that, i.e., pre-eighteenth century. For example, the illusionistic effects of op art are similar to things the mannerists tried to achieve in the late sixteenth century, and I have already mentioned the similarity of certain new movements in drama to medieval liturgy. Unfortunately I do not have space enough here to argue adequately that the aesthetic movements of our time are of about equal significance to the movements of Renaissance art and are in many ways moving in a reverse direction, though I believe this to be true, and part of the vision upon which all that I am writing is based rests upon that condition.

The University as City

However, if we can consider history in such a broad sweep briefly, a fact of some importance for the role of the city in the arts—namely, that the city, which is its patron, has shifted—can be put into significant perspective. It would be fair to say that the organization of men which supported the arts during the pre-modern period was the church, during the modern period has been the commercial city, and during the now-post-modern period is the university. The university is the new city out of which the arts grow. Not only is the university more and more the *locus* of the production of the arts, but it is also the repository of the arts, particularly in those aspects in which the arts are functionally alive, the older city museums being precisely that, storehouses for corpses rather than of materials vitally related to living men. What this means, of course, is that the relative importance of the contemporary university as itself the city in which man's nature comes to its fullest expression is rising, while the commercial and industrial complexes decline in their potency.

To consider that such an important shift has taken place in the contemporary university may seem far-fetched to some readers, but I call them to consider that the university, whether we consider it in its more remote origins from Plato's Academy or from its more scholastic and Aristotelian roots in the Middle Ages, had never been the patron of the arts prior to the mid-twentieth century. And I call them also to consider that the "university" so called is now quite routinely recognized as a university no longer; the proper term is the one coined by Clark Kerr for the University of California, namely the "multiversity," an "environment" of many functions, only one of which is the education of the young.

The role of the traditional university will be played in the future, if it is to be played at all, by the so-called "small college," which is now properly regarded as the true survivor of the Platonic Academy and the inheritor as well of the medieval liberal-arts tradition. By the true university I mean a center of learning where the coherence of man's life can be experienced in a seminal way suitable to his early growth into maturity, rather than the complex environment replete with the full multiplicity of individuated functions which define the traditional city or the contemporary multiversity and which is more suitable to the later and more exfoliated development of man's character. The true university can give some thought to its role in the city, which the university cannot; and it cannot because it is itself a city, one among many contemporary cities. The true university is more important in the reconciliation of man to his own nature than the contemporary city, whether we consider the contemporary city in its traditional form of the commercial and industrial center or the center for the growth and acquisition of knowledge or information which is the form of the so-called multiversity.

The City in Literature

This transformation in our own time of the traditional academy into an actual city brings me to the final consideration of my essay into the aesthetic view of the city, namely, the city in literature. Although the metaphor of the city in literature has important later forms in such books as I mentioned earlier in this chapter, each of these is little more than a minor variant when compared with the city in three great books of antiquity—Plato's *Republic*, Vergil's *Aeneid*, and St. Augustine's *City of God*. Each of these has defined an image which has become an actuality, and they are the three most important "cities" in Western culture—the academy, the imperium, and the church. Symbolically these are the three cities of Athens, Rome, and Jerusalem. These are not absolutely distinct from one another, neither in their ideal nor in their actualized form. For example, St. Augustine's *City of God* is quite clearly an effort to discuss in ideal form the relationship between Plato's divine city and Vergil's city of man. But let us consider each of these three cities briefly in its own original literary setting—that is, as ideals. In the light of these, some interesting relationships in their actualized forms in the contemporary world will emerge.

In the *Republic*, the city, whose forms are described with some fullness, is presented as a mental or intellectual establishment. It emerges into communicable shape through the process of a dialogue between Socrates and Glaucon (largely) and could be said to represent self-discovery. The mental structures as described themselves participate in a prior reality, which Plato regards as divine. Hence the city is not only mental but also a "heavenly" city. The Rome created by Aeneas is not fully described; it emerges as a vague dream or hope from one of the adventures of the hero in his efforts to fulfill the divine call to found the city. The reader already knows the shape of the actual and historical Rome: The story is told in order for him to participate in the making of its destiny. Like Plato's city, Vergil's is said to come from the gods; but unlike Plato's, it is not said to be chiefly resident there, but is chiefly understood to be the actual city of Rome. St. Augustine's *City of God* is a description comparing the two cities of Plato and Vergil, the heavenly city and the city of man, and claims that one may not live in the city of man rightly unless he also lives in the city of God, "these two cities [being] entangled together in this world and intermixed until the last judgment effects their separation."[1]

What attitude do persons living in the contemporary counterparts of each of these three visions of the city take toward actual communities of persons? These attitudes can be easily identified from the character of the city in each vision. Academicians tend to despise the actual world most, at least they do so in their role as academicians. Churchmen tend both to despise and to embrace it, the Christian role being ambivalent. And politicians tend to embrace it most closely and to be least critical of its faults. The characteristic attitude arises directly out of the relative distance between the actual and the ideal city in each of these visions, a distinction which corresponds to the distance between the beast side and the aesthetic side of man. But the words "despise" and "embrace" express only one aspect of the three characteristic attitudes. Another aspect of this relationship can be found in the ethical tone of the persons representing each of the three visions, by which I mean the degree to which they create a pressure to change the character of actual existence; and here, of course, the greater the distance, the greater the ethical drive. Thus, the academic vision sees the most powerful contrasts between the ideal and actual realities. Hence there develops the most revolutionary stance toward actual communal life (when it does not lapse into cynicism or despair), which possesses therefore the most revolutionary drive. Thus schools are more revolutionary in import and character than are churches or political organizations per se. The politician (without learning or meaningful religion) is the least ethical figure, the least concerned to bring about changes, the least disturbed about reality as it is presented to him. And the church man is again the mediating figure, possessing now the ethical drive and now the acceptance, or else both simultaneously in a kind of paradox.

However, in identifying these models with actual institutions, it is necessary to be wary. Reality has a way of being immensely richer and more complex than one's ideas about it, which are suggestive more than definitive. None of the three major institutions I am describing out of their aesthetic sources exists in fact as a pure form without admixture from the other two—not the academy, nor the political community, nor the church—but each contains elements of the other two in varying proportions. Does not the Roman Catholic church continue also the vision of Vergil's imperial Rome and of Plato's Academy as well as St. Augustine's City of God? Nor is the Protestant church free of such admixtures in spite of its effort to "purify" the church from (in particular) the city of man. And what of the political community? Does it not borrow ethical sanctions from the church and learning from the academy? And in the failure to be much concerned with visions, does it not survive on those supplied to it by its sister institutions? And so also is the academy impure in each of its two major American forms—the state-supported and the church-related—as the phrases themselves show. It is interesting that, at the moment, the church-related academy supports *the aesthetic vision* of the state better than the state-supported academy, even while it considers itself separated from the actual state. But this was Plato's characteristic attitude also, so we should not be surprised, since the "small colleges," most of which are church-related, are the true bearers of the tradition of the academy, as I indicated earlier. The state-supported school, on the other hand, is fundamentally an aspect of the actualized state and therefore bears the tradition of Vergil's Rome rather than of Plato's Academy, insofar as it bears any. Complacent about the actual state, which indeed it supports in practice in return for what it is given from that (apparent) source, it supports *the vision of the city* relatively little, whether that be the vision of the political, ecclesiastical, or academic city.

Perhaps these confusions can be summarized and clarified: The more thoroughly actualized one of the three major aesthetic cities becomes, the less does it sustain the seminal model out of which its own destiny has been achieved. Their very successes have threatened their foundations. In spite of the title of this book, it is not merely the survival of the church which is at stake, but of the city itself. And when we speak of the renewal of the city, in any of its three major forms, we must think not only of renewing the cities we know in our direct experience but also of renewing the vision. But I might add, for its particular relevance to the present book's theme, that the renewal of the vision of Jerusalem means, I believe, the renewal of a vision of man in which he may become reconciled not only to a God who may be considered separate from existence but also to himself as a participant in existence. The vision of man in Jerusalem is of a beast who has a peculiar intercourse not only among his own kind but also with God himself— God willing and man willing.

Chapter 6

An
Integrative View

BY MARTIN E. MARTY

The modern who views a city from the air is conscious of disintegration and sprawl. The approach to Los Angeles, seen by many to be the archetypal contemporary city, reveals it to be a plotless area, barely visible through polluting smog. It lacks a center; the roads do not converge on any point in particular. The roads themselves, great freeways, gouge their way through old and new communities. For their sake mountains have been built and leveled, neighborhoods disrupted, vistas obscured. Of course, the limits of the city are not defined; they merge into suburbs which themselves merge into more remote housing areas for scores and scores of miles until mountains, desert, or ocean absorbs them.

The visitor who is able to cope with the visible plotlessness of the post-industrial city will find psychic and spiritual corollaries as he becomes familiar with it on ground level. A wild pluralism characterizes the life of the inhabitants. They do not share common beliefs about ultimate matters, nor do they frequent the same shrines to pursue a religious quest. Indeed, they are under no obligation, external or internal, to be involved with any ritual or ceremony. True, a political order of sorts exists to help organize life, but it is perceived nebulously by citizens who are aware of a bewildering network of governmental forces. Many of them are in seeming competition with one another; federal, state, county, and city elements do not coordinate efforts in such a way that a citizen derives a sense of place from them.

Urban Ruins from the Past

The same modern man finds it possible to become familiar with what appears to be a dramatic contrast whenever he visits urban ruins from the primitive world. If he is not in a position to travel, he can do this visiting indirectly by studying drawings or photographs of the plans of primitive and very ancient cities. A new series, "Planning and Cities," makes possible such an armchair tour of cities of the past. *Village Planning in the Primitive World, Urban Planning in Pre-Columbian America, Cities and Planning in the Ancient Near East,* and even *Medieval Cities* present similar faces.[1]

The cities of the past, so well depicted in these four volumes, virtually seem to exemplify or realize the ancient hieroglyph for the city:

> In the earliest handwriting that we can read, hieroglyphic, the ideogram meaning "city" consists of a cross enclosed in a circle. The cross represents the convergence of roads which bring in and redistribute men, merchandise, and ideas. This convergence entails the quickening of communication which is nearly always a great advantage, but may become a handicap. . . . The circle, in the hieroglyph, indicates a moat or a wall. This need not be materially erected so long as it is morally present, to keep the citizens together, sheltered from the cold, wide world, conscious of belonging to a unique team, proud of being different from the open country and germane to one another. The wall, too, may become an obstacle if it is too high and tight, if it hinders further growth, above all if it frustrates the opportunity for exchanges beyond it.[2]

This ideogram represents the perfectly integrated city. All parts mesh, interlock, relate to one another. One surmises that residents would have had a sense of place and order which might free them to interpret the reality around them and to go about their daily business. Of course, what survives of such cities gives an impression of greater neatness and plan than must have been evident to inhabitants of the past. Foundations, walls, altars, and stony streets are more durable than are shacks, outhouses, jerry-built markets; they are more refined than are the locales of refuse, garbage, and filth which must have made life inside the walls of many a city unbearable.

Yet, given the context of possibilities of ages past, these sites seem to have offered a greater yield for psychic health than do the disintegrative, normless modern cities. The reader pages through the books: The volume on primitive cities shows the schema for a Dogon village in Mali, Africa, with all elements present plus a phallic "village altar" at the center (near a "stone for oil crushing," which represents female genitalia). Cheyenne camp circles on the western plains of the United States differ little, even if their tepees seem like insubstantial walls. An Omarakana village in the Kiriwana district, Trobriand Islands, New Guinea, looks as much like a literal rendering of the ideogram as does an Ambo *kraal* in South West Africa, or a Bororo village in south-central Brazil.

Pre-Columbian America reveals the same integrative riches: Xochimilco, Tenochtitlán, Tiahuanaco—the list of wall-crossroads-center (shrine) sites is endless. Westerners perhaps know best the ancient Near East, because it was the milieu for so much of the biblical drama that was mediated to them through religious instruction. Ur, Babylon, Nineveh, Thebes, Jerusalem, all present similar appearances. At their center are shrines and temples, burial grounds, and sacred hills.

Even as recently as in the medieval cities one comes across the blend of function and idea represented by the walls for protection, the streets for commerce, and—not only in the formal cathedral cities—the place of worship at or near the center or in strategic location. In some of the primitive cities and the cathedral sites it is believed that the urban plan received integration because it was formally designed on the model of presumed celestial cities, but one need not make too much of such an idea of prototype; indeed, in some instances the celestial prototype is manifestly absent:

> A Neo-Babylonian clay tablet in the British Museum shows an ideal map of the ancient world with the city of Babylon located in the center of the cosmos. Literary sources allude to celestial prototypes of Mesopotamian cities. But, surprisingly, no evidence has been found yet in the ancient Near East, unlike the Far East, of a city plan based on cosmic symbolism. Ezekiel's vision of the City of God (Ez. 48:30) implies such a concept, but it remains merely that—a utopian vision.[3]

No matter; whether designed to exemplify celestial archetypes or where the accidental result of functional interrelationships, the pre-industrial and pre-modern cities reveal a high degree of integration, no doubt in part because of an essential simplicity in the way of life of people.

Today the ideogram is only that, the hieroglyph is a romantic curiosity, the idea of a religious center or shrine giving meaning and integration to a walled-and-crossroaded city is only the dream of utopian planners and theologians. In the industrial city,

> Anent the religious sphere in industrial centers, its norms are generally permissive. Actors play divergent, and often contradictory, roles, and the new technology ensures a continuous cycle of change, all of which requires flexibility in the norms. Though elements of the traditional religion remain strong in some industrial cities, "secular religions" like science and nationalism are looming more significant.[4]

The presence of the accidental industrial city has not bred contentment with its plotlessness. Physically, it is ugly; psychically, it breeds crime, chaos, and anomie. The question that exercises urban humanists today is: What can be done about the post-industrial, pluralist city, and—as a corollary to that—is any inspiration or knowledge to be derived from the vision of integrated and integrative cities? Can one gain synoptic and synthetic views of community which can help people who have the technological means to build better cities physically?

The American Archetype for Community

Rather than meander through abstract cities in timeless, placeless dreams, I shall concentrate on three approaches to integration and disintegration in a specific past, that of North America, whose setting will presumably be most meaningful to most readers of this book. For the sake of space and memorability, it will be necessary to condense highly varied and complex historical elements into somewhat overly schematic forms. But from the outlines that then survive, it is possible to see something of the health and the limitations of the integrative symbols, visions, and designs in the life of a particular people.

In the beginning . . . the colonizers revealed numerous apparently conflicting intentions, so far as urban life in the Western Hemisphere was concerned. Some came to find community, seeking India or Cathay, expecting to find passages to shores where gleaming cities already existed, cities which had their own plot and purpose, plus goods to trade. Others came to conquer community; the dream of El Dorado lived also in North America; men were ready to exploit existing cities. But before long it became clear that such cities were not present, at least not on significant, permanent, or rewarding scales. So North American colonists had to build community. They did not come to be lonely frontiersmen, though a few of them were reduced to that by exigency or because of ostracism from early communities. They feared and despised lonely confrontation with nature, the aborigine, the unknown. They had an opportunity, in their errand into the wilderness, to build from new beginnings, to arrange their cities physically and, in a sense, psychically, to allow for order and freedom in balance.

What models did they have? The modern city did not exist in the early seventeenth century. There was, of course, some reminiscence of the one city of late-medieval England, London—though the colonists would not have dreamed of reproducing literally the complex and the sprawl of that early metropolis. A few may have known something of Lowlands cities like Antwerp or Amsterdam, and may have reproduced something of their slightly more integrative elements. But there were not enough satisfactory models from the recent past to be of help for their achievements.

Little can be reproduced from the colonists' urban planning. They did not build enough large cities; by the end of the colonial era, only about five centers could be called urban (20,000–30,000 population or more).[5] Legal secularization with its charter for pluralism did not come in to upset the concept of a single shrine for a century and a half. And secularization in the Durkheimian sense, implying a specialization and division of labor which found God and the priests to be superfluous to many ventures, was not yet present.

People working with remembered villages, a few late-medieval merchant cities, a rejected larger metropolitan center, much practical good sense, and an implicitly shared religious vision have left for us what have come to be regarded as archetypal American forms in the New England village of both national reality and folklore. Physical walls were rare, though New Amsterdam offered strategic possibilities for one for a time. Yet the edges of urban areas were ordinarily well defined by ocean, road, and defensible ranges of houses. In many New England locales people were not free to build beyond a certain point because they could not then be defended, nor could they contribute to defense. Just as there was a wall, so we come across the crossroads, converging on a village commons, a center for merchandise, a village meeting hall. And, as was the case with primitive pre-industrial cities, a sacral center was also built—the New England meeting-hall-and-church combination.

Such a reproduction of the integrative and ideogrammatic city was not always possible. Thus the ecology of Virginia, with its rivers and lowlands, necessitated the development of parishes a score of miles long and a mile wide; these are not the remembered or lauded plans. The New England village or town is normative for most who look back to colonial times. Whether or not this development was a conscious reproduction of a cosmic or celestial city would be hard to determine: The colonists more often spoke of "Zion" than of "the New Jerusalem," and neither image played a great part in planning. But the sacral center, even if it was deprived of much historic symbolism in the form of a lecture-and-meeting hall, was planned. "The colonization of New England, at all events, was on medieval urban lines, as that of Cavalier Virginia and Dutch New York was on an even older feudal pattern of a manorial economy." When Charlestown "threw off" Woburn, as Dedham gave birth to Medfield, and Cambridge to Belmont, each was "no mere scattering of houses, but a civil and religious community, with a central meeting house for religion and a local system of government." In the New World, "the medieval order renewed itself, as it were, by colonization."[6]

It must be remembered that the New England village was a mutation, a throwback, a vestige, and even a retrogression. European merchant cities had moved past what these new urban developers had done. Yet the modern city planner, suburban developer, or religious "church extension secretary," asked to sketch something of an ideal integrative community, will often find himself consciously modeling his work after certain elements of those early and presumably normative communities. Not that all people in those cities themselves accepted the design. Sumner Chilton Powell's history of the formation of a *Puritan Village*,[7] Sudbury, Massachusetts, is a chilling reenactment which shows how small was the interpreting or integrating oligarchy, how limited were its powers and appeals. The meetinghouse at Sudbury was built largely, despite the presence of a despised clergyman, in the face of great political hassles, and after much creative foot-dragging. Yet the result was once again a setting which looks like the wall-crossroads-shrine hieroglyph.

What I have been trying to suggest is that the American archetype for community—almost never realized after the beginnings—is an integrative town, with a single religious interpretive center at its heart. And this archetype was not a mere reproduction of living cities, but a regression, a reversion to medieval and dying patterns, an expression of a faith which was itself on the point of losing its monopolistic hold. A theorist of the era, the Puritan divine John Cotton, conceived of what has been called "the organismic" community.[8] In the mid-nineteenth century Ralph Waldo Emerson was still remembering something of the coziness of life in such communities—even though he neither could nor wanted to embrace their religious core. He reminisced about the ways John Calvin's God had seemed to pronounce perpetual benediction on the doings of his fellow townsmen, all of whom knew their place and found their lives interrelated and informed by the sacral integrating center and vision.

This utopian city, this town in the garden, drew, then, on wisdom and reality from the *past*; it was not oriented toward the future or able to sustain the present realities. The merchant, the trader, the sailor, if not yet the anticipator of the industrialist, all accidentally or consciously conspired to break up the order,[9] to lead to disintegration. None of these had the disintegrating potential of the religious dissenter—as in the case of Roger Williams versus John Cotton. The pre-industrial city's integration depended upon a religious uniformity that was not to survive either as a result of legal imposition or people's free choice. It remains a romantic vision, one which fragments whenever subjected to the tests of actual living in a complex world.

The Futuristic Model

Men did not, however, abandon the integrative dream; somehow they have needed ways to bring order and plot to their view of community and city. The second phase, then, drew its integrating and organismic vision not from past but from future, not from archetype but from eschatology, not from desire for regression to the medieval but from desire to overleap into promised future. If one cannot have a visible city which reproduces the organismic, he can promise a city of the future. He can rescue some brands from the burning, can evoke community of the elect inside the plotless city; he can promise new elites.

This is what happened in the early nineteenth century, when religion had been disestablished, church and state separated, and the voluntary principle born. People could now choose to be religious or to refuse to be so. The characteristic religious figure was no longer the shrine-keeper of the primitive world or the New England minister to whom at least in theory the whole community came for interpretation. Now it was the revivalist who found himself in competition with other revivalists. No longer could he assume that all people in specific communities were to share the same integrating vision; they obviously did not. The physical plans of the new western cities, those which Richard Wade has studied as frontier, merchant, but still largely pre-industrial centers,[10] may still have had downtown churches. But instead of a single meeting house, a number of churches in mild conflict with each other bid for the attention of select elements in the city. Some accidentally served better than others for integration—because of their size, the eloquence of a minister, the social status of the clientele, the strategy of their location, the choices of involvement. But this service, it must be stressed, was accidental; the community as such did not cohere because of their efforts. The new dynamism of the city was commercial, and random populations gathered.

Little wonder that the *future* served as a model, that the millennium was widely proclaimed, that a new Jerusalem and a new people of God were called for. How could one rescue or give plot to existing cities? By the 1840's the rural imagery was prevailing among "Millerites," who became Seventh-Day Adventists. They expected a celestial city to interrupt their rural and village life; they did not find the potential city in the current dispensation of history. The Mormons, or Latter-Day Saints, in the same period dealt with "imaginative projections," the dream of a Kingdom and a city; they found at great sacrifice personally that it was impossible to enact their themes in a pluralist environment and had to migrate to as yet unused space, as in Utah.

The futurist schemes had some practical effect in the towns of

Utah, but for the most part they have disappeared without a trace. The millennium did not begin to appear, the Second Coming did not occur, the futurists did not succeed in displacing or supplanting the pragmatic pluralists who coexisted in secularizing cities. New immigrants came on the scene, further to bring heterogeneity and conflict. The millennial vision was born of wild hopes or of despair for existing community; it had less impact on later interpretation than did the past-oriented, elitist, integrating visions of America's semimythical longer past.

Communitarian Experiments

One other approach to integration came from the American past, to endure into our own time. This was inspired by the *present*, by the promise of community in the here and now. This was the instant Utopia proffered by the Owenites, the Fourierists, the Saint-Simonians, the Rappites, and scores of other community builders of the 1830's and 1840's.[11] These were "heavens on earth," for which one need not wait, or at least not wait long. They were to be perfectly integrated organisms, cities-in-the-garden. Significantly, almost all of them were rural experiments, far removed from actual cities, signs of the abandonment of past cities. One can page through the histories of these communitarian experiments and see once again the dream of reenacting the meaning of the ideogram. Fourierist phalansteries (never realized), plans for Amana, Icaria, Oneida—all were full of order and symmetry. While many of these were heretical or even merely humanist in intention (in an age when such approaches were scandalous to the religious), the analogue to the sacral center was usually present in community buildings. There, through various kinds of meetings, all members of the community would be involved in specific acts of interpreting or receiving interpretation.

By the mid-nineteenth century most of these here-and-now integrative centers had disintegrated. The attempt to make whole communities into elites failed; most of the centers were impractical; tensions and quarrels broke out; the interpretive visions were soon seen to be untrue to reality in both ultimate and proximate senses. Yet, something of the Fourierist models has survived in many of the overly neat town plans of modern suburbia, with their promise of instant heaven on earth and their reality of expression that hell is portable.

I have tried to show that America, though it has lived much of its life in industrial times and though it has given the world religious pluralism in forms that have made spiritual integration difficult, has not lacked models for organismic community. Some of these have been drawn from past, some from future, some from present design orientations. In some senses, they survive because they come to mind at once whenever people wish to give expression to community: What is more logical than defining the limits of community (the wall)? How can one have community without concourse, intercourse, interaction (the crossroads)? How can one make sense of community without a center, formally sacral or at least serving for community-wide interpretation?

The Anomie of Existent Cities

A study of reform, whether by ecclesiastics or secular men, shows that more often than not Americans have reverted to these simple styles of community as being ideal. For some, only rural or village models can suffice if one is to speak of integration. These models may be unconscious; the ties between spirituality and natural community or nature itself are so deep in the history of religion that it is hard for some to conceive of urban sanctity—even if the world offers little future apart from urban life. For others, they are conscious: There must be sparsely populated or small communities if there is to be interpersonality and coherence. They must be simple: To most semi-Utopians, the increase in complexity minimizes the opportunities for integrating disparate and conflicting elements.

Most church men have used the ideogrammatic wall-crossroads-shrine picture. Just as millions of Americans each Christmas send cards depicting the New England village with its central church–meeting house as ideal; just as other millions recognize such community as being somehow more religious than others, as they design or enjoy magazine covers at sacral-sentimental times of the year, so have church planners gravitated to the simple models as if more integration is there possible. At any urban comity meeting after World War II, one could see a headlong dash for each

new suburb, where churches could not only pay for themselves
but where they were planned into village design. Church extension
leaders were more reluctant to work in the ghetto, where the
church had to be in storefronts, in off-center and obsolete buildings, or in temporary space, and where they obviously did not
tower over community. Even more shunned were the affluent high-
rise communities, which embodied the locales for loneliness,
alienation, secularization, and specialization—where churches and
community centers were obviously not central, were rarely planned
in, and, when incorporated, were rarely used.

Few noticed at first that the apparent integrating power of the
suburb or new community was soon to be lost, that disintegration
and anomie were present there, too. Matriarchies, dormitory centers, areas apart from where decision makers made their decisions,
churches could not interpret all of life: they had to be content
with certain crowded aspects of familial, leisure, or personal life.
The church could integrate the "spiritual" sectors of experience,
but not the whole of it; they could work on Sundays to the degree
that they were willing to abandon their sense of involvement in
common life on "the other six days." The attempt, then, to have
the churches serve as integrating centers was not successful in
either traditional or new communities. Little wonder, then, that
some resorted to eschatological and futurist language, to speak of
The New Creation as Metropolis or *The Secular City*.[12] Here were
future cities, secular, but interpreted with biblical symbols, which
would somehow begin to transcend the chaos and anomie of
existing cities.

Pluralism and the Existent Cities of Man

Secular reformers were also often theologians advocating the integrating vision. Paul Goodman envisioned the breakup of the
uncoordinated and dehumanizing university, to see it replaced by
village-model "free universities" where centers of coherence would
help produce interpersonality on a more profound scale. The
black-power reformers like Albert Cleage[13] use explicitly religious
symbols to advocate separate space, separate communities within
metropolis, separate peoples who would find integration around
sacred shrines like his Black Madonna church. They stand in a

tradition as old as Edward Bellamy, Josiah Strong, and other secular and religious promisers of community.

In every case, these Utopians need some sort of walls, to exclude the outsider and to define elites. They need crossroads for "participatory democracy." They imply an integrating center, which may be a formally religious shrine or it may be a locale where the writings of the great leader are discussed, where one is turned on, where he finds the *axis mundi*, or draws his signals.

One can easily see the power in these archetypal plans. It is difficult picturing integration without also some separation; coherence without definition and delimitation; movement of people without interpretation and calls for ultimate commitment and sacrifice. It is just as easy to see the weakness in them. Life is too complex to be reduced to the boundaries set by one or another of the religious groups or Utopian messiahs.

For that reason, many theologians have begun to do an about-face and to speak of pluralism as a fate to be welcomed. Integration must go on somehow inside existing cities of man. Thus the late Father John Courtney Murray: "Religious pluralism is against the will of God. But it is the human condition; it is written into the script of history. It will not somehow marvelously cease to trouble the City. Advisedly therefore one will cherish only modest expectations with regard to the solution of religious pluralism and civic unity. Utopianism is a Christian heresy (the ancient pagan looked backward, not forward, to the Golden Age); but it is a heresy nonetheless."[14]

Similarly, Paul Tillich revealed that, like Murray, he could be an activist in a complex city without resorting to the dream of coherence and perfect integration inside history: his vision stressed the ambiguity of history, the contradiction built into it, the impossibility of realizing Utopia, the rejection of a metaphysics of progress.[15]

The Theologian as Interpreter

The theologian, the church man, the preacher, is in the business of perceiving, interpreting, and—one hopes, in the best sense of the term—manipulating symbols. Inevitably he will be tempted to fulfill his calling by reducing the apparently random or haphazard and certainly conflicting signals people receive into coherent families of symbols. He may then very well grow into the habit of distorting reality by seeing the city in simpler terms than the realistic city is or can hope to be. This in itself may be naïve but not dangerous. It becomes dangerous only if the distorted view builds false hopes, encourages pretensions, stimulates crusades, leads to frustrations, results in dream worlds.

On the other hand, the integrating view is of some aid to the citizens of the disintegrating city. They move by response to symbolic leaders, to images and models, to those who propose a sense of direction. No one can confront all of reality without interpretation; people are fortunate if they have chosen interpreters well. The theologian, then, lives between two responsibilities: He must see enough coherence and integration to offer plot to people in the city of chaos; he must be faithful enough to the empirical city that he does not underestimate its threat or deny its promise.

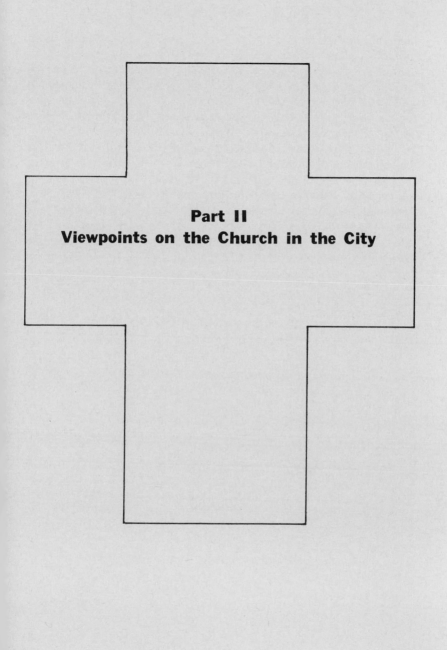

Part II
Viewpoints on the Church in the City

Chapter 7

The City and the Church:
Historical Interlockings

BY ROBERT T. HANDY

Christian churches of many traditions have existed in American cities ever since a few towns on the eastern seaboard grew large enough to claim the status of "city." Church history and urban history have had a continuous interrelationship through the centuries.[1] The story has been one with much movement, struggle, and turmoil as cities have mushroomed and congregations have faced crisis after crisis. The record has many accounts of churches, societies, and missions which served God and man with conspicuous achievement for many generations in the city—but there are also many indications of flight and failure.

Urban historians have not yet put much emphasis on the church in the city. The systematic study of urban history is relatively new; it is just over thirty-five years since Arthur M. Schlesinger, Sr., published his pioneering Rise of the City, 1878–1898. Nevertheless, it is a little disconcerting to find a recent book on urban historiography making no real reference to the churches.[2] Schlesinger himself was much concerned with the life of the churches in the changed environments of post-Civil War America; one of his most famous and oft-quoted articles discussed this in an arresting way.[3] American church historians for their part have traditionally devoted chief attention to such topics as revivalism, the frontier, religious freedom, church and state, and the denominations. It is time for urban historians to pay more attention to the churches and for church historians to focus more on the city; fortunately, there are signs that this is developing.[4]

How does it happen that after more than three centuries of continuous interlockings between Christian churches and American cities that many people are asking the question that gives this book its title, *Will the Church Lose the City?* How does it happen that, after a long history that has delivered thousands of existing urban congregations into the present, such a question is relevant? Though we rightly seek to answer it by considering as precisely as possible the present situation of the church and by assessing as carefully as we can its future prospects, some important perspectives on both the question and its answers can come from historical reflection on the church and the city.

Ingredients of American Protestantism

Even a cursory survey of the annals of American Christianity reveals that one of the reasons that city churches long have had difficulties is a stubborn tradition that religion is at home in the country but alien in the city, and that the patterns of the rural church are normative for the religious life. This attitude has been significant in both Protestant and Catholic history, but because for some three centuries the United States was generally considered to be predominantly a Protestant country, it is appropriate to deal first (and for the purposes of this chapter chiefly) with the very broad spectrum of Christian life that goes under the generic term "Protestant."

There is wide agreement that Protestant churches have *historically* tended to be more at home in rural and town America than in the America of the great cities. Especially in the formative decades of the early nineteenth century, the churches found the atmosphere of rural America congenial, and were significantly involved in and influenced by the culture of the time with its agrarian and individualistic motifs.

The reasons for this involvement are complex, but the broad outlines can be quickly stated. The latter part of the eighteenth century had been a time of serious troubles for the churches. Patterns of church life were in general negatively affected by the onslaughts of the Revolutionary War, by the elimination of some of the state establishments of religion and the weakening of others, and by the hostility of much Enlightenment thought to revealed religion. The forces of religion rallied and fought back, so that in the early nineteenth century a remarkable resurgence of religion was under way. The patterns of this religious renewal decisively shaped nineteenth-century Protestantism, and their pervasive influence persists in many areas of church life to this day.

As is well known, the remarkable religious resurgence of the early nineteenth century was borne largely by revivalism. The churches which most effectively utilized the techniques and theologies of the revival grew to be the giants, often quickly surpassing in size churches which clung to older catechetical methods. The resurgent churches took very seriously the challenge of the frontier; attention was often turned westward to the populations spilling across a vast continent. Home mission and church extension societies were formed to tame the barbarian West with the gospel. Those who led in this thrust of revivalistic Protestantism were committed to religious freedom and to the voluntary way in church advance. The revival significantly increased the pluralism of American Christianity, for in the emotional atmosphere of revivalism denominational splits occurred, while rich resources of land and people provided opportunities for indigenous bodies to form and grow. The pronounced individualism of American life was absorbed into the bloodstream of the revival.[5]

Because those who took part in this significant forward thrust of Protestantism in American life were arrayed in various denominations, and because they said so much about religious freedom, it has been easy to overlook their general adherence to a set of common assumptions and goals for American life. They strove to transform America into a fully Christian nation, building a network of voluntary societies in which the efforts of Christian individuals from many denominations could be blended together to reform the nation. They denied that they were going back on their professions of religious freedom; as they saw it, they were using the opportunities afforded by freedom to win the nation by persuasive means to their drive for a Christian (by which they meant a Protestant) America. They felt they could win America while keeping their denominational autonomies. The Methodists, for example, were not well known for their ecumenical spirit in those days, but in 1844 they could agree that "the spirit of the age seems to demand a friendly cooperation of all evangelical denominations in reforming the world."[6] The reforming zeal of evangelical Protestantism sought a civilization in which Christian morality and values would be taught and respected; the goal was a voluntary but nonetheless real new union of religion and culture. The evangelicals thought that they had given up the medieval ideal of Christendom or a formally Christian culture, because church had been separated from state; actually they had recast and restated the old Christendom ideal for the new situation.[7] Buoyed up by confident hopes in the coming of the millennium, they faced the future with glowing confidence.

The impact on the common life made by this Protestant resurgence was great indeed, and can be traced in many aspects of the society—education, morals, reform, politics. Winthrop S. Hudson has concluded that by the time of Lincoln, "the ideals, the convictions, the language, the customs, the institutions of society were so shot through with Christian premises that the culture itself nurtured and nourished the Christian faith."[8] In a country still largely rural and small-town—by the standard index, the country was only sixteen percent urbanized by 1860—the Protestant resurgence had brought about close affinities between churches and an essentially rural culture. The very achievement seemed to sanctify the association of Protestant values with agrarianism. Revivalistic Protestantism was intensely biblicistic, and the pastoral imagery of the Bible was familiar and meaningful to most Protestants. This tended to reinforce the agrarian leanings and values of the Protestant world. The survival power of these identifications has been high; a recent study of church life in the Midwest has found that "consciously or unconsciously, religion and agriculture are regarded as inseparably related."[9]

Pervasive Rural Orientations

In the latter part of the nineteenth century there came about that dynamic combination of factors which spurred the unprecedented growth of a number of vast metropolises and many smaller cities. It is difficult to disentangle these factors; industrialization, bureaucratization, immigration, and urbanization developed together and influenced one another. Many, probably most, evangelical Protestants, flushed with their triumph in pre-Civil War America, themselves largely middle-class and oriented to rural imagery and habits even though they might live in the city, regarded the burgeoning of great industrial cities with distaste, often with fear. As the streams of immigration began sharply to increase after 1880 and to originate more and more from Central and Southern Europe and hence to bring to the cities vast hordes of Catholics, Jews, Eastern Orthodox, and secularists, Protestant uneasiness about the city increased.

In his famous book of 1885, *Our Country*, Josiah Strong listed immigration as the first of the "seven perils" confronting the United States. He reported that the nation had been invaded by an army that was twice as vast as the estimated number of Goths and Vandals that had swept over Europe and had overwhelmed Rome centuries before. Among the immigrants were numbers of paupers, criminals, illiterates, drinkers, Roman Catholics and Mormons—Romanism, Mormonism, and intemperance were three more of the "perils." Among the throngs of city workers, so many of them immigrants, were increasing numbers attracted to socialism, Strong's fifth peril. The sixth was wealth, which was being conspicuously flaunted in the burgeoning cities; though some Protestants were learning to accept wealth and to praise a "Gospel of Wealth," others who were steeped in traditional rural, middle-class values were troubled by the lavish aspects of city life. The seventh peril was, of course, the city, pictured as a serious menace to our civilization. In the city most of the other perils were enhanced and focalized, as Strong saw it. Noting that while from 1790 to 1880 the whole population had increased twelvefold, he reported that the urban population in that time had increased eighty-six fold. The peril had to be overcome; Strong urged a new Protestant crusade.[10]

Many other Protestant books, sermons and conferences viewed with alarm the growth of great cities. Though of course there was a vast spectrum of Protestant thought and feeling, the deep-lying hostility to the city surfaced at many points. The increase in Roman Catholic strength, the decline of Sunday observance, and the free flow of liquor in urban centers challenged the goal of a Protestant America as it had been long envisioned. Not untypical of the reactions was this statement of the bishops of the Methodist Episcopal Church in 1900:

> The American city is a conglomerate of all races, nations, tongues, faiths, customs and political ideas; and by this fact, and that of an easily obtainable citizenship, it is the menace of the American State and Church. To penetrate this alien mass by an evangelical religion is as difficult as it is imperative. The question of the city has become the question of the race. How to reach the heart of the city and to change its life is, indeed, the question of questions.[11]

The city as a menace to be resisted and redirected into familiar Protestant patterns—this was the predominant understanding among Protestants at the turn of the century.

Such attitudes help us to understand why Protestants found urban religious work so hard to get hold of and so difficult. Joseph B. Clark in 1903 published a work in which he celebrated the triumphant march of home missions westward across America, but when he looked at the record for the cities, he was troubled. He wrote:

> The author makes no claim to prophetic gifts, but he *believes* that organized home missions will not always turn a deaf ear to the bitter cry of the city and pass by on the other side. The boast has been that for a hundred years it has followed the people; then it must seek them within the city gate. . . . The hostile forces that threaten the future of America are not just where they were in 1798, in the new settlements of the West. They camp today in solid city wards; they are intrenched behind miles of tenement blocks.[12]

Men with rural backgrounds and mentalities, however, had serious difficulty in conducting churches into which workingmen encamped in those city blocks could be drawn. Charles Stelzle, unusual among American ministers because he was "a son of the Bowery" who had himself been a workingman, frequently repeated the familiar assertion that the country supplied the church with practically all of her ministers. In one of his books he reported that in a particular conference of a hundred preachers, most with city charges, only two had been born and reared in the city. This partially accounted for the shortcomings of the work among the masses in the average city church, he believed, for "most of our city churches, even among the larger ones, are trying to meet town conditions by an elaborated country church programme."[13] There is evidence that the proportion of men of rural background in the Protestant ministry remains high—ten years ago Truman B. Douglass referred to a study in which a sampling of 1,709 ministerial students found that only thirty-six percent came from cities of more than 250,000 population. "Because of their rural and small-town origins," he concluded, "many ministers bring to their work in a city church a distaste for city ways—a distaste which is the more disabling because it is largely unconscious."[14]

The conviction that the piety and patterns of the rural church are normative for *all* church life has long persisted in Protestant history. The pioneer sociologist of religion in America, H. Paul Douglass, studied 1,044 city churches at the close of the first quarter of the twentieth century, after the churches had had considerable time to think through urban strategy. He found confirmed the hypothesis that "the city church is an evolved rural church."[15] His categorization of urban church types was based on the rural norm—the unadapted church, the slightly adapted church, the internally adapted church, the socially adapted church. Nearly sixty percent of the churches studied were found in the first two categories! The country mentality has long persisted in American Protestantism; many of the hymns, habits, and thought patterns carry the stamp of the "great" century of Protestant advance.

Important clues to widespread Protestant attitudes toward the city emerge from the study of the Prohibition movement. The Prohibition amendment, which went into effect in 1919, was largely supported by the Protestants in the electorate. Joseph R. Gusfield has presented and heavily documented the thesis that the rurally oriented, predominantly native, and Protestant elements in the nation were committed to a culture in which self-control, industriousness, and impulse renunciation were accepted and praised. As this way of life was threatened by the growth of cities with their vast immigrant populations, Prohibition was one way the challenged groups could demonstrate that their way was still the dominant, publicly recognized one. A Christian America, as they saw it, was a dry America. The victory of Prohibition came just at the time when the balance of the nation was shifting from rural to urban; it was a last stand for the old way. "The Eighteenth Amendment was the high point of the struggle to assert the public dominance of old middle-class values," wrote Gusfield. "It established the victory of Protestant over Catholic, rural over urban, tradition over modernity, the middle class over both the lower and the upper strata."[16]

Further evidence on this matter has been provided by James H. Timberlake. He has shown how the Anti-Saloon League, founded in 1895, drew its support primarily from church constituencies. As the fight for the Prohibition amendment reached its climax, it can be seen to a great extent as a conflict between country and city. "One reason for this," Timberlake said, "was the growing determination of the old-stock middle classes to clean up the cities and rid them of their vice, crime, poverty and corruption. Unless cleansed, they feared, the cities would undermine the foundations of American civilization and prevent any further progress toward uplift and reform."[17] The long fight for prohibition and its short-lived triumph revealed and intensified much of the underlying Protestant fear of and resistance to the city. Only slowly have many of these deeper attitudes been modified.

Despite the nostalgia for the country and the clinging to rural church patterns and programs as normative, of course twentieth-century churches in the city (and in the country too, as urban influences have become nationwide) have been deeply affected by the realities of metropolitan development. H. Paul Douglass went so far as to say that "it has remained for urbanization, both in its rural and in its city phase, to give the church the greatest inner revolution it has ever known."[18] Many churches were unable to cope with the changes, and disappeared. Others survived by moving, by following their largely middle-class populations as they moved, often first uptown and then out of town. The pervasive, often unrecognized rural norm was of a church of largely homogeneous people; churches so oriented often followed "their type of people" through several moves. The literature of the city church is full of discussions about the flight of congregations from changing downtown areas. Both the congregations that stayed and those that fled had in fact to make many adjustments to the changing setting, however much old norms persisted. One example is the shift in evangelistic practices; Dwight L. Moody was a conspicuous figure in the transition from frontier to urban revivalism, but after Moody many denominations came to prefer visitation evangelism to mass revivalism. The revolution in church financing from the old pew-rental system to the canvass-pledge-envelope system is another illustration.

The Social Gospel

The most important movement in Protestantism which attempted to deal with the growth of industrial cities was the social gospel. Most of the leaders in the forefront of that movement had had their social consciences awakened as they labored in urban environments—such men as Washington Gladden, Frank Mason North, Walter Rauschenbusch, Charles Stelzle, Josiah Strong, and Graham Taylor. The most fundamental concern of the social gospel was not the city itself, but it was the workingman and his right to organize and to secure better conditions of life and labor. The locus of this concern was most often the city, however, and social Christian leaders gave a lot of attention to the evils of city life and the ways to overcome them. A number of social gospel books focused specifically on the city, for example, Stelzle's *Christianity's Storm Centre: A Study of the Modern City* (1907), and Strong's *The Twentieth Century City* (1898) and *The Challenge of the City* (1907). Those inspired by the social gospel were often in the forefront of genuinely new developments to relate the churches to urban needs. They were especially active in the founding of church federations for social service, in planting social settlements in slum areas, and in building institutional churches. The latter with their large plants and many varied activities for those of all ages were open seven days a week; many theories and techniques for effective work in the cities were first tested and popularized there. Protestant attention to the city was greatly intensified by the social-gospel movement, and its heritage in this respect has been continued in the denominational and interdenominational departments of the urban church.

The social gospel, though it contributed significantly to the awakening of social conscience and to the understanding of industrial and urban problems within Protestantism, was still predominantly oriented to the patterns and hopes of nineteenth-century voluntary Christendom.[19] It strove to "Christianize" (read "Protestantize") immigrant masses and urban structures. Rauschenbusch's *Christianizing the Social Order* (1912) presented the outlines of the program at the peak of the movement's thrust. This "Christendom" perspective hindered the social gospel from recognizing the fact that in the metropolis the transition from the predominantly "Protestant" religious pluralism of the nineteenth century to the "radical" pluralism of the twentieth had already taken place. In the former type of pluralism, the main components were the evangelical denominations chiefly of British background; in the latter type the main components included other types of Protestants (such as Lutherans, emerging out of ethnic enclaves, and the Negro denominations), Roman Catholics, Eastern Orthodox, Jews, and secularists. The social gospel had not fully sensed the significance of the shift, and somehow hoped to overcome the radical pluralism and secularism of urban life. The decline of the social gospel after World War I was occasioned in part by the recognition that such hopes were unrealistic. But the social gospel did make some very important and lasting contributions to the church's confrontation of urban problems.

The Black Churches

The rural orientation of nineteenth-century Protestantism played an important role in one of the most important chapters of the story of church and city in America—a chapter not yet written except in bare outline. The black denominations were born in the northern cities in the early nineteenth century, but they burgeoned with great swiftness in the rural South in the period of Reconstruction. Not wanted in white churches or in white society, the Negroes poured into their own churches, the first public, community organizations they actually owned and controlled. The patterns of piety and of organization reflected much of the familiar patterns of revivalistic Protestantism in which the blacks had been nurtured in Christian faith. The majority of black Christians in America, then and now, were Baptists; Carter G. Woodson reported that in the late nineteenth century they ". . . used the same polity, the same literature, and sometimes the same national agencies as the white

Baptists."[20] Rural imagery and other-worldly outlooks characterized much of the life of southern Negro churches.

Then came a "double migration"—first a slow drift to the
southern cities, though until World War I ". . . about nine-tenths
of the Negroes were still in the South and about four-fifths of those
in the South lived in rural areas."[21] But the war with its need for
industrial workers precipitated the mass movement of blacks into
northern cities. Here the disintegrating forces of ghetto life played
havoc with the personal and family lives of the transplanted blacks
in a way that has become tragically familiar. As in the South, the
churches that were founded to serve the blacks in northern cities
were largely cut off from white church life and served as a refuge
from a hostile white world. A study of Chicago in the 1940's found
that the largest group of churches in the ghetto, the Baptist congregations, "have virtually no face-to-face relationships with any of
their white co-religionists."[22] Of necessity, these churches thought
of themselves as "race churches." Gerhard Lenski's more recent
study of church life in another northern city also found that
". . . the religious and secular activities of Protestants in Detroit
are highly segregated along racial lines. . . . In the realm of
primary-type relationships—intimate relations of kinship and
friendship—segregation tends to be the rule in the urban North
almost as much as the rural South."[23]

Though there are important continuities among black churches
North and South, some important differences soon appeared. In
the North, as E. Franklin Frazier saw it, in varying degrees ". . . the
Negro churches lost their predominantly other-worldly outlook and
began to focus attention upon the Negro's condition in this world."
As the older patterns of piety and morality began to erode, the
emergence of new sects and storefront churches often represented
". . . an attempt on the part of the migrants, especially from the
rural areas of the South, to re-establish a type of church in the
urban environment to which they were accustomed."[24] There were
also movements in quite different directions; some blacks repudiated their Protestant heritage to enter Roman Catholicism, others
to espouse a religion of black nationalism. The whole story of the
transition of black churches in less than a century from an over-
whelmingly rural Protestant environment to a predominantly urban
and secular setting, with all of the attendant strains, schisms, and

emergence of new movements, is one of the most important episodes in the histories of both cities and churches, and one now inviting much careful attention. Other churches which are today floundering in the urban environment may have a lot to learn from them about how to maintain the life of faith in a metropolitan environment, for clearly many black congregations have demonstrated a remarkable religious vitality and relevance. The possible union of black denominations with white if the plan of union of the Consultation on Church Union is accepted could open an exciting new chapter in American church history.

The "Smaller" Movements

There is space only to mention another important area in the historical interlocking of city and church—that of the "smaller" religious movements, often referred to as sects or cults.[25] Some of these bodies were largely rural in origin and apparently remain primarily so, while others have successfully made the transition to the urban environment.[26] Others show a fascinating compound of urban and rural motifs; Timothy L. Smith's analysis of one such small denomination would probably apply, *mutatis mutandis*, to others. He found that "neither the origin nor the subsequent history of the Church of the Nazarene can be understood without a knowledge of the two holiness traditions, urban and rural. The founders came from both."[27] Some of these smaller bodies arose in the urban setting and have made their major contributions there; such conspicuous but differing examples as the Salvation Army, the Christian Science churches, and some of the Negro sects come to mind. The number of the smaller religious movements has greatly increased over the last hundred years, again illustrating that one accompaniment of modern urbanization is increased religious pluralism. Some of these groups have filled needs that the major denominations have largely neglected; they have introduced methods that have been later appropriated by the larger churches. Small and largely isolated themselves, such groups have not been able to deal significantly with the larger world of urban problems. They do provide fruitful points of entry into the study of religious phenomena in the urban context.

Roman Catholic Experience

This chapter has been primarily concerned with the problems which the Protestant churches with their rural backgrounds have had to face historically in adjusting to the secular, radically pluralistic culture of modern cities. It often comes as a surprise to find that Roman Catholicism, too, has often looked toward the rural church and the agricultural life as normative for religion, even though by the dawn of the present century the Catholic church was by far the strongest urban church in the land. Yet many priests came from rural homes, and Catholic seminaries were often located in the country. One of the most eloquent spokesmen for the pastoral harmonies of rural culture was Bishop John Lancaster Spalding. "The farmer is the strongest and the healthiest member of the social body; he is also the most religious and the most moral," he wrote in 1880. "The children of farmers who carry into the cities fresh blood and new energy carry thither also a deeper religious faith and a greater moral earnestness." The farmer, he added, "is not a theorist and cannot give arguments for his faith, but the excellent good sense of which agriculture is the mother teaches him that it is good to believe in God and the soul; that infidelity is a miscreed, begotten of unwisdom."[28] Spalding was not blind to the attractions and opportunities of the city, but when he wrote of it he was especially aware of its evils, of its cruel pressures on individuals and families, and on educational and religious institutions.

There were many Catholics who felt similarly. Father (later Bishop) Francis Clement Kelley, founder of the Catholic Church Extension Society in 1905, felt in his early life that the "real America" was not the America of the great cities, but that which "feeds and sustains the other—the America of the small towns, villages and countryside."[29] The atmosphere within the church in the early twentieth century, especially after the suppression of Modernism, was much influenced by the general Catholic reaction to the French Revolution and its outcomes. There was considerable suspicion of movements which stressed liberalism and the independence of secular forces. Inasmuch as such movements often had their strength in the city, the urban impact was suspect. In the

1920's this mood was reinforced by the view, supported by reference to sociological theories then popular, that the city had a disintegrating effect on all aspects of moral and institutional life.[30] Even such a conspicuous advocate of social Christianity among Catholics as Monsignor John A. Ryan, for years head of the Social Action Department of the National Catholic Welfare Conference, many times "stated his conviction that farm life was more conducive to the development of Christian character than life in the city. In 1920, he wrote that cities larger than 150,000 were, 'on the whole, an evil rather than a blessing.' "[31] And Bishop Edwin V. O'Hara, founder of the National Catholic Rural Life Conference, "continued to regard rural life as normative."[32] Deep into the twentieth century, as Robert D. Cross sums it up, the hold of the rural norm was so strong that many church men still tended "to concentrate upon resisting the city's impact on the Church, instead of upon developing the Church's impact on the city."[33]

In fact, of course, the Catholic church was continuing to grow impressively in city and suburb, and by the time of Pope John XXIII and Vatican Council II many even among the conservatively oriented were modifying defensive stances against the secular city and against other churches. Once again, the possibility of a quite new chapter in the historical interlockings of city and church can be glimpsed.

Urbanization and Ecumenism

This introduces the final observation of this chapter—the impact of urbanization upon ecumenism. It has often been noticed that the effects of the rise of the metropolis on person and institutions are ambivalent: Some react one way, others another. The pluralizing effects of urbanization have been noted; there have also been important contributions toward Christian unity. Val B. Clear has pointed to the ecumenical outcomes of the urban impact on a holiness body of rural background and separatist inclinations:

> Urbanization brought an opportunity to observe the genuineness of person in other religious groups. Honest appraisal of the vitality of the faith and the validity of the works of their neighbors led ministers and laymen alike to revise their attitude toward those of the outgroup. . . .

Cooperation replaced combat. Pastors engaged in interdenominational programs of various kinds, congregations became members of councils of churches, and ministers joined ministerial associations. In the majority of cases, urban Churches of God are now well integrated in local interdenominational programs, with many ministers carrying major responsibilities.[34]

Many churches showed a similar trend to cooperation and ecumenicity. After an overall study of the many currents of Christian unity in twentieth-century America, Robert Lee concluded that "recent developments in American culture, such as population mobility, the mushrooming of suburbia, the trend toward organizational centralization, the rapidity of social change, and the rise of urbanization are among the social sources contributing to the drive toward church unity."[35] There are also religious and theological factors at work in the movements for Christian unity; many would cite them as more important than the social. But none can deny that the problems and challenges the city poses for religion have played an important part in ecumenical history.[36] As the ecumenical circle widens, and churches that have long been isolated from each other—Catholic, Protestant, Orthodox, Liberal, Jewish, black and white—learn to talk, think, and work together, the outlines of a brand-new volume on the interlockings of city and church may be before us. Accepting the radical pluralism and secular life of the modern city as opportunities rather than threats, the churches together may learn to work much more effectively in the urban setting for the glory of God and the good of man.

Chapter 8

The City from a Biblical Standpoint

BY WILLIAM KLASSEN

The biblical narrative begins in the garden and ends in the city. In the centuries that spanned the formulation of the first Hebrew traditions about creation and the writing of the Apocalypse, many different viewpoints about the city emerged. Many influences were at work in the sorting out of these various perspectives on the city.

The Old Testament

For the Old Testament James Muilenburg has given us an introductory study showing the central place which the city of Jerusalem had in the history of the Hebrew people and the major place it had in their eschatological expectations.[1] It had this central place because of the role it played in the early military conquests, the central place it had for cultic loyalty as seen by the presence of the ark there, the importance the person of David gave to it, and the importance attached to it as a place for festal gatherings. The temple hill achieved its prominence not by virtue of political strength but because of religious loyalty and tensions developed when the city absolutized itself as a political entity.

In reading the Old Testament, "one wonders whether the prophets do sufficient justice to the problems of political and economic power and responsibility with which the city is necessarily involved. On the other hand, they cannot be said to condemn the city as such; they are quick to give us a bill of particulars. The city becomes the instrument of exploitation and oppression. . . ."[2]

Muilenburg also notes that the great city (in the words of Lewis Mumford) "is the best organ of memory man has yet created, the best agent for discriminating and comparative evaluation, not merely because it spreads out so many goods for choosing, but especially because it creates minds of large range, capable of coping with them." The great city, Jerusalem, was such an organ of memory, containing the memories of past failures and constituting the focus of future expectations. Through it all it remained the center of festal gatherings for the celebration of joy.[3]

The New Testament

When we move from the Old Testament to the New we find a drastic shift at the very outset. At hand in the Jewish world were the hopes of a future Jerusalem, a heavenly creation which would be of God's own making and which would have some continuity with the present age but would be primarily of an other-worldly nature. Various ways were seen as leading to the realization of that hope. In the Qumran community it was firmly believed that by withdrawal from the wickedness of the temple and the great city, God's own city would be established. His community was being formed in the desert. It could not be shaken by any threat from the outside, and it would ultimately triumph over all its adversaries. This strategy of withdrawal was based in part on the wickedness of the priesthood and the degeneration of the cultus but also had within it some antiurban sentiments.

Philo internalized the idea and by means of allegory arrived at the conclusion that the city of God is really the soul of the wise man. Therefore the city of God is not to be sought in the beyond or within history. It is found in oneself. The dualism between God and world is thus maintained.

The New Testament church took a different approach. The locus of Christ's activity is the city; his disciples are likewise encouraged to do God's work in the cities. And yet there is no promotion of the city per se against the country. It seems that Jesus was interested in people. He was constantly with people; and the rural areas, the wilderness, the mountains, and the sea were places of refreshment and retreat for him. There is no withdrawal from human relationships in the message of the New Testament, and Jesus himself took his place within the urban structure of his time without any basic critique of it. God's activity was to be found within the structures of human life, and not a trace of asceticism is to be found in Jesus, nor is there any element of withdrawal in his approach.

The early church followed this approach. The center of the growth of the church as portrayed in Acts was the cities. Paul seems to have assumed that if he touched base in the cities he had proclaimed fully the gospel of Christ from Jerusalem to Illyricum (Rom. 15:19). No city was considered too difficult: Jerusalem, Antioch, Corinth, Ephesus, and Rome, all in turn become places where the "good news" was proclaimed, and all in turn became centers of Christian influence.

Max Weber is correct in asserting that early Christianity was an urban religion and that "its importance in any particular city was in direct proportion to the size of the urban community."[4] He goes even further to suggest that "It is highly unlikely that an organized congregational religion, such as early Christianity became, could have developed as it did apart from the community life of the city (notably in the sense found in the Occident). . . . What is more, the specific qualities of Christianity as an ethical religion of salvation and as personal piety found their real nurture in the urban environment; and it is there that they constantly set in motion new stimuli in contrast to the ritualistic, magical or formalistic re-interpretation favored by the dominant feudal powers."[5]

After the beginning of the Christian mission the theologians of the early church began to formulate their positions toward the city. The most specific attempts at this are made by the writer to the Hebrews and by the writer of the Apocalypse. We shall therefore devote our attention to their views of the city.

Before considering their view of the city we must remember that for these writers the altar and the marketplace were closely related. The people lived within the shadow of the temple, but the two institutions were closely related to each other. We must not therefore too sharply differentiate between the "spiritual" and the material or "this-worldly" dimensions of their language. Most likely they did not sharply distinguish between secular and religious institutions but rather looked at life from a holistic point of view. They definitely rejected any approach which placed God outside of the world which he had made. While God retained his independence, he also continued to be intimately involved in the affairs of the world. This is after all the crux of the incarnation— that God could become a part of a messy world, associate with messy people, and by such participation give men hope to live with new purpose and joy. Consequently William Baird fundamentally misrepresents the situation when he says "the problem of the Corinthian and the contemporary churches is how to live in the world in response to the God who stands outside it."[6]

It is a fundamental conviction of the early church that God was among them in Jesus Christ. The interplay between heaven and earth is hard for us to grasp, but unless we grasp it we miss a very important dimension of the New Testament message.

The Letter to the Hebrews

The theme of the epistle to the Hebrews is the pilgrimaging people of God. This theme is developed with reference to the place of Jesus Christ as the leader of that people and his superiority to all other leaders God has given to his people. It is developed also with reference to the continuity that the people of God have with the people, which came into being through the faith of Abraham. Genesis 2 describes the daring act of men who wished to build a tower reaching to the heavens, thereby securing their existence for perpetuity and making a name for themselves. Their effort was so puny that God had to go down and see it (11:5), but even this act of hubris failed, and the narrative forms then a fitting background for the story of Abraham, who built instead on faith and answered God's call to move (Gen. 12). He left his country, departed from his clan, and obeyed the call of God, not knowing where he was going. For the Israelites this separation from his roots became the foundation stone for their existence. As an early creed expressed it: "A wandering Aramean was my father" (Deut. 26:5). To trans- late that into modern language, we would say: "A homeless hippie was my father." The Israelite creed then stressed the rootlessness and detached character of Abraham their father. He built himself no enduring culture, no great city, or even a great palace, but dwelled instead in tents, staking all that he had and was on the promises of God. God's exodus people began with a refugee, a displaced person who saw in his uprootedness a call from God.[7]

The writer to the Hebrews explains: "For Abraham was waiting for the city which God has designed and built, the city with permanent foundations" (11:10). And Abraham began a people who, like him, were rootless, keeping their eyes on the goal toward which they were moving, they "admitted openly that they were foreigners and refugees on earth" (11:13). They kept looking for a country of their own, they did not keep looking back but kept looking forward, longing for a better country, the heavenly country, "and so God is not ashamed to have them call him their God, for he has prepared a city for them" (11:16).

Those who would argue that the church has a hard time today because people are mobile and do not set down roots in a community would do well to ponder this fact. The people of God came into being when Abraham moved. The essence of the church is to grow, to change, to adapt. Mobility is not what is destroying the church today; rather it is the apparent inability of the church to take seriously the fact that it is a pilgrim people, committed to move. The structures of the church and many of its patterns of life are committed to stability. It builds cathedrals and not tents. It builds its own towers desiring to reach up to heaven and does not strike out in new directions looking for the city which has foundations.

And where is that community with sure foundations to be found? Again the epistle to the Hebrews clearly indicates that it is found wherever the people of God meet in serious assembly. A difficult, and in some ways obscure, passage, Hebrews 12:22–29, forms the high point of his argument. Indeed, what follows after that may not even belong to the sermon proper, but in any case is not a part of the essential argument of the book. What, then, does he say at the end of his homily?

After having told his readers that they do not approach Mount Sinai as did their forefathers, he tells them positively what the center of their life is. The usage of his terminology should not confuse us. Nor should we dismiss it as useless typology, for what he says is of profound significance for the church and its convocations today. Schematically he says:

You have come:
to Mount Zion

to the city of the living God
  the heavenly Jerusalem
  with thousands of angels
to the joyful gathering of God's sons
to God, the Judge of all men
to the spirits of just men made perfect
to Jesus, who arranged the new covenant
to the sprinkled blood that tells of better things than Abel's blood.

When we analyze the first group of these categories, we are immediately struck by the prominence which political categories have here. Just as Jesus did not shy away from the use of political categories (kingdom, loyalty), so Hebrews, along with Paul and other New Testament sources, sees the Christian commitment and loyalty in clearly political terms. Let us not summarily spiritualize these categories and thus eviscerate them. For Hebrews the assembled believers constitute a political entity—they are a city in which the living God dwells, which in fact he has constituted. It has continuity with the past (Mount Zion) and looks forward to the future (the heavenly Jerusalem), and the presence of angels indicates that God is directly involved in its present meeting. But above all it is a joyful gathering of God's own people right now, confident of their ownership by God (names written in heaven), even in spite of the persecutions that have already come and those which still threaten.

In the concrete assembly of believers, God is present. Nothing so permeated the conviction of the early church as this: When they gathered, God was present. Whether or not it goes back to a saying of Jesus can be disputed, but Matthew mirrors the conviction for his group that Jesus will be present wherever the sins of a fellow believer are taken seriously and where the forgiving action of the church is taken (18:15 ff.). Paul also saw clearly that when Christian worship is conducted rightly, with an equal concern for mutual edification and for the outsider, then God is really among the believers (I Cor. 14:25).

What separates us from the New Testament writers is the way in which they intermingle religious and secular categories. They can speak of the church as a city without any embarrassment, and we should not move too readily to assume that what is involved here is a typology foreign to the modern mind.[8]

What is important for us in a study of this material is not only
the ties which Hebrews seeks to establish with the Old Covenant
but also the way in which we see our own continuity with that
people. For when Hebrews intermingles the divine and the human,
when he interdigitates the transcendent with the immanent, the
earthly and the heavenly, he is really saying that the incarnation
has made all such categories obsolete.[9] For when the assembly
meets, God is present, Christ is present, speaking words of forgive-
ness and grace in contrast to the words of vengeance spoken by
the blood of Abel.

From this he draws the conclusion that we as listeners to God
speaking within our assembly have an ever greater obligation to
receive what he says. Although he describes him as speaking from
heaven, again the spatial category is not primary but secondary.
The main thing is that God is speaking, and in reinforcing his
point he refers to the prophecy of Haggai, who lived in a time when
a temple was being built, but which had to be built in the awareness of a great shaking that was about to come. A shakedown is
coming, he says, which will involve not only the earth but also
heaven, and all that has been created by human hands will be
destroyed. All that will remain is that which cannot be shaken.
What is that? The kingdom (the political community known as
the church), which we are in the process of receiving.

In this reference to an unshakable kingdom, the author is picking up an idea often found in Hebrew literature. How does one
build so that the foundations of the community will not be shaken?
Isaiah, writing in the period of the Assyrian threat, castigated his
contemporaries who sought their security in their wine (28:1–13)
or in their political alliances (28:14–16). Alongside all that
others were doing, God was laying a cornerstone and building a
community in which justice was the plumbline (28:17). He who
has faith in this activity of Jahweh will not be shaken (28:16). At
Qumran this verse from Isaiah was read as referring to the community which they were building, and their towers for self-defense
were seen as means whereby they would secure their community.
The early church, however, saw Isaiah's pronouncement as supporting their insistence that men who place their faith in God
have a security not obtainable through any other way (Rom. 10:
11, I Pet. 2). Nevertheless, they did not individualize this faith, for

the men who believed formed a community. This community aspect gave the early Christian witness strong inroads into the urban centers of its time, for men were looking for community. The breakup of the city-state and twin themes of cosmopolitanism and individualism which characterized the Hellenistic age gave birth to the growth of many guilds and societies in which men could achieve their identity and find themselves, their fellow men, and a god who would see them through the difficulties of life.[10] Christianity survived over its contemporaries because of its political dynamic, for Christianity threw its liturgical symbols into the violent process of translation, and its social dynamic became political. In other words, Christian faith stressed more the importance of change than it did the security of the past. It could be argued that even the verse from Hebrews 13:8, "Jesus Christ is the same yesterday, and today, and for ever," does not necessarily imply that he never changes but rather indicates that he will always be what he was yesterday, namely an agent of change. Therefore the church finds its security in its relationship to Jesus Christ, the greatest agent of change the world has ever known. The foundation that cannot be shaken is not the social structure in which the church lives, but the relation that it has to Jesus Christ. Any church that sees itself in this context and finds continuity with the people who gathered around Mount Sinai, and those who met in house churches in the Roman Empire, will find that its mission will inevitably give it pertinence and relevance to the urban situation today.

The Community of the Future

The book of Revelation also has much to say on the theme of the city. It is firmly rooted in its culture and addresses itself to the problem of a church under persecution. The churches to which it is addressed live where Satan dwells (Rev. 2:13) and have experienced bloodbaths. The writer aims to instill hope in them for faithful living in their day and to give them a perspective on the future. This is, however, no sentimental consolation gift provided for those destined to lose the battle. No theme is so prominent in the book as the theme of victory, and there is every indication that even in this book the tension is maintained between earthly and heavenly

—which would clearly mean that we cannot assume that he projects victory into the beyond.[11] He also clearly sees a degree of continuity between the city of men and the city of God, for he does not see one age as following upon another. Rather he sees the events of one age as sharing in the character of another age and believes that eventually there will be a new heaven and a new earth. Both the old heaven and the old earth have within them the seeds of their own obsolescence. The fact that even the old heaven will be destroyed indicates that this author too does not think in terms of the earthly as heading for destruction while the eternal order remains secure. All that opposes the purpose of God will ultimately perish. One may call this "triumphalism" if one desires, but it surely is not a naïve optimism. For the "great city" is the scene of the church's witness, and the Lamb's triumph must be won there by the faithfulness of her witness. Unless the church remains constant in its devotion to the Lamb and his commitment to nonviolent change, God's purposes will never be realized in history.[12] To the one who conquers is promised a prominent place in God's own temple, and he will be inscribed with God's own name and the name of the city of God, "the New Jerusalem which comes down from God out of heaven" (Rev. 3:12).

There is a constant battle in history between the city which God is seeking to build and the city which is built upon the waters (Rev. 17). Both strive to obtain the allegiance of men, but the union of economic and political forces eventually brings about the ruin of the great city, and every effort to save her fails. For the judgments of water pollution (8:9), air pollution (8:12), of poverty and famine in the midst of affluence (6:6) all do not bring her to repentance—which seems to have been the main goal of these events of history (Rev. 9:20–21).

Babylon the great city is thrown down with violence (Rev. 18:21), and with that the deck is cleared for the coming of the new city. This holy city, the new Jerusalem, is the bride, 'the wife of the Lamb. It is clear that the seer is here speaking of the church, and yet how startling that he should use the imagery of the city.

What is he trying to tell us? Surely that the political metaphysic of the city is important in that which God is trying to do in history.[13] What a strange city it is! All the values of life are inverted, and the most precious metals are commonplace. Although he describes the wall as "great and high" (21:12), it is really very puny by comparison with the height of the city (fifteen hundred miles). Even making some allowances for the size of an angelic cubit (21:19), at most the wall would be two hundred fifty feet high. To make it even more absurd, the gates of the city are never shut, and with all those valuable jewels, protection would seem to be in order! But the strength of the city is its purity and the presence of the Lamb, whose example of overcoming evil through suffering runs throughout the book. Far from abdicating the question of political control, the throne is at the center of the city with (for the first time in the book of Revelation) the throne of God and of the Lamb brought together (22:1). Issuing from this city, coming from the throne, is a stream of healing for the nations (22:2), and the kings of the earth shall bring their glory into it (21:24).

One of the reasons the city exists in history has now been overcome. No longer do men need to protect themselves with walls or by doubling the police force. For the strength of community is now so great and the presence of the Lamb so pervasive that no protection is any longer needed. All the benefits of this society are equally open to all.

Far from projecting this kind of hope into the beyond, the church felt that in its very existence the foundations for this city were being laid. Were not the twelve apostles the foundation (Rev. 21:14)? Driven by this conviction, the early church lived its life, and this same conviction can control our attitude toward the city. The biblical material gives us no ground to glorify the secular city as the goal of God's purpose in history.[14] Rather, what the church stands for can best be achieved in the city. It is easier to build the church in the city, because the essence of the church is caring relationships that are not defined by blood, race, or cultural ties. It is easier to be the church in the city, because no false bases for community exist there.

The fact that the church has given priority to the city in the centuries when it made the greatest advances should indicate to our generation that we must also follow that route. We are in a position to develop a different alternative than that pursued in previous generations. During the first few centuries, Christians, whether by choice or necessity, withheld themselves to a large extent from public life. Then, during the Reformation attempts were made to unite public domain and the church in such a way that the interests of both could be served. This experiment ended in disaster at many places, and where it met with limited success, as in Calvin's Geneva, it sacrificed the right of dissent.

Today, with our conviction that the Gospel is social as well as personal, that Christians are on the side of the oppressed and in favor of change, there is renewed reason for Christians to confront the problems of the city with the joyful courage that has always been a hallmark of God's people. Here the community of God's people can be built, here the structure of power can be challenged and redeemed, and here the triumph of God's justice (Matt. 12:20), for which Jesus gave his life, can be accomplished. This can come about as we recapture a theology of purpose and the conviction that God is in Christ now renewing all things, including the structures of man's existence, the city. Once we have seen the city as a part of God's gift to man and embrace it without fear, such communities of commitment will arise—indeed, they have already arisen—and in them we see indications that the church will not lose the city, for the Lord of the church, who wept over his favorite city, still watches over every city, not because the city with its mass of steel and concrete is a special object of his love, but because every man who lives and dwells within the city—be he mayor, councilman, subway operator, slum landlord, prostitute, dope pusher, gangster, clergyman, or social worker—all are objects of his love and capable of redemption by him. For all of them the community life of the church is available, and as that community life is established, the other levels of urban life fall into perspective.

Chapter 9

The Churches and the Challenges of Poverty

BY LYLE E. SCHALLER

"Perhaps it's time for the poor people in the inner city to pick up their belongings and go out and squat on some of the vacant land in suburbia. We can't seem to get any decent housing for poor people built in the inner city. Maybe what we need is to see about a dozen Resurrection Cities spring up in the suburbs all around the city. This might help break the stalemate." The speaker was a $25,000 a year, middle-aged, white professional in the housing industry, and he was addressing a church-sponsored conference called to focus attention on the issues of poverty, community planning, and housing.

"No wonder this country is in the mess it's in," was the whispered response of a locally well-known Presbyterian layman to the Methodist minister sitting next to him. "When presumably responsible leaders such as this fellow talk like that, is it any wonder that we're on the road to anarchy?"

This episode points up several of the problems confronting the churches as they seek to respond to the challenge of poverty in an affluent American society.

First, what was it that touched off the negative reaction in this Presbyterian layman? Was it an image of poor people erecting plywood shanties in the park across the street from his $45,000 home in the wealthy suburban neighborhood in which he lived? Or was it an image of black people invading an all-white suburban neighborhood? Or was it the advocacy of the further spread of deviant behavior across geographical, social, and economic lines by a person with whom he had thought he could identify in educational, income, and religious terms?

In nearly every city in the United States these three concerns—race relations, poverty, and the spread of deviant behavior—are inextricably woven together. The church man who is concerned with one cannot ignore the other two.

A second important consideration highlighted by this episode is the geographical concentration of the urban poor in the inner city. In nearly every metropolitan area in the nation the poor are concentrated in the older sections of the central city, while the middle- and upper-income families reside in the newer housing in the outlying sections of the urban regions, where also are found the new schools, the new retail shopping facilities, and the greatest amount of open space.

Detailed statistical data for such an analysis will not be available until 1971, but it appears that the residential segregation of the urban population along racial lines is decreasing, while the residential segregation along income lines is increasing. In 1950 in the nation's two hundred and twelve standard metropolitan statistical areas the median family income in the central city was ninety-six percent of the median family income in the suburbs; in 1960 it was down to eighty-three percent, and in 1970 it may be as low as sixty-five or seventy percent. In dozens of metropolitan areas the proportion of residents in the central city who receive some form of public assistance or who are below the "poverty line" in terms of income is three to ten times the proportion found in suburbia. Unless this pattern is sharply altered—and Christian opinion can be one of the most important forces in helping to reverse it—the churches will default on a remarkable opportunity for ministry and witnesses.

A third point illustrated by this conference is that there is a wide difference of opinion among church men on how the nation should respond to the problems created by an unequal distribution of resources, wealth, and income. At this particular conference about two-thirds of those present applauded the remarks of this speaker, although with varying degrees of enthusiasm, while another one-third were conspicuously quiet. The existence of this diversity of opinion must be recognized by those who think of the churches as natural allies in the "war on poverty."

A fourth point lifted up by this opening illustration is that the churches are not newcomers to this struggle. Any evaluation of the churches' involvement in the current struggle to eliminate poverty should recognize that unlike government, the universities, and business, the Christian churches have expressed great interest in the subject of poverty for centuries.

Two Traditional Expressions of Concern

Two expressions of this interest have relevance here. On the one hand, for over nineteen centuries Christians have been actively involved in dealing with the plight of the poor and the blight of poverty. In the early church, deacons were selected to minister to human needs. Soon the churches were expressing their compassion through the "seven corporal works of Christian mercy"—feed the hungry, clothe the naked, shelter the homeless, care for the orphan, tend the sick, visit the prisoner, and bury the dead. The establishment of church-sponsored hospitals, homes for the poor, and orphanages were among the most highly visible evidences of this concern by the churches.

Within the past century in this country the churches were there to educate the freed slaves in the South, to respond to the plea in Lincoln's second inaugural address, ". . . to care for him who shall have borne the battle and for his widow and orphan," to help the poverty-stricken immigrants from Europe in the cities of the North, to assist the victims of the dust bowl in the Midwest, and to aid the American Indian in the West. Several years before Michael Harrington wrote *The Other America*, and nearly a decade before the Economic Opportunity Act of 1964 became legislation, the churches were focusing attention on the "pockets of poverty" scattered across America.

In addition to these and many other domestic ventures, the churches also have been actively engaged in a continuing war on poverty on other continents. Much of the overseas missionary activity of the Methodists, the Presbyterians, Lutherans, and other mainline American Protestant denominations has been directed toward raising the educational level of the people, eliminating hunger, treating the sick and the injured, eradicating disease, improving the productivity of agriculture, and in other ways reducing the impact of poverty.

In nearly all of these ventures, both domestic and overseas, the efforts of the churches have been concentrated largely on treating the results of poverty and on working toward the elimination of some of the more obvious and less controversial causes of poverty.

A second historic expression of interest by Christians in this subject has been to exalt the state of poverty. Throughout the Judeo-Christian tradition the poor have been metaphorically linked with the humble and the meek. By honoring the poor one honored God. In the Beatitudes poverty is depicted as a much less precarious state than wealth. When the rich young ruler came to Jesus inquiring about eternal life, he was confronted with the demand that he become poor. The Qumran sect of primitive Christianity apparently practiced voluntary poverty. In many of the orders in Christianity a vow of poverty has been a condition for entrance. Martin Luther praised poverty indirectly by noting that "rich folks' children seldom turn out well." For centuries it was assumed that the man who entered the full-time professional ministry in the United States was electing a path of poverty for himself and his family; and for thousands this was and is still the case. In 1968, for example, a survey of the salaries received by fifty *full-time* Negro clergymen in Cleveland revealed that forty-one of them were below the "poverty line" as defined by the Social Security Administration.

In recent years the attitudes of the churches in both of these areas of concern have changed. Less dramatic, but longer in duration and greater in scope, has been the move away from the traditional exaltation of the state of poverty.

While still articulated by many Christian pietists, it seldom is intentionally practiced by either the clergy or the laity. For the person entering a religious order in an affluent nation such as the United States in the twentieth century, the vow of poverty no longer is comparable to a vow of chastity or a vow of obedience. The *white* graduate of a Protestant seminary who is ordained and enters the pastoral ministry probably will find that his total remuneration is as large as, and often may exceed, that of his high-school friend or college classmate who has had two or three years of post-graduate professional training for a career in the law, social work, teaching, public administration, or some other person-oriented field of endeavor. Likewise in most of the larger predominantly white denominations the combination of the denominational pension system and the mandatory requirements of Social Security are greatly reducing the chances that a pastor will spend his retirement years in poverty. Literally dozens of surveys and studies of the vocational migration of ministers reveal that the dominant pattern is from the denomination that is relatively low on the socioeconomic scale to the denomination that ranks higher on such a scale. The institutional church in America apparently does not regard poverty as a basic requirement for the vocation of clergyman.

This same pattern has been prevalent for an even longer period in the relationship between the institutional church and the layman. This can be illustrated by the spread of the "Puritan ethic"; in the influence of the wealthy layman in the decision-making processes of both the congregation and the denomination; in the location and scheduling of denominational, and especially of interdenominational and ecumenical, meetings in a manner that tends to bar the participation of any layman with less than an upper-middle level of income; in the naming of Protestant churches and seminaries (especially in the nineteenth century); in the allocation of funds in denominational budgets and in the geographical location of the new churches organized during the new-church-development boom of the 1950–1965 era.

For at least two centuries the trend in American Protestantism has been away from an exaltation of poverty and toward an acceptance of the power and pleasures that are inherent in wealth.

During the past two decades there have been a few minor countertrends within this general pattern. Three merit mention here. One was the glamorization of "inner-city" ministries that began in the 1950's. In many respects this resembled the surge of interest in foreign missions that spread across American Protestantism in the nineteenth century. The second was the picking up of the civil-rights issue by white liberal churchmen in the late 1950's and early 1960's. The third was the widespread effort that dates back to about 1965 to secure representation from the "poverty community" on various ecclesiastical boards and committees. The motives for this effort were mixed and ranged from tokenism and a desire to be "in" on the latest fad, at one end, to the surprised discovery and sincere acceptance of the idea that the poor might have some unique insights to contribute to the churches' mobilization for the war on poverty.

While each of these three countertrends is important, it certainly would be premature and probably would be misleading to suggest they represent either a return to an exaltation of poverty or a shift from paternalism to participation. In examining what the churches are doing today and the implications of these actions for tomorrow, it should be remembered that this is occurring within a frame of reference in which the churches have been and are exalting wealth, not poverty, and within a tradition in which the primary emphasis for centuries has been on helping the victims of poverty rather than on changing the conditions that perpetuated poverty.

From Social Welfare to Social Change

Without question the most important element in the churches' contemporary response to the challenge of poverty has been the shift from an emphasis on social welfare and direct services to a new focus on social change.

This shift in emphasis has taken place in a comparatively brief period of time. It has been initiated and implemented by a very small minority within the churches. It runs counter to the centuries of tradition of helping the poor by providing services *for* people. It abandons both the historic exaltation of poverty and the more recent actual exaltation of wealth in favor of an exaltation of the right of self-determination. This shift in emphasis from social welfare to social change is susceptible to widespread misunderstanding in an era when the rising demand for the right of self-determination and the struggle for racial justice are often confused in the mind of the general public with an increase in deviant behavior and with a sharp rise in the number of persons receiving some form of public assistance. Perhaps most significant of all, this change is occurring when there is nothing approaching a consensus among church members as to what type of changes are desirable— or even whether promoting any change in the status quo is an appropriate function for the churches.

To a very substantial degree the impetus behind this shift in emphasis came from developments outside the churches—the most significant being the growing alarm in the late 1950's over the rise of deviant behavior among juveniles; an increasing awareness of the economic, political, and social conditions underlying the plight of the Negro; and, subsequently, the drafting and administration of the Economic Opportunity Act of 1964.

The Evolution of the War on Poverty

In the late 1950's and early 1960's there emerged the belief among a few executives in the Ford Foundation and several upper-middle-level bureaucrats in Washington that one way to cope with the growing problem of juvenile delinquency was to build a program around a "community-action" component that would channel the sense of helplessness and despair of inner-city youth into a constructive expression of self-identification, self-determination, and self-expression. This concept was the central element in the development of "community action for youth" programs that came into existence with a combination of federal, local, and foundation financing in sixteen cities across the country in 1961. It is especially significant to note here that Attorney General Robert F. Kennedy was greatly intrigued by this concept.

This basic concept, which several federal officials urged should be *the* central element in any national antipoverty program, actually became only one of several titles in the package that came before the Congress.

Like many other bills, the final draft of the Economic Opportunity Act of 1964 actually became an amalgam of several programs and proposals with "something for everyone" in the package. As a result, the original legislation provided people in the local communities with two very interesting possibilities. One alternative was to look at that part of the package which really was built around the traditional social-welfare concept of direct services to the poor. This included the popular Head Start program, the Job Corps, and various other training programs for women and young people.

The second alternative was to focus on social change. Title II of the Act departed from the tradition of federal grant programs by allowing the local community the alternative of setting up a private nonprofit agency to administer the community-action program. It was this part of the Act that included the famous phrase calling for "the maximum feasible participation of residents of the areas and members of the groups served." This later was incorrectly abbreviated by many to simply "maximum feasible participation of the poor."

To its originators, and to a rapidly growing number of people in cities all across the nation, the community-action program was a radical new concept which would enable the poverty-stricken to throw off the shackles of apathy, racism, and despair by gaining a meaningful degree of control over their own destiny. Three out of four of the first five hundred and thirteen community-action agencies organized under this legislation were private nonprofit agencies, and one-fourth of the members of the governing boards were drawn from the ranks of the poor.

To many of the existing local leaders this concept had the potential of producing undesirable conflict, competition for patronage, and a possible redistribution of power. One way to defuse this bomb was to interpret the purpose of the community-action concept as simply a new method of coordinating the resources and goals of local public officials with those of the leaders from the private voluntary agencies and of representatives from the "poverty community." This interpretation usually gained at least the partial approval of officials in the Office of Economic Opportunity in Washington and eventually was officially accepted by the federal government.

During the next four years the original concept of community action as a means of getting at the root causes of poverty gradually was abandoned, a new thrust in finding jobs and providing job-training opportunities for the adult male was added, and a substantial amount of the financial resources were directed to summer programs for Negro youth in the hope that this would help counter the rapid increase in urban violence during the "long, hot summers."

It is but a slight oversimplification to say that five years after the President called "for a national war on poverty," the emphasis had regressed from the earlier one of stimulating and encouraging social change back to a concentration on direct services and to reducing deviant behavior among young urban males.

The Response of the Churches

While there are exceptions to any generalization, the response of the churches to the ideas and programs embodied in the Economic Act of 1964 was just the reverse of that of most governmental and secular voluntary agencies.

At first the overwhelming response of the churches was to enlarge and extend their programs of direct services. Parishes, denominational agencies, and interchurch groups took advantage of this source of funds to launch Head Start programs and day-care centers, to expand their work with migrants, and to provide new employment opportunities for ghetto youth.

As the months passed, as the community-action program bogged down, and as the difficulties of achieving the goal of "maximum feasible participation" became more apparent, the attitude of church leaders involved in antipoverty programs changed.

Gradually the emphasis on direct services decreased and the churches began to allocate more of their own resources, especially manpower, to self-improvement programs. Some, such as the retraining programs initiated by Leon Sullivan in Philadelphia, gained widespread favorable publicity and were copied in dozens of cities. Others, such as the Delta Ministry in Mississippi, were far more controversial and attracted much less support.

Many different efforts to enable the poor to help themselves were initiated and supported by the churches. Some, such as many of the church-sponsored housing ventures, tended to be low on actual involvement of the poor in the decision-making process and also frequently did little to help the poorest of the poor. Others were geared to gain "a voice for the voiceless and power for the powerless." These included a wide array of efforts in community organization, in gaining meaningful representation for the poor on the local antipoverty board, in supporting the demands of young Negro males, and in organizing welfare mothers.

By 1967 and 1968 many church leaders were beginning to support the concept of black power, black capitalism, and black control of businesses in the ghetto. Operation Breadbasket, under the leadership of Martin Luther King, Jr., and Jesse Jackson, was an outstanding effort in this respect which gained widespread support among white church men.

Increasingly the national boards of home missions of the larger white denominations began to give first priority to those proposals which were geared to accelerating the pace of social change. The traditional programs built around direct services were relegated to a lower priority, which often meant they were not funded at all. In several denominations comparatively large sums that had been appropriated to support or extend the work of the parish ministry were reallocated to new ventures in supporting social change. Major national fund-raising drives were undertaken in the United Methodist Church, the Lutheran Church in America, the Christian Church (Disciples of Christ), and other denominations to mobilize the resources necessary for an enlargement of this effort.

In addition to a change of emphasis from social welfare to social change and the resultant reallocation of resources, church leaders also began to show a new interest in the philosophical and economic aspects of the problem of poverty. Robert Lampman has pointed out that the United States has used four different strategies in meeting the needs of the poor and reducing poverty. He listed: make the system work; adapt the system to the needs of the poor; adapt the poor to the system; relieve the distress of the poor. As church leaders became more interested in developing a strategy of social change to the issue of poverty, it soon became apparent that there was more support for the general idea of change than for any single strategy or even for a combination of strategies. The divisions and tensions produced by these differences in political and economic philosophies first became highly visible in 1968— unless one goes back to read the debates of the social-gospel era!

What Are the Implications and Consequences?

At this point in history it is impossible to list all the implications of this newest development in the churches' response to the challenge of poverty. It is possible, however, to suggest that the consequences of this accent on social change will be felt in at least three places in the life and ministry of the churches. These include the implications for the church leaders involved in this new emphasis on social change, the possible ramifications in the institutional life of the churches, and the possibilities that emerge for direct-action programs.

It may be helpful to conclude this chapter by suggesting a few of these implications. It should be noted, however, that these actually are not mutually exclusive categories and several of the suggested implications could be placed within two or three categories.

A. Implications for the churchman favoring social change

1. This new emphasis on social change runs counter to both the historic exaltation of poverty and to the actual exaltation of wealth. Since it suggests a need for the redistribution of wealth, it will be threatening to those who uphold either of these conventional traditions.

2. This new emphasis on social change runs counter to the traditional and relatively noncontroversial emphasis of the churches on direct services. Thus it will be threatening both to those who believe the social-welfare activities of the churches should not extend beyond limited direct services and to those who favor an extension of the programs of direct services.

3. This new emphasis on social change already is requiring those advocating it to gain a new and more sophisticated understanding of the process of planned social change. A relevant illustration of this is that many of the early enthusiastic supporters of community organization are now beginning to see the vast difference between organizing for power and organization as a part of the process of planned social change.

4. This new emphasis on social change as the major element in the churches' response to the challenge of poverty is requiring church men to acquire a more sophisticated understanding of economics. For example, it is becoming increasingly apparent that the key employment statistic is not *how many* people are unemployed, but rather *who* are the employed. Likewise, in working on the problem of poverty, patterns of underemployment and subemployment, while less visible, often are more important than patterns of unemployment. Similarly, it is important not only to know that the average wage paid by cigar manufacturers was $1.39 per hour in 1968 compared to an average of $2.51 per hour paid by cigarette manufacturers, but also to know *why* cigar manufacturers pay such a comparatively low wage and *what* are the alternatives for action.

5. This new emphasis on social change means that church leaders will be more actively involved in lobbying in state legislatures and in the halls of Congress. This also requires a high degree of sophisticated knowledge on proposed legislation and on the probable consequences of various alternatives. An illustration of the need for such a sophisticated understanding was emphasized in 1966 and 1967 when a great many national church leaders came out with unqualified support for proposed legislation on rent supplements and the model-cities program, both of which tend to continue the concentration of the poor in the central city, while neglecting alternative legislative proposals, such as the rent-certificate program, which would disperse the concentrations of poor people.

6. Perhaps the most serious question confronting the proponent of social change is whether he will choose to work for reform of the system or for overthrow of the system. Should he be a reformer or a revolutionary? This is a real choice for the proponent of social change and one that seldom confronted his predecessor who specialized in direct services to the poor.

B. Implications for the churches

1. It was and is relatively easy for a single parish or for a lone denomination to carry out a program of direct services unilaterally. It is comparatively difficult to execute a program of social change unilaterally. The shift from social welfare to social change also is a shift from individual action to collective action. One of the most important lessons learned by students of the social change process is the importance of the coalition. This lesson applies to the churches. This shift in emphasis will reinforce the pressures for interchurch cooperation in efforts by the churches to combat poverty.

2. In granting this high priority to social change, the churches also are moving in the direction of the "professionalization of reform." One implication of this is the addition of a new group of highly trained specialists to the payroll of denominational and interchurch agencies. The change agents join the evangelists, the professional educators, the church administrators, and the missions executives as specialists in the hierarchy of the churches' bureaucracy.

3. When the churches moved from an emphasis on direct services to supporting social change as their primary response to the challenge of poverty, this meant that they were moving from a relatively noncontroversial type of response to a very highly controversial type of response.

4. In moving in this direction, the churches subjected themselves to some very divisive pressures as programs move from generalities to specifics. The goal of self-determination appears to be a nondivisive and unassailable objective when presented in general terms. It becomes more divisive when presented as a supporting argument for black power in the United States, and even more divisive when applied to the churches' attitude on conditions in South Africa or in Nigeria.

5. In this shift of emphasis the churches cannot help but be involved in what many status-quo-minded churchmen will label as deviant behavior—or at least the support of deviant behavior. This ranges from peaceful protest demonstrations to the employment of change agents who may engage in unconventional behavior dramatizing a point to the comment quoted in the opening paragraph of this chapter in which a prominent church leader proposed an unusual solution to the problem of reducing the concentration of poor people in the inner city.

C. Implications for direct action

In shifting from a program of social welfare to an emphasis on social change as their most appropriate response to the challenges of poverty, the churches also have shifted from a "them" to an "us" focus for their efforts. This can provide a strong foundation for a variety of new church-supported direct-action programs. Three examples will illustrate this point.

1. In addition to supporting a general extension of the minimum-wage laws, the churches could begin to pay the minimum salary and provide the normal complement of fringe benefits (pension, health insurance, paid holidays, sick leave, etc.) to their own clerical and nonprofessional employees. Less than one congregation in ten pays a salary and provides the fringe benefits for its lay employees comparable to those provided by private industry.

2. In those economically heterogeneous communities where the membership of each local church tends to be drawn from a socioeconomically homogeneous group, there might be some new ventures that would encourage the congregation to be an agent of reconciliation *and a vehicle for assimilation* within its own community.

3. Instead of white suburbanites traveling into the inner city to serve as volunteers in direct-service programs, some of these white suburbanites might be enlisted as change agents in their own community. A high priority for change would be to "open up" these communities to the construction of housing (or the use of existing dwellings) for low-income individuals and families who now are confined to the central city. This change might be accomplished directly by encouraging the local officials to approve the necessary enabling legislation. Or it could be accomplished indirectly by making it unnecessary to secure such approval for federally subsidized housing in these suburban municipalities.

In shifting to an emphasis on social change as their primary response to the challenge of poverty, the churches are opening the door to many changes, and perhaps the most crucial of them all is the one which will find the most resistance in many congregations —the breaking up of the growing concentrations of poverty-stricken families in the inner city and a reversal of the increasing compartmentalization of the urban population along economic lines.

Chapter 10

The Black Church in Search of a New Theology

BY GAYRAUD S. WILMORE, JR.

The new black movement came into national visibility and prominence when Stokeley Carmichael and the leaders of SNCC raised the cry of Black Power in 1966 during the Meredith march from Memphis to Jackson, Mississippi. In the three years since that time the magnetic force of the slogan and the ill-defined but slowly developing ideology which lies behind it have permeated and reshaped almost every institution of the black community. Public education, sports, music, the theater, black writers and artists, the culinary arts, home furnishings and decoration, wearing apparel and hair styles, professional associations, fraternal orders and societies, business, politics, community organizations, and college and university students and faculty—all of these, in one way or another, have been co-opted by or enlisted into the new black movement which has taken the place of the old civil-rights movement.

The New Black Mood

Today in black ghettos from Harlem to Watts there is a renaissance of everything black, or everything African, quasi-African, or pseudo-African. In short, everything that belongs to Afro-American history and culture is being lifted up, examined, and, if possible, renewed in the search for black identity, pride, and power. It is, altogether, a remarkable phenomenon in the history of American race relations, without parallel except for the period of Marcus Garvey and the Harlem Renaissance of the 1920's.

It was inevitable that the black churches would sooner or later reflect the new influences sweeping through the urban ghettos of the North and West, and to a lesser extent through the cities of the South. Indeed, anyone who had observed closely the role of black churches and churchmen in the civil-rights movement, how that movement itself became a kind of noninstitutional, underground church, could have anticipated the deep religious implications of black power and its revolutionary effect upon the largest and most substantial of all ghetto institutions—the Christian church.

The driving force of the civil-rights movement under the leadership of Martin Luther King, Jr., himself a Baptist minister, was the religion of social justice. Infused with what Joseph Washington in his *Black Religion* called "the American Negro folk religion,"[1] it seethed with the fervor and emotionalism of protest and resistance. Carried on mainly outside of the institutional structures of the black denominations, the southern-oriented, clergy-led civil-rights movement (as differentiated from that part of the movement led by CORE, SNCC, the NAACP, and the Urban League) became a "church" in its own right. It was characterized by a feeling of divine vocation, an evangelistic message and mission, an internal discipline and mutual love among the brethren that was molded and tested in the fellowship of suffering. There was the spirited gospel music of the rallies and marches; the down-home liturgy and revivalism of the great mass meetings; the charismatic teaching ministry of the voter-registration drives and economic boycotts; the stylistic, Baptist-type stewardship in fund raising for subsistence salaries and bail bonds; the missionary network of churchmen related to SCLC; and above it all, the apocalyptic vision of King, the high priest and true prophet, as characterized by, for example, his "I have a dream" speech at the March on Washington in 1963.

If 1963 was the high-water mark of the interracial, crusading, religion-oriented civil-rights movement, 1966 was its lowest ebb.[2] In going to Chicago to begin his confrontation of the great power structures of the northern cities, Dr. King, as it were, went to Jerusalem. White power in Albany, Birmingham, and Danville were not to be compared with that of the industrial-financial-political complex of the Democratic machines of the great metropolitan areas of the North. The Daley forces in Chicago were as entrenched as the Sanhedrin and no less impervious to the encroachment of an outsider from the hinterland.

The inability of King to mobilize the masses of Chicago Negroes against the Daley machine signalized also the inherent weakness of the southern-revival-meeting, nonviolent-direct-action techniques when pitted against the secularization and anomie of the black ghettos of cities like Chicago, New York, and Los Angeles. The coordinated plan for the desegregation of metropolitan area housing which came out of his Chicago campaign was little more than a victory on paper. The real fact was that Dr. King and his southern-based SCLC staff had experienced their Good Friday in Chicago, and there was no resurrection on the third day.

National Committee of Black Churchmen

During the early summer of 1966 a small but influential group of black clergy in New York City, led by Benjamin A. Payton, Robert Spike's successor as the executive director of the NCC Commission on Religion and Race, organized a new group known as the National Committee of Negro Churchmen. Its hidden agenda was to provide for the big cities a noncompetitive but effective alternative to the social-action strategy of SCLC in the North. More importantly, this group was determined to uphold and hopefully influence the emerging movement for black power which King had all but repudiated, much to the relief of the white religious establishment.

Since its inception, the National Committee of Negro Churchmen raised important theological issues which provided the substance of a continuing controversy and dialogue, both within and outside of the organization. Some of these issues were introduced by the very existence of NCNC. For example, some white Lutheran churchmen asked whether or not the latent purpose of the National Committee was schismatic, contrary to the dominant spirit of the ecumenical movement and corrupted by a serious distortion of the concept of the unity of the Body of Christ. Some black Baptist churchmen, on the other hand, looked askance at the new organization because of what they suspected was a propensity to further institutionalize black religion by directing it toward a radical secularization in the context of black power, therefore challenging the traditional churchmanship of the five major black denominations.

Other questions, both theological and ethical, were raised in various statements and deliverances of the NCNC and in formal and informal discussions at its meetings. From the beginning, the theological program of the Church of the Black Madonna in Detroit has been a constant challenge to NCNC members—especially that congregation's view of the irrelevancy of the New Testament and the color of the historical Christ. Also the escalation of riots in urban ghettos and the implication of black churchmen in these "acts of rebellion" forced NCNC members—as well as others—to ask whether or not a theology of limited violence were possible and how it should be articulated and implemented within the black Christian community.

It was, of course, inevitable that the coming together of mainly northern black churchmen from diverse theological and ecclesiastical traditions would force the consideration of difficult whys and wherefores—the search for a theological base upon which to stand. But the fact that this group was formed in the hurricane eye of a black revolution unprecedented in American history and at a time when the credibility of the Christian faith was being severely tested in the black ghettos of the nation created an even more intense climate of inquiry and concern about theological and ideological foundations than may have been generated in calmer days when black clergymen came together to form ministerial alliances for mutual edification and preaching contests.

When the National Commitee of Negro Churchmen came on the scene in 1966 (the name has since been changed to Black Churchmen), it represented, in one important respect, a schism in that interracial, nondenominational fellowship that was King's civil-rights movement. It was the result of the first serious impact of black power upon that "church." The now-famous Statement on Black Power issued by the new group and published Sunday, July 31, 1966, as a full-page ad in *The New York Times* was not merely a critique of the faltering white liberalism of the day. It was also a critique of the idealistic theological liberalism of Martin Luther King, Jr., the man to whom it nevertheless acknowledged loyalty and without whose inspiration and leadership it could not have come into existence.

But black power had at last infiltrated the black churches, particularly those of the North, as God's own judgment, in secular disguise, not only upon a faithless black church leadership that had abandoned the masses for a whitenized version of an irrelevant spirituality and institutionalism, but even more profoundly, a judgment against all Christian churches and Christian theology in particular.

The Search for a New Black Theology

What is today called the search for a new black theology that is shaking up the traditional black churches and fomenting black caucuses in the predominantly white denominations is the radical response of those black clergy who followed King from the rural South to the northern ghettos. Men and women still loved him and honored his memory, but found the theological wineskins of the institution that was the civil-rights movement unable to contain the new wine of the religion of black power which authenticated itself to northern black churchmen with power through the charisma of Carmichael, McKissick, and the young black militants who called for revolution rather than reform, pride and power rather than a hat-in-hand, foot-shuffling integration.

A generation of black ministers and seminarians reared on Brunner, Barth, and Niebuhr were now reading Frantz Fanon, Malcolm X, and Ron Karenga and asking themselves what did those pale-faced American and European theologians of a racist-dominated religious establishment know about the souls of black folk or the realities of the black ghettos where black men saw, in the mutilated face of a rat-bitten child or a drug addict bleeding in a stinking alley, the image of the crucified Lord.

White theology has well served the white church. Bonhoeffer, Barth, Niebuhr, and Tillich have all described the substance and style of a contemporary faith for white, Western men of the post-World War I Europe and the United States. We do not doubt that we can and have learned something from them that is important and true. But probably for the simple, almost absurd reason that they are white, they have never been lowered into the murky depths of the black experience of reality, where the black Christ walks the dark streets—out of a job, busted, and emasculated, and where he speaks to black people in the idiom of 125th Street and Lenox Avenue.

They have also never, to our satisfaction, resolved the deep ambivalence American blacks have about the American Christ. This ambivalence of belief and nonbelief, reverence and outrage, was hewn out of the peculiar experience of being at once coddled and betrayed, patronized and rebuked, called to be a moral black man in an immoral white society.

Of this ambivalent attitude toward the white man's religion, Vincent Harding writes:

> It was ours from the beginning. For we first met the American Christ on slave ships. We heard His name sung in hymns of praise while we died in our thousands, chained in stinking holes beneath the decks, locked in terror and disease and sad memories of our families and homes. When we leaped from the decks to be seized by sharks, we saw His name carved on the ship's solid sides. When our women were raped in the cabins they must have noticed the great and holy books on the shelves. Our introduction to this Christ was not propitious. And the horrors continued on American soil. So all through the nation's history many black men have rejected this Christ—indeed the miracle is that so many accepted him. In past times our disdain often had to be stifled and sullen, our anger silent and self-destructive. But now we speak out.[3]

White theology has just not presented us with good theological reasons why we should not speak out of this ambivalence of love and rage, nor has it taught us, if indeed we should speak, how to speak and be heard. Nor has white theology been able effectively to reconstruct either for us or for the white church what came down to black people as the Christian religion deliberately adulterated, defused, shorn of its most relevant and immediate ethical insights and implications for revolution.[4] Presented to us as a religion of contentment in the state of life in which one found himself, it sought to make more tolerable the terrible anguish of the present and prepare a deprived and subjugated race for the joys of the world beyond.

What we black people have had is a religion which avoided

questions about personal dignity, collective power, freedom, equality, and self-determination and concentrated on worldliness and immorality—the terrible sinfulness of chicken stealing, lying, laziness, uncleanliness, drunken duels with switchblades on Saturday night, being late for work on Monday, and sexual relations with any white woman—at the pain of death. In short, the religion that was given to black people was carefully tailored to fit the purposes of their oppressors, corrupted in language, interpretation, and application by the conscious and unconscious racism of white Christians, from the first plantation missionary to Billy Graham. White Christianity has been what the ghetto militants call the "religious trick bag," and with practically no exception the theology black ministers learned in the white seminaries (and in the black seminaries which tried to be their carbon copies) was unable, either by conscious intent or powerlessness, to interpret the profound meaning of this intellectual and spiritual disservice, to correct it or to extricate us from it.

It should come, therefore, as no surprise to anyone that what the black revolution mandates for the preaching, teaching, and witnessing ministries of the black church in America has forced a search for a black theology beyond American white theologians and beyond the quasi-Gandhian, theological liberalism of Martin Luther King, Jr.

Today a few young black scholars and pastors are breaking ground that has never before been traversed by mainline white theologians. Nathan Wright, Joseph Washington, Vincent Harding, James H. Cone, Preston Williams, Eric Lincoln, and others whose names are not so well known are beginning to produce an increasing quantity of articles and books out of which these new directions will eventually take shape as a theological program for the black church, not only in this country but also in Africa, where a few black theologians like John Mbiti in Uganda and Bolaji Idowu in Nigeria are working on similar themes related to the indigenization of Christianity in the cultures of Africa.

It is perhaps much too early to try to detect the main outlines of a system or systems of theology in the varied and rather uncoordinated work that has been done during the last two or three years. Taken together, however, a few published and unpublished writings begin to lift up certain recurring ideas and emphases which suggest the freedom and flexibility with which black churchmen are approaching sacrosanct and traditional themes in theology and ethics which are relevant to the purposes of a militant black church.

The Black Experience: Liberation of the Oppressed

First of all, black religion is seen by many of the younger churchmen to be a religion for the present with a strongly instrumental character in relation to the black revolution. Does the black church, the perspective through which it views the faith and acts upon it, have any authentic, unique, and authoritative meaning to assign to blackness and the black experience (as does, for example, black music, art, literature, and drama) which sets it apart today as an indispensably viable institution for the liberation of all black people—indeed, all oppressed peoples—and for the humanization of white civilization? That is the question for which an affirmative answer is presupposed as prolegomena for further exploration— for example, the statement by James H. Cone, "The blackness of Christ is a theological concept. As I see it, Christianity is a religion for and of the oppressed."

The idea certainly is neither new nor startling. Vittorio Lanternari in his book *The Religions of the Oppressed* notes how a subjugated people refashions a religion received by forced acculturation and makes it answer its need to liberate itself from the oppressor. "Thus the religious cults have taken from the Bible such terms and messianic ideas as seemed to validate their own yearning for religious freedom and political independence. The cults actually transmute the hope for a spiritual Kingdom of God held out by the Scripture, into a hope that political, social and cultural autonomy and progress may be enjoyed by the natives now, on this earth."[5]

What is important in the discussions now in process in the black church is the willingness to face this possibility self-consciously, without embarrassment, and not only to discard certain portions of the Bible if they do not serve this purpose but also to seek openly the kind of rapprochement with Black Muslims, Islam, and other non-Christian religions wherever they express the same revolutionary concern for liberation from exploitation and oppression.

As a religion for the present and for the pragmatic possibilities of the present, black Christianity has no sense that present formulations or present strategies have eternal validity or relevance. Historically the churches have in every generation revised and reformulated their creeds and confessions in view of the particular needs of the time. The architects of the older theologies would be amazed at the beliefs of the contemporary churches. Those who lived as recently as the nineteenth century would judge that monstrous injustices have been committed against basic dogma and fidelity to the Scriptures by Bonhoeffer, Niebuhr, and a long list of present-day professors of theology who have great prestige and influence in their respective denominations.

This is only to say that the white churches, particularly in America, have no serious qualms about reshaping the faith to conform with modern scientific discoveries, new cultural realities, or new ethical insights and understandings. The argument of some that nevertheless "the faith once delivered to the Apostles" remains fundamentally unaltered by the contemporary statements of faith and reigning theologies is less than candid and wholly unconvincing.

The black church has even less compunction about entertaining radically different theologies than those of the past, not only because its needs today are so vastly different from those of the late eighteenth and early nineteenth centuries, when its style of devotion and belief was formed, but also because it has always been characteristic of white people to require of black people adherence to standards and values to which they themselves pay only lip service.

Brother Malcolm: Liberating Truth

"The God who spoke by the prophets and in the fullness of time by his Son, *now in this present time* speaks to us through Brother Malcolm." This is what some black churchmen seem to be saying. What this really means is not altogether clear, but it does point to one important conclusion. It is that this pierced and tortured young man, who was not a Christian, discovered something about the meaning of blackness and the essence of the American reality that conveyed such a profound and liberating awareness to the souls of black folk, inspired such a feeling of human nobility and the power to struggle against "the slings and arrows of outrageous fortune," that it is impossible not to believe that the essential truth of what God is doing and demanding in the contemporary world is revealed by Malcolm's life and works.

It is possible, at least for black folk, to believe that the God of Malcolm X, especially toward the end of Malcolm's life—no matter what Malcolm called him—was none other than the God the Father of our Lord and Savior, Jesus Christ. The God of all oppressed, subjugated, and emasculated men was revealed to oppressed, subjugated, and oppressed black Christians by a man who knew himself to be a servant of Allah! That may seem incredible to white theologians—it is not so incredible to black.

Serving a religion of the present, the new black theology will unabashedly incorporate present truth, relevant truth, wherever it is to be found, wherever it liberates people from the shackles of oppression. Nor will there be in this theology any speculative eschatology to recall the pie-in-the-sky promises that were so much a part of traditional black religion. The emphasis is on the relativities rather than the absolutes of divine revelation, on the here and now—the secularity of the in-breaking Kingdom of God, where shoes, and square meals, and decent houses are the symbols of a beatitude wrested from conflict with principalities and powers which, it must be acknowledged, may yet become in the hands of the oppressed the instruments of new oppression.

In this religion, therefore, the truth is always with the oppressed in the present condition of oppression. Social justice becomes the primary if not the sole basis for justification, and sanctification is the state of grace which gives freedom for men to take whatever means are necessary to secure their humanity as sons of God.

Because such a religion sees its own cultural context as the variegated expression of the people's revolutionary situation, it seeks concrete indigenization in black culture—in its music, its art, its social life, and its folklore. As a position paper of the Council of Black Clergy of Philadelphia puts it:

> The function of the religious force is to organize those customs, practices and understandings that the community has embodied as its most important reality. . . . The truth about the history concerning black people is the tragic irony that insti-

tutions functioned in the black community not for the needs of black people, but rather for the needs of white people; and the religious institution, together with other black institutions, failed in its responsibility to develop a viable culture.[6]

Thus black religion, as Joseph R. Washington contends, becomes a religion of the people, not of an ecclesiastical institution. In the traditional black community the church was at the center performing its integrative function. For the new theology the term "religious force" suggests the decentralization and proliferation of the church *qua* institution, while retaining the distinctive cultural vocation of religion as the inherent dynamic of the black community as a whole.

A Reconstructed Doctrine of Man

A second group of formulations in the new black theology clusters around what may be termed a reconstructed anthropology or doctrine of man oriented to the concept of blackness as a unique experience and gift which, if properly understood and used, can open up for all men in this time a more profound meaning of the nature and potentiality of true humanity.

Related to a developing doctrine of man is the doctrine of the humanity of Jesus in whom we see not only the transcendent reflection of ourselves as men—what we can become—but also, existentially, what we are. Thus we have in the work of Albert B. Cleage, Jr., and an increasing number of black ministers the contention that the historic Jesus was black and that the risen Christ relates to black people as a black Savior.[7]

While it appears that most black theologians have not as yet acknowledged the historical accuracy of Cleage's conclusions about what happened to the color of the Jews during their Egyptian sojourn, many do validate a black Christ on the basis of an expedient and effective pastoral theology.

Father Lawrence Lucas, a member of NCBC and the Roman Catholic caucus of black priests, writes:

> While the historic elements of the Christ figure include pigmentation and the probability of hair "like unto lamb's wool," this does not make such normative. The fact that Christ was so real to Sallman that he made Jesus a man of his own culture

and race is a fact that must be paralleled in all races and cultures, if we seriously mean that he is to reign over all and that his lordship is universal. . . .

In our present context, we are involved more with the resurrected, living Christ, rather than or more than the historical Christ. The historic circumstances under which the Christ figure first appeared must be considered eternally, universally authentic, valid, normative, revelatory, etc. However, it is under the present circumstances that this Christ is now being Himself. In so far as white "Christians" have distorted this Christ into a white Christ interested only in subjugating, exploiting black people, I think it is valid to speak, in terms of present realities, of a black Christ to correct this distortion.[8]

There is at present little or no theorizing about the Fall of Man and the origin of the races of mankind, although any synthesis with Black Muslim theology or African religions would certainly force certain issues of this genre to be raised and clarified. There is, however, much discussion about "soul" as the special instincts and sensibilities of the "natural man," for whom sin is the contravening of his own intrinsic nature as one made for fellowship with his neighbor rather than disobedience to externally prescribed and transmitted laws of God governing multifarious and inapposite aspects of behavior.

The idea of "soul" is difficult to grasp and more difficult to define. As the term is employed by black writers today, it signifies a style of life characterized by warmth, wit, and practical wisdom —the ability to comprehend, to have compassion for others, especially for those who suffer or are in need, and to identify with and "feel into" their situation. It is that peculiar artistic and emotional freedom of black people which has its roots in the African heritage of communalism but is reformed and reshaped in the ghettos of America and is opposite to the style of life formed by the structured, unfeeling, scientific rationality of white Western civilization.

Soul is the naturalness, the spontaneity, intuition, creativity, and nonconformity which gave birth to the distinctive styles of dress, food preparation, music, ways of feeling and acting of a people who have known the terror and tragedy of a dehumanizing oppression, but also the beauty of a life together in the black ghetto—the affirmation of the simple pleasures of the natural life and the joy of discovering how to keep life human under the inhuman subjugation of a racist society.

The concept of soul which black artists and writers have lifted up and shaped out of the quasi-mythical ethnic and cultural context of black America gives to many black theologians a clue into what contemporary theology may be reaching for in what it vaguely calls "true humanity." The question that black churchmen are asking is whether true humanity is possible in a system dominated by the profit motive, by a seemingly uncontrollable technological reason, and by a white racist mentality which are perceived as the marks of imperialism and conservatism by revolutionary peoples all over the world.

The affirmation of soul leads black theologians naturally to the affirmation of pride—in some even arrogance and hostility toward the oppressor—and has rehabilitated the concept of self-love as an indispensable characteristic of manhood for an exploited, subjugated, and emasculated people.[9] The case is made that the idea of love as white Christianity has understood it has emphasized subordination, passivity in the face of injustice, and self-abnegation. Moreover, the conventional concept of Christian love has assumed the absence of power and conflict inherent in the real world and therefore has become to the faith of black people a stumbling block which no longer should be regarded as revelational.

The Coherence of Love and Power

Lawrence Jones in a sermon at Union Seminary echoed what one hears frequently from black pulpits when he said:

> Power is the condition of the energy that delivers love from vapid sentimentality; it is also the judgment that delivers those who use power from falling victim to its inherent capacity to corrupt. Some such understanding of the Christian meaning of love and some appropriation of the essential uses and possibilities of power linked to and judged by love, seem appropriate to the Gospel in the ghetto. The most loving service a citizen may perform for his society, for his neighbor, or that groups of citizens may perform on behalf of their nation would be to confront them with the ways in which both the overt power of the state and the covert power are used to undermine the ends of justice and are found in preserving an unjust status quo.[10]

This coherence of love and power is a continuing theme in the search for a black theology. The National Committee of Black Churchmen declared in its first policy statement:

> We regard as sheer hypocrisy or as a blind and dangerous illusion the view that opposes love to power. Love should be a controlling element in power, but what love opposes is precisely the misuse and abuse of power, not power itself. So long as white churchmen continue to moralize and misinterpret Christian love, so long will justice continue to be subverted in this land.

Paul Lehmann, among several well-known white theologians, has recognized the neglect of an adequate understanding of power in the white church. In an article which many black churchmen will commend as a contribution to their own thinking, Lehmann shows that he well understands the dilemma of the black churches in the United States and Africa.

Related to the question of power and revolution in the search for a black theology is the question of violence as a legitimate instrument of social change in the hands of Christians involved in just revolution. Many younger black clergy in NCBC have found themselves caught up with ghetto riots in such a manner that they felt obliged, if not to participate in violence, to support and protect those who did.

Part of the new theological program is to deal positively and affirmatively with the issue of self-defense and to broaden that everywhere-accepted but rarely acknowledged concept to include or intersect concepts of limited violence, violence against violating property, the disruption of the machinery of oppression, and counterviolence.

Fanon's familiar argument that the oppressed man fulfills himself through the violent act has a certain attraction for black theologians, although there has been no attempt yet to deal systematically with the idea. A few people have sought to rehabilitate theologically the passages having to do with divinely ordained or approved violence in the Old Testament and to lift up such passages in the New Testament as Matthew 21:12 ff., 10:34–35; Luke 12:49, 13:6–9; and Revelation 20. Whatever approach will be taken, it seems likely that the militant black church will not assume that the tradition of nonviolence is the normative or only valid form of Christian resistance to individual and systemic violence. Many will agree with Lawrence Lucas:

> Violence does play a role in social change. The Christian sometimes submits himself to violence knowing that every human action is involved with the contradictions of sin. Faith in the goodness of God is not to be equated with confidence in the virtue of man. The Christian therefore sees a good God working his will even in and through violence. A crucified Christ is a momentary defeat but not an ultimate victory. When systems tend to destroy rather than help life, they must be destroyed. . . .
> There are situations where Christians may become involved in violence as an ultimate recourse which is justified only in extreme situations. The use of violence requires a rigorous definition of the ends to which it is used, and a clear recognition of the evils which are inherent in it and it should be tempered by mercy.[11]

Thus the concept of soul as the unique experience and gift of black people pointing toward the meaning of true humanity, the principle of self-love as a necessary precondition for loving others, the coming together of love and power in the creative struggle for justice, and the tactical uses of disruption and counterviolence as legitimate means of revolutionary change are all basic and recurring themes in the discussions now in process in black churches and seminaries over what should be the main lines of a black theology.

Together they form what is not a new but certainly a radically different view of the nature of man and society than the predominantly white churches have been accustomed to. Black theologians will seek to develop and fortify these perspectives by whatever biblical material is available—a frowned-upon but not unknown practice among white theologians as well—and perhaps shape them into doctrinal formulations that can be readily utilized for homiletical and didactic purposes in the revolutionary black church.

Nature and Purpose of the Black Church

A third development in the current thinking among black churchmen has to do with nature and purpose of the black church. As early as 1956, Ruby F. Johnston in her *The Religion of Negro Protestants* indicated a diminution of nonempirical elements in the life of black congregations and the increasing coordination of religion with various aspects of the practical life:

> Practical religious action is an outcome of subordination of the supersensory. Therefore, it is expected that in the successive stage of religious development (the trend toward experimentalism, being presently considered) practical programs are not as outstanding as the decline in emotionalism. Though nonexperimental and emotional religious actions are closely related and often accompany each other, the change from the former in some respects is not as noticeable as a departure from the latter. As there is further deterioration of nonexperimental beliefs, religious action will increasingly acquire a social quality reflected in group living. Altered religious attitudes indicate a close relationship with the community. Religion is significantly conceived in terms of the principle of group welfare. Religious ideas are directing interests in practical action.[12]

Today this secularization of the black church is positively construed by many pastors and seminarians. Perhaps the most noteworthy characteristic of a survey taken in 1968 among a group of black churchmen was the emphasis upon the church as a social institution which should be dedicated not to the salvation of individuals but to the pursuit of freedom, justice, and material well-being of all people in the society; hence, the devotional life of God's people, the liturgy and preaching, as well as the institutional life of the congregation should be oriented toward collective participation in the renewal of the black community and the organization of that community for economic, political, and cultural power and self-determination.

The purpose of the new black church, therefore, is to project a new quality of secular life which boldly expresses that cultural heritage and those operative values which are rooted in the peculiar experience of a people whose life has been a struggle with psychological and physical suppression and subjugation. In the words of the April 5, 1968, statement of the NCBC on urban mission, the call of God is to "the development of the black church, not only as a religious fellowship, but as a community organization, in the technical sense of that term, which uses its resources, influence, and manpower to address the problems of estrangement, resignation and powerlessness in the political, cultural and economic life of the black community."

The problem for the new theology, of course, is that with the exception of individuals like Henry H. Garnett, Absolom Jones, and Adam Clayton Powell, the Negro church has been, by and large, a conservative institution dominated by a politically quiescent, status-conscious black bourgeoisie and governed by paternalistic, domineering pastors, bishops, and ecclesiastical bureaucrats. Black religion in this new day must break with those debilitating structures and the patterns of institutionalism which have sapped the vitality of the white church with respect to needed changes in church and society.

As Joseph Washington has warned in his reply to critics who repudiated his earlier view of black religion:

> Greatness is in black people *qua* black people. Their institutional expressions may not measure up to their greatness, but radical change will come about through the people who are black, irrespective of their allegiance vis-à-vis ideologies, analogies and philosophies. Defensiveness of black ecclesiastical institutions is a misplaced emphasis . . . attunement must be made to black people and not institutions. Those who place priority on black institutions over black people or who hold that the two are inseparable are defending the wrong substance of black power.[13]

Insofar as Washington is still promoting social integration and church integration as the highest priorities for black churchmen, one wonders to what extent he is really committed to the solidarity and self-determination of black people through their churches.

Here Washington breaks with what appears to be the main direction of the new theology as it is being developed by the official statements of NCBC. There is a great deal less talk about integration among this group. It is not assumed that the unity of the human family and the mystical unity of the Body of Christ is shattered by the communal integrity and institutional unity of black people. To the contrary, many black theologians are now saying that the total assimilation of blacks within the dominant and (for the foreseeable future) racist white church and society makes impossible the preservation and enhancement of precisely that personal sense of self, dignity, identity, and collective responsibility that helps a people to heal the scars of the past, empowers them and gives them an awareness of being called to the service of that universal justice without which the oneness of humanity and the church cannot become an operative reality.

Oneness in Plurality

That reality consists not in the sameness of the mythical melting pot and the deracination of one people while another people continues to make particular ethnic characteristics the defining context of acceptability. That reality rather consists in each group bearing those peculiar gifts, wrought in the various life experiences of a historical people, which are gratefully received and respected by others and which make for the creative diversification and enrichment of the whole human family.

Such a view of the oneness-in-plurality of the People of God and, for that matter, of the human race makes racial integration, in the best sense of that greatly perverted term, a by-product of the total humanization process in a society rather than an unconditional mandate and rigidly conceived goal of almost ontological status to which everything else must be sacrificed at all costs.

As far as the black church is concerned, the emergence of the black-power ideology out of the militant secular milieu of the ghetto, despite the intrinsic deficiencies of ideologies, may be the last opportunity for the church to break out of its symbolic commitment to the illusory goal of one-way integration and permeate the black community with a positive concept of power and a sense of transcendent vocation that will serve the purposes of justice and freedom in a pluralistic society.

The idea of the black church as a "community organization" (albeit different from the mass-based Alinski type) whose nature it is to unveil the reality of God's grace and righteousness in a people's constructive use of cultural, political, and economic power is gaining currency among black clergy and is seen as the secular analogy of the divine election and servanthood motifs in Christianity which have been hopelessly spiritualized by the white church in America.

The Reality Beyond Blackness: True Humanity

How to describe the nature and purpose of the black church as an organization mobilizing community resources for political and economic power without falling into the trap of a conforming ideology and institutionalism which discourages freedom and creativity will remain one of the difficult problems faced by the new theology.

If, as some of the black theologians are saying, black people are today God's Chosen People who have a special cultural vocation, the question must be raised whether or not the institutional church, or organized black religion, is indeed coterminous with "black people" or "the black community." A debate on this question is going on today, and it is becoming apparent that the fundamental issue is between those who desire to retain a bond with historic Christianity and its institutional forms and those who ask for a more poetic and mystical conception of the church as that invisible body of oppressed people (who happen to be disproportionately black in America) whom God has chosen to be the instrument of his judgment and grace for all mankind.

Already one hears talk in this debate of "the reality beyond blackness." Cone and Harding, to mention only two of the younger men, are probing the issues beyond the secular mission of the renewed institutional black church to envision the breakups of the American- and European-dominated world civilization with its flaxen-haired white Christ and its oppressive and dehumanizing societal structures. The call of God to the black people of Africa and America, they are prepared to say, is the call to cultural renewal and to a true humanity which the old order of white supremacy has all but obliterated. Only when this renewed and true humanity is possible for black people will it be possible for any people. And until it comes, there is no real hope and no true reconciliation for the world.

Chapter 11

Religion, Church, and Culture

BY WILLIAM HAMILTON

In my morning paper, I read of Mr. Nixon's visit to the Marble Collegiate Church in New York, where he heard the distinguished minister say: "God doesn't want anyone to be hungry or oppressed. He just puts his big arms around everybody and hugs them up against himself." It's going to be an interesting four years for us all.

Definitions

I mean something fairly specific by the three terms of the chapter title. I take *religion* to mean: a practice or discipline, with some sort of intellectual structure, offering a description of man's present experience of himself in relation to his world. It then focuses on the critical or negative portion of that experience in the name of some other reality—transcendent, ultimate, or historical—and develops a means of moving from a present dissatisfaction to a more desirable status, attitude of life. Thus, I am not using "religion" in Barth's sense as identical with "sin," or in Bonhoeffer's sense as a project for imposing needs or wishes on a world. And I am not using it in a sense that its opposite could be "secular."

Culture, then, takes its place within the above definition, as a collection of social, intellectual, and aesthetic forms of man's present experience of being in the world. Perception of culture is the beginning of the perception of religion; criticism of culture is the beginning of the criticism and purification of religion.

By *church* I mean those Christian organizations, institutions, and assemblies devoted to an examination of the changing relationship between man's experience of himself and the gospel.

Theological Options

When a gulf is perceived between man's experience of himself and the nature of the gospel, the church's theology has a number of options. It can devise ways of bridging the gulf: It may decide that man's present questions are really the questions of the gospel; it may decide that the gospel's questions are really the same as man's present questions; it may shame us out of modernity, laugh at our anxious relevance games, and lure us back to the gospel, ignoring the gulf. Or it may invite us to leave the church whenever the problem of relating gospel and world, in either thought or action, is believed to require styles of thought and life for which the church has no precedent.

Protestant thinking on the relation between gospel and world, Christ and culture, achieved a masterful historical and normative summation in Richard Niebuhr's *Christ and Culture* (1951). In spite of the author's great sensitivity to the partial validity and even necessity of the several various Christ-culture relationships throughout Christian history, it was clear that he was able to persuade us that our faithfulness in the twentieth century required that the church once more undertake the task of the transformation of culture. Thus, "Christ as the transformer of culture" became the motto for our theoretical ethics and practical action, and to some extent still is.

"Christ, the transformer of culture." What has happened? Nothing seems especially wrong with this, when we look at our New Testaments, or when we focus on certain golden ages in the past. But somewhere along the line, and fairly recently, the idea that once persuaded us and that worked so well in so many aesthetic, political, and intellectual contexts now seems empty, pretentious, and absurd. Do we dare talk this way anymore, when we all know that the real issue for the Christian community is not how it can transform something, but how it can stay alive? The church, which in our rhetoric is the revolutionary spearhead of the gospel in the world, is increasingly devouring its wisest and most loving chil-

dren, draining their valuable inner and outer energies in just the
process of staying inside. The church, always effective in transforming the content of its pronouncements to suit the times, can
hardly lay any present claims to transform the world when it is so
impotent in the prior task of transforming itself.

Specious Attempts at Relevance

The relation of the church to culture today? None of any importance, except as an instance of specious attempts at relevance
("God and the Hippies," "Jesus Is What's Happening, Man," "The
Prophetic Voice of Bob Dylan") or as a reflection of that fear of
change which is the true enemy.

It is my conviction that we are at the beginning of something
like a genuinely revolutionary situation in the field of religion in
America, and that by and large this is a revolution going on outside the church and a revolution that will ultimately pass the
churches by in most of their present forms. The function of religion, then, is that of discernment of this revolutionary situation in
culture, and of finding some means of clarification, understanding,
and action on the basis of what is found. To examine "the problem
of church and culture," then, is to discern this revolutionary situation, and to try to understand why it is largely bypassing the
church.

Is there any way of defining this revolution? Can a revolution
ever be defined, or do we just have to live with it—to get with it,
or to reject it? I would like to try to propose a conceptual scheme
by which this revolution can be understood. For if we do not try
to do something like this, we are at the mercy of the undereducated
journalists and the threatened religious leaders for both our data
and our responses.

I do not think the Reformation is a helpful model for the revolution we are in. It is, in fact, as unhelpful religiously as Munich
is politically when used as an event to justify America's immoral
continuation of the Vietnamese destruction. For the Reformation,
oddly enough, was a decisive and fast-moving thing. One could
point to dates, times, and persons. This is not the case with our
religious revolution (though if any document could possibly be
the ninety-five theses of our revolution, it would almost certainly

be Dietrich Bonhoeffer's letters from prison). What is happening to us is actually more like the Renaissance, which was recently defined as an attempt to find a compromise formula for those who wished to live with Christian convictions and classical forms. Our revolution has a similar problem—the attempt to find a means whereby one may live in one's religious place as a fully contemporary man or woman.

A Proposed Scheme

Let me propose a scheme that may help us see what is going on. I take it that we can understand the Western religious tradition, in terms of three ages, three periods.

We may provisionally and roughly date *the first age* from Abraham to Luther, and we may say that its main problem was the naming of God—who art thou? This is the time of the Jewish-Christian tradition, the classical Christian era. The monuments and works of this age are simple to state: Catholicism, Scripture, Chartres, the *Divine Comedy*, the saint.

The second age, from Luther to Freud, or perhaps Sartre, has another main problem. Not the naming of the gods, but the naming of the self. Not the look upward (Gothic), but the look within. "Who am I?" This age has also familiar characteristics—Protestantism, the hero, the explorer, bourgeois man, self and identity problems, pietism, experience, psychoanalysis, existentialism, goals, values, the performance principle.

And *the third age*, from Freud or Sartre, from yesterday or today to—when? And here we have again another central problem. The naming of the neighbor, the world—who are you? Who is my neighbor? God cannot save (the first age's solution), man cannot save himself (the second age knew this but thought it was an argument for the truth of the first age), for only communities can heal. The concern of the new age is the shaping of healing communities, just as at the close of the second age we were given a superbly fashioned therapy (psychoanalysis) to save us from our sick communities—family, nation, church. The characteristics, models, heroes of this age are harder to see, for we are just beginning to feel what it is like to live partly in it: Marshall McLuhan; style as our desire, rather than goal or value; cool; the

Beatles; the New Left; "what's happening"; transcending the self-world distinction; post-historical, beyond Jesus, post-Christian.

Now, everybody knows that historical periods, if they exist at all, never fit neatly together. There are always overlapping edges. The problem of the self is radically posed deep within the first age in St. Augustine's *Confessions*, and decisively at the close of the age in lay mysticism and nominalism. It can, therefore, be suggested that mysticism is the religion-event that gets its genuine power by standing at the juncture of the first and the second age, the buffer between both, drawing from both, a help and a threat to both.

The problem of the world is, of course, raised profoundly in the second age—fundamentally, we can say, by the eighteenth-century political revolutions. In this sense the French Revolution is the true start of the third age, and the third age contains thus the idea of the death of God, and Karl Marx as chief interpreter.

Our religious revolution is defined, I am claiming, by the fact that we are somewhere at the edge of the second and the third age, and further by the fact that the fundamental theological and religious problem in this interlocked situation is political: Where are the healing communities to be found?

The Role of the University

It is my conviction that the religious revolution will be played out, in the future, largely in the American university, and scarcely in the church at all. Thus the traditional problem of the church and culture must be translated to the new context of the university. But how the university is thus becoming "religious" needs some clarification.

I am persuaded that the really new thing about our common life is not that people fail to follow the old ways, and not that the old rules are any more flawed than usual, but that the institutions, structures, and methods by which the norms are passed along are no longer merely modestly ill, but impotent, and more and more unable to perform their transmitting functions. I am thinking primarily of the special illness in the three great moralizing institutions of the modern West—family, church, and nation. The new fact with which we have to reckon is that an increasing number of

Americans are experiencing these institutions as dangerous and sick, so that our main moral work seems often to be one of extricating ourselves from the damage done to us by these old and honorable structures which once determined the shape of our moral lives for us, and which often seem today either not to do it at all, or when they try to do it, do it so badly.

Family, nation, and church are not equally sick, or sick in the same way, or equally sick for all. But they are sick enough to mark an important new situation and to require of us some hard and dangerous thoughts.

If these institutions are not terminally ill, then our task is easy and easily stated—cure, effect the modest changes necessary to restore them to their old moral functions. The liberal and conservative alike would agree here that this is sufficient for the day. But if the illnesses are more serious, and possibly terminal, what then is our moral task? Is it simply to kill, or to let die, these sick communities that bedevil us? This is the answer the Freudian revolution has bequeathed to us, whether we have been analyzed or not. The Freudian analysis has as its main function the liberation of man from his sick communities, whether family, church, or nation (mainly family, of course, in Freud's own work), and it has performed this liberation often with a deeply impressive skill.

This is where the battle lines really get sharply drawn. Is devotion, say, to a sick nation really sick; is not courage the name for a devotion to a flawed nation coupled with a desire to cleanse? Or, may it not be true that devotion to a sick nation is true sickness (the peace movement), while moral health demands that we withhold devotion and give only dissent to a sick nation?

If the family, nation, and church no longer possess their power to bear or to pass on viable religious and moral standards for Western men, then it would seem that they should be killed, ignored, or allowed to die. And this precisely for moral reasons.

But what is to be put in their place if we decide to allow them a decent and dignified death? Freud did not fully face this issue. For if he saw, with a clarity that still has the power to overwhelm us, that some communities have made us ill, he did not really see that only the community can heal. (This is perhaps the true meaning of the religious aphorism, "Outside the church there is no salvation.") The only healing community that Freud could propose to pit against the ailing one of the bourgeois family was the doctor-patient relation, and the only civilization he could envision was one containing inevitably sick communities. They could not, he said, be made fully well; what we can do is to instruct man how to deal with the inevitable damage they will always inflict.

In this sense, Marx saw something Freud did not. Marx saw our sickness and concluded that only the community can heal. The old ones cannot, so new ones must emerge.

Freedom from Sick Communities

But what actual communities can heal us, if the traditional ones cannot, and if Freud's doctor-patient relation and Marx's proletariat are inadequate? Is there anything we can do, beyond a necessary rebellion, against the sick communities? Rebellion, however necessary, is not enough. We must press beyond the necessary freedom from sick communities that Freud has made possible for us, and we have to find, as Philip Rieff has suggested, a way of combining Freud's critique of the sick community with something like Marx's search for the healing community.

Good rhetoric—but how? What healing community, if not nation, family, or church; if not the sexual, political, and religious communities already at hand? Here we come to the point, I think, where something new is taking place in our moral and religious life, at least here in America. For it appears that the university is, almost by default and certainly inadvertently, taking over the value-passing functions once traditionally exercised by nation, family, and church. Here is the place where the young discover what is in their past, and how they propose to make use of what they discover, by simple acceptance, by transformation, or by negation. Our moral situation *is* revolutionary at the point where values are being passed along. In this sense, the university is functioning *in loco parentis*, *in loco ecclesiae*, and *in loco patriae*. It is beginning to do by default what parent, priest, and president no longer have the power to do.

This is why the university is such an exciting, bewildering, and creative moral community today, and why the press and the media are taking to the university with such lascivious glee. The real life of the university is increasingly not academic, but religious and moral: It is a search for a healing community, a search for comrades, for those who share your secret, your style of life, your hair style, your paperback tastes.

This is why the young are so often not interested in the academic life, but in the good life, the full life; more zest, more joy, more vitality than we teachers manage to show. This is what "student power" means, for they rightly discern that not only their minds, but their whole lives are being shaped, and they want in on the shaping, to undo or neutralize the damage they rightly suspect we have the power to inflict. *Gaudeamus igitur, iuvenes dum sumus*, they sing, and they mean it. This quest for new values, new communities within which the old values can be tested, new styles of life, leads to many strange places—to the street, to living in the ghetto, to jail, to the Sheep Meadow, to LSD and pot, and often, to bed. Sometimes our classes and seminars help; often they do not.

On the campuses the religious revolution is here. The pop governors like Reagan and Kirk cannot wish it away; they do not like it; they should not, for it is a threat to them. But, with all of its terror and promise, can it break out of the campus and into the streets, the halls of Congress, the corridors of power, into the rest of this bewildered and sick nation? Is it a "cop-out" or a "takeover" revolution? And can the ferment restore, or will it somehow replace, the troubled church and distintegrating family?

It depends. Will the new ways in which the old values are being passed on lead to new values? Will the new media give us some new messages? Will the medium here, as elsewhere, become the message? It will certainly not be enough to improvise new ways of stating and passing on the old songs and stories. (The old songs are good songs, sometimes; their names are chastity, fidelity, patriotism, faith, love.) If we are really to be effective revolutionaries, we will need not only new media, but new messages, new songs. And they will have to be as good as or better than the old, as "All You Need Is Love" is better than "When Your Heart Goes Bumpety-bump, It's Love, Love, Love."

If the university scene is just a new place for doing an old thing, then we are hung up on the sterile struggle between rebellion and conformity. If we are to shape something genuinely new, something probably beyond our present Christian and Jewish allegiances, then much is required of us—patience, time, discipline, and a trust that we can learn from one another, and be wrong.

Chapter 12

Leadership for Change
in Church and Society

BY GEORGE W. WEBBER

The purpose of this chapter is to propose a plan for the education of the clergy that takes into account the fundamental missionary purpose of the church, the reality of contemporary urban society, and the tasks appropriate for the clergyman.

A severe malaise is presently infecting the ranks of the clergy, Protestant and Roman Catholic alike. The steady stream of men leaving the ordained ministry, increasing in volume each year, is more than matched by those who remain in parish positions, but at the price of a deep sense of frustration and discouragement. Customarily this sad state of affairs is blamed on the rigidity or irrelevance of present ecclesiastical structures, the superficial commitment of many church members, or the present state of confusion in the churches over their mission and ministry. In this chapter I want to leave aside these traditional criticisms, however valid, and focus on one other significant factor—that to some significant degree the clergy are not equipped personally and professionally for faithful and effective ministry in the contemporary world. Sometimes they still hold to an understanding of the nature and purpose of the church that grew up in small-town or rural America, a world that no longer really exists. Sometimes they apply old models to a situation where these are largely irrelevant. Other times they lack either the personal maturity or the skills that are required to give shape to an appropriate expression of their function.

Insofar as such factors as these account for the discontent among the clergy, they are matters that can be dealt with. The purpose of this chapter is to suggest a program for the education of the clergyman that starts with his first approach to the seminary and continues to the end of his ministry.

Pre-Seminary Education: A Moratorium Period

Perhaps more than any other vocation, the ordained ministry demands a coherence between a man's life and the work he must do. Personal maturity, Christian commitment, and professional competence are all clearly demanded. But the fact is that few men presenting themselves to seminary are likely to have even come close to fulfilling their potential in terms of maturity. Entrance into seminary is not the answer to this issue, but a further postponement of a solution.

Several years ago, the faculty of a leading seminary spent the two days of its annual retreat discussing the present student generation. Four able members of the Bachelor of Divinity student body were present for the first session to indicate as honestly and fully as possible where they stood in terms of faith and vocation. After listening to their discussion, a psychiatrist from the Harvard College Health Services was asked to interpret what they were saying (the students having been packed off home). His response was that these students were going through what Erik Erikson called an "adolescent identity crisis." They were struggling valiantly to discover their own values as persons, their faith commitments, and their vocational direction. This was not meant as a judgment upon the students, but a recognition that the American middle class programs children and young people in such a manner through family, school, and church that they arrive on the doorstep of the seminary still seeking their own identity. I am convinced that this generalization holds true for a good percentage of the students at the leading Protestant seminaries and increasingly is characteristic of Roman Catholic seminaries as well. Unless theological education starts from this situation of their students, it will clearly fail to create the context for effective education. Until a man believes that Jesus Christ is important for him, why study the New Testament? Unless he has some likelihood of entering the ranks of the clergy, what will motivate him to undertake field work in a parish or to study homiletics?

The seminary must provide the opportunity for a man to face the questions of faith and vocation as the heart of his agenda and in an appropriate location. I am convinced that the time is between college and formal seminary years. The *locus* is a job in the community, from Peace Corps and military service to the kind of job the man might have begun out of college if seminary had not been in the picture. One structured program with five years of experience is the Metropolitan Intern Program developed by Union Theological Seminary and the East Harlem Protestant Parish, now administered by New York Theological Seminary, New York City. The rationale is derived from Erik Erikson, who suggests that the achievement of maturity for the young person can best be attained by a "moratorium" period.[1] Having been programmed by adult expectations and direction all his life, the young person needs a time to drop out of these systems, earn his own living, and determine his own values, goals, and style. The Metropolitan Intern Program provides such a context. The five-part program involves living in an inner-city neighborhood with another student or two, undertaking the widest possible range of secular employment, and relating to the community and to the church as a resident, not an embryonic clergyman. The only formal requirement of the program is that the student meet with a group of ten twice a week for reflection on his experience. Even this is not a traditional academic seminar. Responsibility for using the time effectively is in the hands of the group, with the formal leader acting primarily as convener and resource person. This context enables the students, with the help of their peers, to explore the meaning of their involvement, examine their own commitments, test their understanding of themselves and their world, and work toward clarity about vocation.

Now that some one hundred and sixty men and women (including twenty wives) have finished their intern year, it is clear that such a moratorium has dramatic effect. Almost without exception the year has meant an impressive development in personal maturity, sense of vocational direction, and clarity in faith. In perhaps thirty percent of the cases, the men or women do not go on to further seminary training, although a high percentage of them do appear to be motivated by a strong concern for others and clear Christian commitment.

I suspect that if no students were allowed to begin formal seminary education until they had lived and worked in the world for a year or two, we would transform the seminaries in one blow and provide for the church in the future clergy with far greater maturity and competence than at present.

The Metropolitan Intern Program provides another important clue for the training of the clergy. This involves the role of the men who are assigned to function as conveners and resource consultants to each group. For a young person to decide on a vocation, he needs men before him whose work evokes a positive response. Men become doctors when they see what a doctor does and believe that is what they want to do. In our day models of ministry that attract able men to the seminary are singularly lacking. Once they begin the seminary course, the most attractive model is the seminary professor, operating in the classroom, but this model is simply irrelevant to most situations where ordained clergy are needed in today's world.

Thus, in the moratorium period the student needs to be confronted with vocational options that reflect the best in the clergy today. The key is his own unit leader. This man dare not fall into the traditional role of teacher, pastor, or supervisor. His one mandate is to help the students to make maximum use of their own experience, that is, to accept responsibility themselves for reflection on their year. He is a catalyst, a convener, a theological resource person, whose function is to share in the learning process as a participant with his own unique contribution, but not at one pole in the learning process with the students at the other.

The reader should be clear that I am affirming such a style of ministry as increasingly normative for the clergy role in the future. Today, as Christian laymen become the only effective servants of Christ in the world, the fundamental bearers of the mission of the church—when, for each of them their whole life must be a witness to Christ—then the function of the clergyman is precisely that of a convener, a catalyst, who enables them to reflect on their experiences and search out paths of faithfulness as they wrestle with the ambiguity of mission. In a wide range of situations today— industrial chaplaincy, parish pastorate, community organization—

clergy are discovering that the words that express their function are enabler, equipper, catalyst. Their unique contribution comes as a participant, not as a leader or professor, bringing to bear for the whole group their own knowledge of scripture and tradition.

The pre-seminary intern, working with such a man, has steadily before him a model for ministry that gives him an authentic basis on which to decide for or against the vocation of clergyman.

The Theological Seminary: "Doing Theology"

At present, during three years, the seminary attempts to provide its B.D. student with a classical theological education in which he is asked to master the basic biblical, historical, and theological disciplines and, at the same time, attempts to provide him with the professional tools he needs for the specific functions of the clergyman. Here I would argue that the latter task is impossible from the vantage of the seminary and can best be done effectively when the man is located in one of the specific forms of ministry that are emerging. The former task, as now conceived, is no longer relevant to the best insights of mission theology and does not equip a man for the essential task of theological resource for the Christian community. The fundamental purpose of the seminary years should take shape in training a man to "do theology." This is admittedly a tricky and ambiguous term, but in this chapter I want to try to give it explicitness.

Theological education has been laboring under a static conception of revelation. "Jesus Christ, the same yesterday, today, and forever," was taken to mean that there was a deposit of theological truth in scripture (and in tradition) that had to be learned as the basic substance of theological education. The student had to master as best he could the whole corpus of biblical, historical, and theological material. As a clergyman he would have the task of interpreting or translating this faith to his own people and time, but even this severe communication problem was not of much concern to the seminary faculty outside the practical field.

Today many powerful voices are arguing for a dynamic and contemporary understanding of revelation. To affirm a God of history is to make history the locus of self-understanding for the church, not the past, however important. In the very real history of today, though surely in the light of scripture and tradition, the Christian must seek the revelation that becomes real for him. In the words of Gabriel Moran:

> A series of events in that past that delivered a set of revealed truths not only does not restore validity to history, but seems to be a direct denial of it. . . . Strictly speaking, therefore, revelation is found in completeness neither in scripture nor tradition but in the human consciousness of the risen Lord.[2]

There is nothing novel about this approach to Christian life. Church history is the story of emerging new demands in society which lead to response in the churches and only in the final place to theological reformulation or justification. To state it another way, "We do not know what we do not do." Learning takes place in relation to involvement and responsibility.

But, for theological education, this line of thought demands a virtual revolution. No longer can one be content to give major attention to transferring to the student a vast load of accumulated theological knowledge and thus provide him with the equipment he needs. Truths announced to students by the teacher cannot be truths that set men free. They must be discovered and understood by students in communal experience as the truth for them. "It is in human history that God is revealed and there is no other place for the student to discover revelation except as a reality given in his own life."[3]

I am suggesting that the fundamental task of the seminary must be to teach a man to "do theology," that is, to understand the events of contemporary history in the light of a biblical faith, to recognize the claims both of a prophetic and a servant ministry in the concrete occasions of his own time and place. The remarkable report to the American Association of Theological Schools entitled "The Curriculum for the '70s"[4] makes "doing theology" the central thrust in the task of the seminary, but without making any real attempt to define the term. Perhaps it can best be described as a process with a number of interlocking elements.

To be as specific as possible, this process involves taking with equal seriousness both scripture and tradition, on the one hand, and contemporary events, on the other. In the dialogue between these two, the meaning of faith for our time and the concreteness of obedience may be discovered. God is at work in the world; he is Lord of history; he calls men of faith to join in his mission; our knowledge of what he has done gives a perspective for analyzing the present and shaping the future. To "do theology" means to live in the world with eyes of faith. Two illustrations point in the direction of what this might mean; in no sense are they exhaustive.

(1) In recent years the engagement of the church in the world has raised severe questions about the basic purpose of mission, focused particularly on the nature and meaning of conversion. In effect, poor and black men all over the world were saying to the church and the missionary that they were not interested in having their scalps taken or their souls "saved" by the white man. Clearly, on grounds of effectiveness alone, traditional styles of evangelism are in trouble. To "do theology" means that the basic task is not to find new ways of doing the same thing, but to take the serious challenge of the world as a question with which to search again in scripture and tradition for the meaning and purpose of evangelism. In this case, careful reflection leads to a drastic reformulation of our conceptions of mission and ministry, long taken for granted. As one simple example, it becomes at once apparent that American evangelists have taken the biblical word "witness" to mean "win" and set out to conquer the world for Christ in a style that has no biblical basis whatsoever. In a word, God through the events of history is always raising issues which demand that the church reformulate in the light of continuing revelation the faith which it affirms and the purposes which it serves.

(2) Again, to "do theology" is to understand quite secular events in terms of biblical perspectives. This can require the prophetic task of seeking out the myths of every human society and every person, with no ax to grind, accepting the task of "seeing it the way it is and telling it like it is." Or it can be to read events in the light of God's activity. Several years ago I had occasion to spend four days at Daytop, a rehabilitation center for narcotics addicts. The most remarkable fact of those days was the discovering of the quality of life displayed by many ex-addicts— joy, openness, freedom, selflessness, in other words, the fruits of the Spirit. In trying to understand what made Daytop so powerful, I suddenly realized that they not only had made their purpose, "to create new human beings," a thoroughly biblical task, but were

actually living in a community of nurture that expressed to an unusual degree a number of basic biblical insights: "love your neighbor as yourself"; "bear one another's burdens . . . for each man will have to bear his own load"; "now there are varieties of gifts, but the same Spirit"; and "rather, speaking the truth in love, we are to grow up. . . ." Here, in a totally secular setting, one can only affirm that the Spirit is at work and rejoice. Here truly one discovered a sign for the times, part of the meaning, surely, of "doing theology."

A number of seminaries are moving in the direction of a curriculum that is focused on helping men learn to be this kind of theologian. In a joint program begun in the fall of 1967, the Roman Catholic Seminary at Maryknoll, Union Theological Seminary, and New York Theological Seminary, all in New York, offer a semester program that seeks to be an experience in "doing theology." Each Wednesday afternoon and evening, working in groups of ten with one faculty member as a fellow participant, the students are assigned to dig into one aspect of the urban scene. The semester might be spent in getting at the dynamic forces in the Ocean Hill-Brownsville school situation, the war on poverty in East Harlem, or the ferment among youth in the ghetto. This is an exercise in understanding God's agenda, or simply learning to do urban analysis. But the main point is to initiate a process in which the issues that emerged from their urban involvement are examined to see what challenges and questions they raise with which the church in its mission and ministry would have to deal. Much of Thursday morning is spent in lifting up the points where traditional theology and practice are being questioned. The hope, of course, is that these issues will be taken back to the regular seminary courses and provide a basis for the urgent study of biblical, historical, and theological materials for their insights and perspective.

A program such as this is only a feeble step toward the seminary that will make involvement the core of its whole curriculum, and restructure teaching in the traditional disciplines in terms of their usefulness in the process of "doing theology." The program also demands teachers who are prepared to accept a new style, again that of enabler, resource person, catalyst, partner in learning, and not the authority in some area of knowledge.

Continuing Education: On-the-Job Training

While the theological seminary may give particular attention to the task of "doing theology," this responsibility is normative for mission and ministry. Therefore the imperative for continuing education is unavoidable. Seminary begins the task that must be continued throughout a ministry. Therefore I would argue that theological seminaries can relax about trying to do the total job of equipping men for ministry and leave part of the preparation to others, specifically as part of continuing education that takes place in relation to the particular ministry to be undertaken.

In the urban technological society of today a wide range of specific patterns of ministry is emerging, many demanding the presence of seminary-trained men and women. But the tools and training for the specific work to be done can hardly be acquired in a seminary. They must be learned on the job or in relation to the very specific demands of that ministry. No seminary can do much in the way of "practical theology" or teaching professional skills in the face of such pluralism.

There is no longer a normative "general-practitioner role," for even the parish pastor is a specialist. Clearly, on-the-job training must be the locus in which a man develops the skills for his particular work. The myth that a man gets his education in seminary must be killed. There he only begins what is a lifelong process of continuing education. A doctor, lawyer, or scientist who is not engaged in an ongoing process of education becomes a quack in five years. So also, with the rapid change in mission and ministry, the clergyman must accept the normative character of continuing education.

For the argument here, let me examine the rationale for the training process for an urban parish clergyman as it has been developed by the Metropolitan Urban Service Training facility (MUST). The task to which he is called is to enable his congregation to discover and engage in the mission to which God calls it in the particularity of its own time and place. The first step is to define this mission through the process of investigation and analysis. The clergyman needs help in learning, himself, and then in enabling others to engage in this process. When the man is lacking in this skill, he is almost inevitably driven into maintaining patterns of institutional introversion that ignore the claims of mission.

In the second place, the pastor needs competence in understanding the dynamics of his own congregation, its history, commitment, and potential. He must be able to do a "systems analysis" of his resources. In recent years a whole generation of young clergy have gone forth into parishes, filled in seminary with "renewal theology," and determined to make their new parish into a congregation in mission. They imposed a dramatic and wonderful vision that, more often than not, bore no relation to the reality of the situation with which they had to deal. If the many sociological studies of congregations by Peter Berger, Gibson Winter, and others are correct, it is simply foolish to expect the typical parish ever to become in any corporate sense a congregation in mission. Rather, the clergyman needs to look for the gold that is hidden in the vein, those who within the congregation are ready to respond to the claims of Christ and venture into mission. He is a miner, hopeful that the vein might assay out at five or ten percent gold. MUST has discovered that much of the anxiety and frustration of clergy is relieved when they are helped to understand the real forces which are at work in their parish and in the institutional structures of their denomination. Then they are able to decide to continue to work within these structures, with all their limitations, or to make the decision to work elsewhere. In either case, they no longer are confused and baffled by forces they do not understand and with which they are thus not able to deal.

This leads to a third area of competence for the pastor. He must be a politician, able to mine the resources of his situation effectively. This takes a quite different set of skills from the traditional pastoral roles of preacher in the pulpit, teacher in the classroom, and counselor in the study. The irrelevance of each of these roles as traditionally exercised is obvious in the urban parish. Preaching as the basic style of opening up scripture is ineffective in a TV-saturated, spectator-oriented, post-McLuhanite age.

The effective teacher today is not the lecturer, but the enabler in the learning process for students, with whom he remains one in the game. The counselor function in even a small urban parish is utterly impossible for even three men, when conceived as meeting the personal and spiritual needs of people. The preaching office must be seen in a style of dialogue which enables Christians to discover and employ a biblical faith in their own lives; the teacher must help men face the issues of decision and obedience and find the strength and wisdom to take the consequences in their own lives. The pastoral office is primarily the job of equipping laymen to fulfill their mission in the world. These all demand skills and sensitivity that can be learned and developed. They are skills which inspire, unlock, enable, and equip the faithful for their mission and ministry.

In its continuing education program, MUST has worked in collaboration with New York Theological Seminary. The basic component is a weekly workshop on the practice of parish ministry in which no more than six clergy meet for four hours of intensive reflection. The agenda is each man's own practice of the parish ministry. The first question is this: "What are you doing in your ministry, and why?" They are asked to define their own model of ministry and justify it in terms of their own tradition and the needs of their parish. The second question is: "What, in fact, is happening in terms of your goals and purposes?" This is the issue of honest feedback and evaluation, almost always avoided by clergy. Does the man have a way of checking his own performance? Is he doing what he claims? Can he be clear about the results? We have been amazed at how few men really can handle this question, but it is relatively simple to come up with fairly clear evidence. For example, if preaching is his major emphasis, it is easy enough to ask his key laymen to sit down on Sunday afternoon before a tape recorder and talk about what the sermon said and meant. For the preacher to listen to the tape is usually extremely painful.

The third question for the workshop is: "In the light of this appraisal, what needs to be changed in your theology and practice? What is a responsible model for your ministry, and how can you develop both the requisite skills and the necessary feedback mechanism to function with integrity?" In this third area there is material for many months of work for each of the men. The hope in the course of one semester is to make clear to each the inescapable necessity of such a continuing workshop pattern in his own ministry as the best hope he has of keeping alive and relevant in the face of the ambiguities and frustrations of urban ministry.

We have discovered that the key skill for clergy in these programs turns out to be the same as that for the seminary teacher and the leader in the intern program. They find themselves as enablers, trainers, equippers of the saints. Their function is to help people to learn, to reflect, to plan, and to act. This demands the ability to work with groups, to use experience and involvement for learning. The essential competence to match this skill is that of theologian. To the involvement of the laymen, the clergy must bring the resources of scripture and tradition, not as proof texts, but as genuine elements in decision making. It is his job to help the laity "do theology," that is, relate faith to obedience.

For the long haul the clergyman needs to work continuously on the skills his specific work requires, to find the time for reflection that provides perspective, and to attain collegiality with his peers that forces him to honest appraisal of his performance. The workshop experience under the tutelage of a seminary may be helpful, but there is no excuse for any clergyman's avoiding a regular involvement in such a workshop pattern with other pastors in which they together continue the process of education.

Chapter 13

The Church in the City
as a Locale
for Humanizing Life

BY HOWARD MOODY

The question asked in this volume's title—*Will the Church Lose
the City?*—by now may well be merely rhetorical. Perhaps the
church lost the city a century ago.

The diminishing role of the church in the urban centers of our
nation probably should prompt us to ask: "Will the city lose the
church?"

The life of the city and the life of the church in America are
inextricably bound together. Only if both the city and the church
fulfill their true reason for being will there be even a chance for us
to survive the future burdens of existence.

Lewis Mumford, one of the more controversial urbanologists,
suggests that "We must restore to the city the material, life-
nurturing functions, the autonomous activities, the symbiotic associations that have long been neglected or suppressed. For the city
should be an organ of love, and the *best economy of cities is the
care and culture of men*"[1] (italics mine). This, I would suggest, is
the true reason for the city's existence. It is the only rational justification for enduring the hardships and struggling against the human and mechanical elements that threaten the very life of the city.
Cramming eight million people together in unbearable proximity
so that we stand on each other or shove each other but seldom
embrace one another must have some believable justification. And

the only real reason for the existence of cities must be the "nurturing of life functions" and "the care and culture of men." Our cities must be more than carefully planned monuments to massiveness sprawling aimlessly over the countryside in disconnected entities. We must remember that people are the subjects for whom and around whom cities should be built.

Whenever I travel from my magical island of Manhattan to the mountains or the ocean, I wonder why people insist on living amidst all the unbearable problems and the polluted environment that threaten to destroy our physical bodies—even before the Bomb does! What "sickness" draws me to endure the metropolis? The only sense I can make of it is that I live for the challenge and the promise of the city. The *challenge* is that the city might be changed from death to life, from decay to renewal. The *promise* is that it could exist for the care and culture of men.

Church-City Parallels

It seems that in the life of the church there is a parallel to Mumford's definition of the cities. In trying to define and redefine the mission and meaning of the church's existence in the last decade, we were drawn to Paul Lehmann's statement that God's mission is mankind and keeping human life human. For this the church is at best an agent.

When we have been courageous enough to recognize that the church's reason for existence is not merely to save its own hide or to guarantee its own perpetuity, but mainly to be at the task of "humanizing life," we have discovered a reason for staying in the church—despite its collective hypocrisy and apathy. If the city itself is to be a place for "the care and culture of men," how much more the church ought to be a locale for the humanizing of life. That we have not understood what this entails constitutes the most important factor behind the diminishing size, significance, and influence of churches in the city.

Just as many city planners and builders thought that all buildings, capacious projects, extensive networks of highways, and mountains of manufactured goods were what make a city important, so many clergy, leaders, and planners of the Christian churches thought that preservation of church buildings and church organizations, or that doctrinal purity and theological uniformity, were what made the church. This is a natural enough mistake, but its impact is far-reaching. To paraphrase Mumford, the *church* should be an organ of love—and the best economy of *churches* is the making and keeping of life human.

If this is true, then the way of the church in the world is indeed inadequate. The city planner must keep in mind that physical and material planning enables people to create a civilization; likewise, developers and leaders of the church must recognize that the physical environment, the programs, the activities, and the liturgical practices must serve the purpose of humanizing life.

How can we turn sectarian enclaves of like-minded people with similar beliefs into an open and universal community of accepting and accepted persons? This is no mean question. T. S. Eliot puts the question to city dwellers as well as church men in his chorus from *The Rock*:

> Though you have shelters and institutions,
> Precarious lodgings where the rent is paid,
> Subsiding basements where the rat breeds
> Or sanitary dwellings with numbered doors . . . ;
> When a stranger says: "What is the meaning of this?
> Do you huddle together because you love each other?"
> What will you answer? "We all dwell together
> To make money from each other?" or "This is a community?"[2]

Toward Symbiosis

Let us again refer to Mumford, as he speaks of restoring the "symbiotic associations that have long been neglected or suppressed." The biological understanding of *symbiotic* is the "living together in intimate associations of dissimilar organisms." This is one of the unique and precious distinctions of urban life—the amazing diversity of human beings, of all shades of color and of all varieties of ethnic and cultural backgrounds.

As this is true of the city in terms of its real nature, it must be even more true of the Christian community in the metropolis. The church must be able to hold together in creative conflict the real diversities of humanity, the clear differences in theology, and the truly distinctive moralities. The universality and the inclusiveness of Christian vision somehow must be incarnated in the visible reality of the church in the city. Our buildings often seem like closed turf reserved "for members only"; our worship and ceremonies often exude exclusiveness; our statements and resolutions frequently have the arrogant ring of theological and ecclesiological necessity. The agnostic, the believer, the half-believer, the atheist, the Catholic, the Protestant and the Jew must link together, must test each other's presumptions, must challenge each other's behavior—leaving the residue of our faith/unfaith upon each other. Only then may we have a vital, living community of faith. Christians who live in a homogeneous environment of believing comrades may enjoy a kind of sectarian security (and it may be possible to do in certain rural and small-town communities), but it is a luxury not permitted the church in the city.

One of the most important ways of making life more human is to liberate men from the gnawing fear of and insecurity about difference and diversity. With the recent school strike and its escalation of anti-Semitic and white racist slogans, New York City, the great melting pot of America, has suffered a most serious rupture in ethnic minority relations. The church in this city has been almost completely impotent to address or in any way ameliorate the racial and religious tensions tearing at the fabric of *civitas*. This comes in no small measure from the ecclesiastical isolationism of the church, and the ethnocentrism of our theology.

Another characteristic of the city is that it is a place of great flux and change. The city is constantly decaying and dying at the same time it is being born and renewed. This constancy of change that characterizes the city is also descriptive of our whole world. Men living in the midst of these alternating tides must be nurtured and prepared for these cataclysms that keep interrupting the stability and familiarity of "life as we know it."

The Church and Revolution

The church, historically associated with metaphors of eternal, unchanging, and absolute, seems least prepared in the city to deal with change and turnover. Yet it is precisely at this point that I think the church must be prepared to break new ground. This change and revolution, most visibly seen in the tearing down and rebuilding in the city streets, is a necessity for the growth of people. And one of the most important tasks the church could have in humanizing life in the city is to relate to the revolution that is permeating every social and political institution in our common life.

Let us be clear about what the church can and cannot do in the crisis of social change. It seems that the most effective way for the church to tie into those revolutions is not to lead them (we relinquished that right a long time ago) or to baptize them, but to service them—just as the Quartermaster Corps in the military furnishes the troops with the items needed to keep alive in the struggle.

To clarify what I understand is the church's place, consider the black revolution. This is typically one of the significant areas of rapid social change, highly relevant to the life of the city. The churches became relatively involved in the civil-rights phase of the black revolution but lost their thrust in this field with the rise of "black power" and "violence" during the post-Watts period. When separatism seemed to replace integration as the aim of the movement, Christians became uneasy and alienated. This is despite the fact that the church has been just about the most practicing separatist in the whole of society.

Our task now—as individuals and as churches—is to be what our black brothers ask us to be, advocates among our own people for the abolition of white racism, seeking to tear down the walls of hostility that keep us apart even when we're together and helping our people to understand the causes of colonization and suppression of black and poor people in this nation of affluence.

I believe that in the time ahead black separatism (some people call it an "interim ethic") will be on the wane, and whites will be tested not by their color but where they stand on white racism and their willingness to risk their necks with and for black brothers in the struggle for justice and equality. To help in their revolution we have to be willing, as one church executive said, "to put our money where our P.R. is." Where the churches are found in the urban revolutions of our day will largely determine whether the city is lost to the church.

The Urban Drama

There is another theme in Mumford's monumental work on the city in which he lifts up the significance of urban drama. It is his feeling that the great dramatic occasions of urban life—the courtroom, the arena, the parliament, the council meeting—are what give meaning to so many activities of the city. Out of this ritual and dramatic action has come the dialogue which is the ultimate expression of the city. I am deeply impressed with a new artistic development (highly urban), the "street theater," where social and political problems are lifted up and dramatized right on the street-corner before the *polis*. In it, drama breaks another barrier of communication (the theater building) and takes its words directly to the people.

The church has a special opportunity as a community uniquely concerned with drama (the mass, worship services, ceremonies) to help create those situations where ritual and cultic acts can open up dialogue in the community. Traditionally in the Christian church, worship has been seen as the dramatic enactment of the work of life (*liturgia*). It has been a way of innovating and making real the struggles that we carry on in the world. Its limitation has been its confinement and its esoteric quality, which for the most part made it an "inside exercise" for believers. The space, the language, and the accouterments of worship made them appropriate only for the enclave.

The church in the city, attempting to be a locale for humanizing life, must see that part of its task is in nurturing and caring for the urban man's symbolic need for communal rituals to evidence a universal drama dealing with urban living. When one speaks of secularizing worship I would think of those kinds of rituals, both memorials and celebrations, that are inclusive of the whole populace. These are times when the drama of worship escapes the narrow strictures of theological exclusiveness, and even the physical limitations of the sanctuary, becoming instead a celebratory event for the community.

To illustrate, this past year Judson Church has been the scene for several memorial services for assassinated victims in our national life. These events, one nationally televised, were more than church services where the Word is spoken or Bread is broken. They were public rituals of grief and thanksgiving which called for the setting aside of normal services.

Also I recall a few years ago the effort we made, at a terrible risk, to place our Easter-morning worship in Washington Square Park, a natural staging area in front of our church building. We elected not only to put it outside for the community, but to expose this most sacred of our ecclesiastic and theological rituals to the secularizing process. We put Easter worship in the vehicle of an early-morning "happening" in the park and let our most incredulous Christian affirmation be seen and spoken in the form of metaphorical vignettes about life and change. And we topped this dangerous exercise by inviting *everyone* to breakfast with us at the church.

The church in the city has amazing opportunities to open up places and times of drama and dialogue, using the natural proclivities of the Christian church in the service of all the people. Why don't we make all outstanding civic events the cause for celebration and festivals, in which the whole community has the opportunity in drama and ritual to pay homage to times of renewal and redemption? We might, with imagination, replace the unbelievably dull and repetitious events that pass for commemorative occasions in the life of our cities.

The "flower children" of several seasons ago (how I do miss them) pointed in some important directions with their "love-ins" and "be-ins." They may have frightened us and made us uneasily anxious, but when our guards were down, we knew that something beautiful and different was happening, erupting through the routinized dullness of our collective existence like some epiphanies of joy—allowing us, even for one day, to be human to each other. How telling it was that this kind of event didn't originate in the churches, but even sadder we did not take the children's cue and make these celebrations of our human life periodic occasions. Rather, by joining the Establishment "put-down" of these events as simply opportunities for pot-smoking and exhibitionism, we never saw the beauty of their potential.

Why do dedications, commemorations, and other civic ceremonies have to be composed of unbearable speeches with leaden words, the music of the sanitation-department band, and meaningless prayers from tripartite religion? The church could give leadership in developing occasions for real drama and "happenings" that could transfer community rituals into festivals of joy and surprise.

Marks of the Humanizing Church

If the church, *for* the city and *in* the city, is to be a locale for humanizing life, there are several marks that it will bear:

It will be a *place* for the *displaced*. I hope Christians have finished that period of breast-beating and *"mea culpas"* over the fact that they own buildings. We should never have been trapped in that disincarnate spiritualism that pretended the church was like some floating angel unattached to any concrete place. We should not be ashamed of our buildings (however big or ugly or old), only of what we have done with them—turning them into mausoleums or well-kept landmarks, or bastions of respectability rather than places of life and human warmth and contact.

The church must be a place, but a special place, for all the displaced people of the city, swarming over its face, uprooted, unsettled, and highly mobile. The church can be a human, communal sanctuary—not meaning a holy and special place where holy and special things are said and expected, but a *commune* where all things may be said; a human waystation where modern pilgrims of all kinds could stop to visit, protected there from the pressures and conformities of this world that urge us to end the journey and close the search. In a world where painful exactions and unbearable stereotypes are made of persons, the church could be a place where the expectations are *only* that we be tolerant of each other's search. Where the only blasphemy is a hurried or frenetic pressure that people embrace some abstract gospel or liberal ideology or vocational commitment. Where the only heresy is the failure to share with another (when it is desired). Where we are in the pilgrimage. Like the desert Bedouins gathered around the campfire of an oasis, people need a place in the city—a commune, a sanctuary where we tell each other our life stories, share our anguish and joy, our fears and hopes.

Another mark of the church as a locale for humanizing life is one of *radical openness*. By this I mean that in the services rendered, in the meetings held, and in the worship conducted, they are done without ulterior motives, hidden agendas, or guile of any kind. The church must be sure that the people accepted and served are not manipulated ideologically or sociologically. There must be nothing but the situation that is given and the relationship that grows out of people caring for each other and helping one another to grow by love and acceptance. This openness of which I speak does not come because we do not believe anything, but because the church believes some important things, namely, that we live in a dynamic world still in the process of creation and every human life is analogous to that world-in-creation. Secondly, it believes we are only men, not gods or God. To play God with truth or with determination of another human's life is the final blasphemy.

Something More Than Success

This radical openness is not an easy posture. It has in it a risk of failure which stems from the deep conviction that there are some things more important than success or even survival (not many, but some). Openness means you have relinquished complete control of persons and situations: Outcomes can't be guaranteed. It means that churches and congregations will have to put their institutional life on the line at some points. Radical openness means that neither the fear of change nor the dread of catastrophe must prevent us from being, with integrity, what *we* are in dealing with other humans, being as *they* are. For what will it profit a church if it converts the whole city and loses its own authentic spirit?

A further mark of the church as a locale for humanizing life is that it will be infected with a "spirit of liberty." In a world enslaved by fears, chained by anxieties, informed by calculating prudence, and smothered by a debilitating consensus, it is a breath of freshest air to breathe freedom. The church so often is a proclaimer of freedom—but not an exemplar of freedom. It is those people called Christians who have been supposedly liberated that are slaves of their own morality, their own rituals, their own laws, their own theological systems.

It doesn't mean that any church is completely free, but that what it does and what it preaches are tested by that spirit. It is the burden of our faith, and the freedom, of which we speak; it is not license without limitations, but it is the "liberty of the Christian man," i.e., "that slave of no man, the servant of everyman." Bonhoeffer's prototype Man of Freedom, with all its attendant dangers and possibilities, is the kind of church we're talking about.

If life is to be made more humane, that sense of liberty must rule our lives, so that we do not simply preach about freedom but rather act as if we're free persons. The city which is bound and cribbed in by so many fates and necessities needs such beachheads of freedom to sustain persons in their hope and break open to them the possibilities of a new life and a renewed city. In such liberty we may discover that the church is not just a traditional institution of ancient rituals and symbols by which we are bound to the past, but the Christian community (in its fullest sense) is something that happens like Christmas (where something special is born) or like Easter (one who is dead is now alive).

The church is not just a religious sector carved out of the city. It is a "happening" in the city, and when it occurs in authenticity it is a miracle and a surprise to believers and nonbelievers alike. For those who are very sure they know what the church is and exactly where it is found, the idea is a little bothersome. But then, the same people would never pick a stable or a cave for anything special to happen in.

But thank God for the surprises by which he turns our knowledge into folly, and our certainties into absurdities.

Part III
Actualities and Prospects

Chapter 14

What Are the Churches
Actually Doing
in the City? I

BY DAVID W. BARRY

This could be a very misleading chapter. It could list literally hundreds of new forms of ministry that churches are developing in response to the crises on the American urban scene and leave the reader with the impression that the city church is vibrantly alive, flexible, innovative, and relevant. Indeed this is the impression conveyed by much of the denominational press, which is never able to resist becoming a public-relations arm of the church for the mission boards.

In fact, however, the churches of the American cities for the most part are doing what they have always done—carrying on the largely traditional forms of worship and Christian education, serving population groups they have historically been related to, trying to survive the waves of population movement that bring unfamiliar people to the neighboring streets, trying to capitalize on the "favorable" population movement to suburbs, and reserving more radical responses only for situations of obvious institutional failure or crises of the intensity of the recent riots.

Migration of Population

The big sociological fact that dominates all others on the American urban scene is the movement of black citizens from the rural South to the cities, North, West, and South. Accompanying this has been the smaller but still very sizable movement to the city of Spanish-speaking groups (Mexicans, Puerto Ricans, Cubans, and others) and Indians. As they have moved in, the more affluent white population has departed for the suburbs, with a drastic effect on the churches of the city, Protestant and Catholic, and on the synagogues as well.

Population figures for New York City dramatize the magnitude of the change. The Department of Church Planning and Research of the Protestant Council makes the following estimates concerning that city's Protestant population:

	Total Protestants	Black	Spanish-American	White
1940	2,010,000	430,000	not available	1,500,000
1950	1,750,000	700,000	35,000	1,015,000
1960	1,752,000	1,000,000	130,000	622,000
1968	2,042,400	1,382,000	146,000	514,400

Thus in the past quarter-century the nation's largest city has lost a million white Protestants and gained a million black and Spanish-speaking Protestants. On a smaller scale numerically, but often with an even greater proportionate effect, the same story can be told of other cities—Washington, Chicago, Newark, Cleveland, St. Louis, Gary, Los Angeles, Oakland, and many more.

And with the newcomers, of course, come all the liabilities America imposes on its dark-skinned citizens—poverty, inferior education, deteriorating housing, rising welfare rolls, unemployment and underemployment, and the associated ills of the poor.

So the primary answer to the question, "What are the churches actually doing in the city?" is this: They are reacting to the tremendous social change in the city brought about by ethnic population movements. For the predominantly white Protestant denominations this has meant great trouble: It is estimated that fully half of such churches in New York City are barely surviving and have little capacity to do anything else. A few show bright promise—not generally through racial integration, the hopeful strategy of the 1950's, but through identification with the new racial groups. On the other hand, the black denominations are thriving as never before, with churches multiplying, growing, and building, and are turning their eyes to new fields to conquer—housing, community control of schools, economic development, political organization, and other new forms of ministry relevant to the needs of their people. And the Spanish Protestant churches, especially the Pentecostal churches, are perhaps the most dynamic evangelical churches to be found in the city today.

The strength of the white denominations—again Protestant, Catholic, and Jewish—has fled with the white population to suburbia, where the religious institutions of white America are prospering, despite a growing evidence of anguish of conscience over the racial separation. There are numerous but rather sporadic instances of efforts to relate white suburbanite Christians to black ghetto Christians, but none that has effectively changed the population flow. One of the most spectacular was a project in the spring of 1968 headed by Monsignor Robert J. Fox of the Archdiocese of New York, called, "The Thing in the Spring," which brought thousands of suburban volunteers into fifty slum blocks in Manhattan and the Bronx for a day of clean-up, paint-up, and beautification.

The historic "power structures" of the churches have been slow to reflect the changing nature of urban Protestantism. The predominantly white denominations still tend to be headed by white leadership, as do the councils of churches. There are instances of change: The Council of Churches of Greater Washington, D.C., recently called a black executive; in New York City the Presbytery of New York City and the New York Conference of the United Church of Christ now have black clergymen in the top executive roles; and the Episcopal Diocese of Long Island has a black suffragan bishop. But for the most part such ecclesiastical structures are still white in leadership and style, and as a result attract minimum participation from the black church community. Increasingly, black churches are setting up their own interchurch structures outside the white church establishment and are forming black caucuses within the denominations that have a racial mixture.

New Mission Efforts

The context of the ministry of the city church today, then, tends to be business as usual in the face of mounting urban crisis and drastic social change. Church budgets continue to flow through the old channels for familiar purposes. Obviously this cannot continue indefinitely, and church leaders are concerned, bewildered, and looking for new shapes and styles of ministry relevant to the changing urban demands. New experiments are popping up everywhere—usually ecumenical, usually related to the racial situation, usually employing specially raised "crisis" funds or foundation or government funding rather than the regular budgets of the church. Consider the following random selection of new mission efforts reported in the church press in 1968.

Chicago, Illinois: The Wellington Avenue Church of Christ (a church in the West Side ghetto) mortgaged its building for ten thousand dollars to support Operation Breadbasket, an economic enterprise of the Southern Christian Leadership Conference.

Detroit, Michigan: Four hundred Protestant and Catholic women pounded the streets for three months to prove that the poor pay more for less and that a housewife's skin color affects the price she pays, in a project called Focus: Summer Hope, financed by New Detroit, Inc., a civic and business group founded after the 1967 disorders.

Kansas City, Kansas: The United Presbyterians founded a church with membership based on a concern for social issues rather than place of residence.

Portland, Oregon: Seventeen churches in downtown Portland, including Roman Catholic and Missouri Synod Lutheran churches, sponsored a project called Hub-CAP, which includes the Clarix coffee house and the Outside Inn, havens for alienated and estranged young people on the loose.

Pittsburgh, Pennsylvania: The Episcopal Church of the Holy Cross bought a food market in the Hill District, scene of racial disorders following which thirty groceries closed down, and is selling shares in the new cooperative at ten dollars each.

New York, New York: The Judson Memorial Church opened a residence and community program for the "hippies" and runaway youngsters of Greenwich Village, with the help of several foundation grants.

Menlo Park, California: The City Council approved the setting up of a cooperative grocery store in a ghetto neighborhood by a group headed by A. W. Williams, pastor of the Second Baptist Church of San Mateo.

Denver, Colorado: The Executive Cabinet of the Colorado Council of Churches endorsed the goals of the strike against Kitayana Brothers Greenhouses, the state's largest producer of carnations, the strike issues being union recognition, higher wages, and better working conditions.

Washington, D.C.: One hundred and fifty Protestant, Catholic, and Jewish leaders from nineteen states attended an Interreligious Legislative Conference to press for legislation supporting the goals of the Poor People's Campaign and recommendations of the National Advisory Committee on Civil Disorders.

Kansas City, Missouri: The Metropolitan Interchurch Agency operated a command post during the riots (including Roman Catholics, Southern Baptists, Lutherans), requested a public apology for police use of tear gas, and succeeded in getting the municipal stadium opened for a "talk-out."

Chicago, Illinois: Baptists, Lutherans, Presbyterians, Episcopalians, and Roman Catholics joined to form an academy for black high-school dropouts (Christian Action Ministry), financed by government funds.

Minneapolis, Minnesota: General Assembly of the United Presbyterian Church voted to raise a ten-million-dollar crisis fund and directed its agencies to allot thirty percent of their reserve budgets for inner-city seed money. Most of the other major denominations took similar actions at their annual meetings.

New York, New York: Protestants, Roman Catholics, and Jews (denominations and welfare agencies) set up an Urban Crisis Ecumenical Task Force to be prepared to react to summer crises, and trained fifteen hundred volunteers in thirty "clusters" to understand the racial crisis and discover a role to play.

Bergen County, New Jersey: Church Women United working with the National Council of Churches set up a program to help certain New Jersey adults acquire literacy.

New York, New York: The Ministers' Interfaith Association (Central Harlem) and the East Harlem Cooperating Christian Churches each opened an office to give churches and groups of churches technical aid in sponsoring housing and urban-renewal projects.

Chicago, Illinois: The Chicago City Missionary Society changed its name to the Community Renewal Society and began a drive for three million dollars to invest in the renewal of a selected ghetto neighborhood through a black-white coalition.

Chicago, Illinois: The Northside Cooperative Ministry, including twenty-eight churches, opened their churches to feed and shelter demonstrators at the Democratic National Convention, and their clergy stood with the demonstrators under police attack in Grant Park.

Houston, Texas: The new president of the Southern Baptist Convention announced he is no longer a segregationist, and the Convention called on Southern Baptists "to resist prejudice and to combat forces that breed distrust and hostility."

New York, New York: The Interfaith City-Wide Coordinating Committee against Poverty involved three hundred and eighty-two churches in poverty areas in the employment of two thousand six hundred seventy-five young people, mostly Neighborhood Youth Corps enrollees, with a youth payroll of almost a million dollars, and supervised seventy-eight VISTA volunteers in community projects.

New York, New York: PEDCO (Presbyterian Economic Development Corporation) announced that its loans to ghetto-based business and housing enterprises now total over one million dollars.

Now, this listing of church actions is obviously not typical of what city churches are doing; if these were normal church activities, they would not be reported as news. But out of them, one can get a sense of the direction in which city churches are heading.

Churches of every theological persuasion in the cities are moving to address the human problems and issues of today's cities, although they are not at all clear as to which issues churches can best address—community organization, political action, education, economic development, housing, job opportunities, racism, labor organizations, youth alienation, or others.

The preservation of small and struggling local churches is no longer a significant priority of mission.

Local churches are learning they cannot address urban problems in isolation, but must join neighboring churches (and secular agencies) in ecumenical efforts that have the potential of having an impact on a community.

The urban church will not much longer tolerate national denominational structures which drain off the benevolence dollar into national bureaucracies, headquarters buildings, conference and travel budgets, national programs, and self-serving denominational literature in the name of Christian mission, and return only a pittance for urban mission in the field.

Black church leadership is beginning to emerge into positions of power on the urban scene.

Former scruples about the church's use of government funds are rapidly disappearing (and never existed in the black church), and city churches are turning to government programs as well as private and foundation sources for resources to conduct relevant human ministries.

Models for Mission Strategy

With denominational structures proving largely irrelevant to the new tasks in which many churches are now engaging themselves, there is much discussion and some experimentation in new forms of church organization for metropolitan mission. Almost without exception, these forms assume that a metropolitan mission strategy requires an interdenominational or ecumenical organization with the capacity to put together denominational budgets and staff to conduct programs formerly left to denominational auspices as well as new programs and programs formerly conducted by councils of churches. A recent Presbyterian survey shows the following models of organization for effecting a metropolitan mission strategy.[1]

A. Councils of churches and their divisions

(Example 1) Council of Churches of Christ of Greater Cleveland, Cleveland, Ohio. After much study, this council was reorganized by the denominations in 1966 as a joint instrument for urban mission. It works through three commissions: (a) Metropolitan Affairs (war on poverty, social-welfare program), (b) Ecumenical Education (stressing training the laity to serve in the world), and (c) Public Witness (mass communications and public relations).

(Example 2) Board for Urban Ministry of the Rochester (New York) Area Council of Churches. This is a new structure through which eight denominations have agreed to plan, administer, and staff all their new urban work in the Rochester area.

B. Para-council agencies, including groups outside council membership

(Example) Interreligious Council on Urban Affairs, Chicago, Illinois. This is a service agency comprised of representatives of Protestant, Catholic, and Jewish groups established to "augment the contribution of organized religious bodies to the solution of urban problems."

C. "Joint Action in Mission" structures at metropolitan levels

(Example 1) Collegium for Ecumenical Action, Los Angeles, California. This is a group of Protestant denominational and ecumenical agency executives who began meeting without formal structure to plan together for metropolitan mission, then in 1966 agreed to consider themselves a single Protestant staff of thirteen to do planning, reflection, coordination, and communication.

(Example 2) Joint Action in Mission, New York City. This is a covenant relationship among Protestant denominational and agency executives to meet regularly, plan together, and use existing staffs for ecumenical action rather than create new ecumenical structures.

Which of these models, if any, will prove to be most effective, time alone can tell. All of them find great resistance to the reallocation of budgets and staff to new thrusts in mission, or to set hard priorities that require discontinuing the funding of low-priority projects in order to have resources for new and high-priority programs.

Ecumenical Mission Structures

The counterpart of the emerging ecumenical-mission structures at the metropolitan level is the ecumenical interparish structure at the local-community level. In New York City the decision was made in 1968 for a radical reorganization of the Protestant Council of the City of New York, the new organization to be based on "church-community associations," or ecumenical associations of churches at the neighborhood level, inclusive of Roman Catholic parishes. As the Council proceeded to study the city's neighborhoods, it became clear that a number of such organizations had already come into being without any stimulus from overhead agencies. The Ministers' Interfaith Association in Harlem and the Interfaith Community Services of Brooklyn (Bedford-Stuyvesant) had been organized in response to the riots of 1964 to conduct ghetto youth-employment programs; included Protestant, Catholic, and Jewish (Orthodox) participants; had incorporated; had scraped together budgets from foundations, antipoverty programs, and their own members; and were operating programs not only in youth employment but in health care, college assistance, welfare client organization (with VISTA workers), mental health, senior citizens, and employment—as well as occasional mass ecumenical services, as on the day after Martin Luther King's assassination. These interchurch organizations and others from East Harlem, the South Bronx, the Lower East Side, South Jamaica in Queens, and other poverty areas had banded together in the Interfaith City-Wide Coordinating Committee against Poverty, which had contracted with the Neighborhood Youth Corps and VISTA for the largest such programs in the nation. While this had the endorsement and participation of the denominational executives in Joint Action in Mission, it was the clergy of the black and Puerto Rican churches, with minimum support from the "standard-brand" denominations, who had created the organization and located sources of support.

This pattern of neighborhood interchurch organization for mission effort is developing in a number of cities, as in the Northside Cooperative Ministry in Chicago previously referred to. It is found especially in neighborhoods where poverty is a problem and where the old-line denominations are in trouble. They are emphatically nontheological; the ecumenical partnerships derive from a common commitment to get a job done in a troubled community, not from a moral conviction that they must implement Christ's prayer "that they may be one." In the more affluent communities where churches are not under pressure to survive, they more often seem content to express their ecumenicity through ministers' fellowships, union Thanksgiving services, and such verbal ecumenical efforts as living-room dialogues. Increasingly these are interfaith, in line with the new ecumenical mood.

Another increasingly familiar pattern is the neighborhood organization in which churches are closely involved, and often were instrumental in founding and staffing, but which involves nonchurch groups and is not considered a church effort. Such, for example, is the well-known TWO (The Woodlawn Organization) in Chicago, or BOMB (Better Organization in Mid-Bronx) in the Bronx, or COINS (Christians and Others United in Neighborhood Service) in Brooklyn.

There are also urban programs which were begun by churches and which continue to be largely under church control, through the composition of their boards, but which are addressed to urban problems that have not historically been considered church-program concerns. Perhaps the best known is Opportunities Industrialization Centers, Inc. (OIC), which began in Philadelphia under the leadership of a Baptist clergyman, Leon Sullivan. Together with several hundred other black clergymen, Sullivan decided to attack the problem of racial discrimination in employment through economic boycotts of products sold by companies which practiced racial discrimination (the boycotts were euphemistically described as "selective patronage"). Through effective use of the pulpits of black churches ("First we talked about Jesus Christ; then we talked about Taystee-Cakes"), the churches opened up a number of skilled jobs to their black communities. They then found they did not have the trained personnel to fill the jobs. Sullivan thereupon started a skills-training program, using black volunteers and stressing (a) motivation for work, (b) concentration on skills relevant to specific jobs, and (c) training for definite jobs that would be available at the end of the training program. It worked so well that the Ford Foundation, the Department of Labor, and business itself eventually brought financial support to this program, and today there are OICs in some eighty cities in the United States.

A somewhat similar program under the auspices of the Southern Christian Leadership Conference is Operation Breadbasket, headed by Jesse L. Jackson, which uses the economic power of the black consumer as the entering wedge to secure jobs and economic power for the ghetto resident.

Finally, individual churches by the hundreds are undertaking programs that ten years ago would not have been considered the business of the church. Tutoring programs are very popular as one way in which concerned volunteers can help to remedy the deficiencies of urban educational systems serving black children.

Head Start programs have gravitated naturally to churches, which often have the only available classroom space outside the public schools in ghetto communities. The Housing Act of 1966, as revised in 1967 and 1968, is obviously designed to encourage churches (nonprofit agencies in general, but in the ghetto this means churches) to get into the business of sponsoring housing for low-income people, and a rapidly increasing number of churches are trying to take advantage of this legislation. The antipoverty programs have opened up many new possibilities; there are churches in Harlem, for example, that have in effect turned over their premises on weekdays to antipoverty programs, reserving only Sunday for "religious" programming. And in very, very rare instances, individual churches have made the decision to defy the traditions of institutional behavior and accept the necessity of radical change to become relevant to the urban crisis. One example is the historic Broadway United Church of Christ in Manhattan, which, finding its edifice condemned, decided not to rebuild, but to lease its valuable land to commercial interests, use the income for programs related to urban problems, and accept the invitation of a neighboring Roman Catholic parish to use its facilities for Sunday worship.

The Anguish of the Church

What we are seeing, clearly, is the anguish of the church as it faces the anguish of the urban world. Seen in historical perspective, the denominational systems of Protestant America were at least in part a device to avoid direct confrontation between an uncompromising gospel of love and justice, supporting the stated aims of American democracy, and the realities of injustice and inequity among races and classes in American society. The denominational device allowed each class and ethnic group to have its own "church," and thus kept the contradictions of social injustice outside the framework of any given religious community. The restlessness within the urban church seems to be signaling the end of the denominational system. Across the country the youth of the nation are announcing that they will not tolerate what they see as the hypocrisy of an older generation that proclaims one set of values and practices another. The dark-skinned ethnic minorities are announcing that they will no longer tolerate second-class citizenship. And within the church the younger clergy in particular are saying that either the church becomes an instrument for social change, or they will desert it for some other institution or movement that will. It is a time of testing for the church, with most of the action occurring in cities. It would appear that the church must either rise to the challenge or be written out of history as one of God's instruments for the redemption of mankind.

Chapter 15

What Are the Churches Actually Doing in the City? II

BY G. H. JACK WOODARD

In Shakespeare's *Julius Caesar* we are reminded:

> There is a tide in the affairs of men
> Which, taken at the flood, leads on to fortune;
> Omitted, all the voyage of their life
> Is bound in shallows and in miseries.
> On such a full sea are we now afloat;
> And we must take the current when it serves,
> Or lose our ventures.

Future historians are certain to call this era a flood tide for the churches in the cities. Tide and time are beginning to run out for the old ways and attitudes. We must dare to cast off and set sail on new and risky voyages of servanthood into the unknown, or be left high and dry on the mudflats of history. The name of the sea on which we are afloat is "the urban crisis."

That crisis is the result of the greatest migration in the history of mankind. In every nation of the world huge masses of people are demonstrating they prefer poverty in the city slums to poverty on the rural soil. Urbanization is a phenomenon that is not geographic. It cannot be thought of as simply a problem of the cities. It affects the societal structure of jungle villages in Africa and bustees in Calcutta equally and drastically. The growing of pine trees supplants the farming of cotton in Alabama, and black families leave their enforced idleness to move to Harlem. But their migration leaves an acute problem in Alabama as much as it creates a problem in New York. There is an "urban crisis" in Alabama and an "urban crisis" in New York—and in every other corner of the globe. And it is a godsend to the churches because it is absolutely unavoidable.

No amount of rationalizing or of theological erudition will alter the fact that the churches have lost their ability to maintain the status quo of a salaried clergyman in every hamlet or an ornate edifice every few blocks in the cities. Drastic change is inevitable. The only question is whether it will be voluntary or involuntary, constructive or destructive.

The churches need the urban crisis more than the urban crisis needs the churches—just as was true in the now-dead days of the civil-rights movement. Unavoidable crisis is the mother of renewal. God must see his churches like the farmer saw his mule, which had to be hit in the head with a plank to get his attention so he could be trained to do the job for which he existed on the farm. The churches have to be hit with a crisis in order to embrace change.

But whatever the motivation, the churches are indeed changing drastically—not just in the cities, but everywhere. Forty-nine of the fifty-five Episcopal parishes on the island of Manhattan could not operate as they do without dead people's money in endowments, and so there are islands of insularity to change. And such islands are likely to exist for many years. But the Lord God is bringing a whole new church to birth in these times. What is now called (with unfortunate accuracy) "the underground church" is likely to become *the* church. At the least, the underground church is a sign of the marks of the *new* church of God. The central issue for the church as we have known it is not whether it will change—it inevitably will. The issue is whether it will prove capable of changing fast enough and radically enough to be a part of God's new church rather than a historical curiosity left behind by the blinding, joyful pace of God's creative activity in these years.

The significant question is not "What are the churches actually doing in the city?" but "What is God doing everywhere, the city included, and what is the response of the churches?"

Let the People Decide

"I am come that they may have life and have it more abundantly." Biblical texts like this one have found expression in mission and ministry for centuries. But almost never on the basis that the "unchurched" man knows best what the church should do for him. The churches have designed one mission program after another with the presupposition that the churches know what is best for those whom they would serve. And underneath much of the rhetoric has been paternalism. The churches, consciously or unconsciously, have served as instruments of control of the poor. "Rice Christians" have been produced by the thousands in the ghettos as well as in Asia.

But a historical shift has begun to take place. Here, for example, are the policies (adopted in September, 1967) which control and shape the urban mission program of the Episcopal church:

> Resolved, the House of Bishops concurring, that in the execution of any and all grants contemplated by the "Crisis in American Life Program" of such General Church Program, the Executive Council acting for and on behalf of the Episcopal Church, either alone or through coalition with other churches or agencies approved by the Council, shall be responsible to the Episcopal Church, in accord with proper stewardship, for the following aspects of each such grant:
> (1) Initial appraisal of the purposes and ends sought to be obtained by the proposed grant recipient;
> (2) Initial appraisal of the ability of the proposed grant recipient to attain such purposes and ends;
> (3) Proper accounting by the grant recipient for the proceeds of such grant and audit thereof in accord with customary procedures;
> (4) Evaluation of the administration and execution of the grant and of the progress towards the attainment of the purposes and ends sought thereby;
> (5) The programs contemplated by this Resolution Number 6 shall be administered, implemented, and carried out without regard to race, creed, or ethnic origin.
> Otherwise, neither the Episcopal Church, nor the Executive Council or any officer or agency thereof, shall undertake to exercise any supervision or control whatsoever over any grant

once made, or the administration and execution thereof by the
recipient, or the ends and purposes sought to be attained thereby;
Provided, that none of these funds may be utilized for the benefit of, or in connection with, the activities of any individual
or group which advocates the use of violence as a part of its
program.

What a revolution lies within these policies! "Let the people
decide" is their presupposition. They mean that a church has
decided to be an enabler of what the poor and the dispossessed
want—what they think is best for themselves. Do they want the
power to make a city government do what they want done in their
neighborhood? Then the church will provide funds without strings
attached for community organization. Do they want a chance to get
their own side before the public in a controversy? Then the church
will buy space for them in the press and time on television without
editorial control. Do they say they are being economically exploited by outsiders? Then the church provides skills and capital
for the development of economic power. Is there a flicker of new
determination among the lowest of the labor low—the domestic
servants? Then the church provides funds and training for union
organizing to enable them to form a union of domestics.

The urban mission program of the churches begins to become
something very simple and yet extremely different from what it has
been. It begins to become what its supposed beneficiaries say it
ought to be—not what the providers of the money say it ought to
be. And often the effect is that the providers of the money discover themselves and their institutions and their businesses and
their social structures the objects of attacks made possible by
their own money.

Not surprisingly, resentment grows and retribution is serious. In
the first full fiscal year after full implementation of those historic
urban-mission policies by the Episcopal church, national income
of that denomination fell by nearly twelve percent. When the rate
of inflation is taken into account, that is a drop of more than sixteen percent in one year. It would be simplistic to say all of that
decline is due to hostility toward that church's style of response to
the urban crisis, but a significant part of it certainly is due to just
that factor. Similar situations exist in other mainline denomina-

tions whose urban-mission policies have been somewhat the same—United Presbyterian, United Methodist, United Church of Christ, and others.

There is a real question about whether these denominations will prove able to sustain "let the people decide" as a new foundation stone for mission program in the cities. Much of the outcome will depend on the staying power of their leadership more than on their future balance sheets. Church leadership in these days of continuing crisis has already learned existentially the meaning of "leadership fatigue." It is one thing for a national church leader courageously to walk the plank at a major conference or convention and to elicit a response of the moment in the form of an affirmative vote by the delegates present. It is quite another thing for him or her to maintain vision and perspective and energy to outlast the storm of opposition which surely arises after the delegates return home and the church constituency begins to realize what has been done.

But the tension and the financial crises have great value in opening denominational structures to real renewal and change. There begins to be a merciless and long-overdue examination of church priorities. The extreme difficulty of sustaining the essential vigor of leadership until aged retirement begins to be faced and talk arises of reasonably limited tenure for top leadership. The fact that "let the people decide" should apply within the churches as well as outside them begins to be realized, and reforms aimed at achieving participatory democracy within the churches begin to gather momentum. Time-honored church institutional forms such as exclusive dependency on the parish as the fundamental unit begin to be exposed as houses of straw, and experiment aimed at discovering and testing more viable forms begin to be taken seriously. Clergy begin to be *obviously* ill-prepared for the roles they are expected to fill, and reform of theological education and training begins to gather momentum. The ministry of the laity suddenly becomes more than rhetoric, and action-training movement grows. Ecumenicity leaps to the fore as necessity in action rather than the abstract discussion forum it has been through most of this century.

What Are the Churches Actually Becoming in the City?

Let us then turn to an examination of what the churches are becoming in the cities. The nature of these times and their blinding pace of change make it essential to look beneath the catalog of today's doings and try to discern the trends that are marks of becoming.

Two very significant shifts are taking place. First, the traditional financial base of the churches is crumbling. This is far more than merely an effect of hostility within the membership. The denominations have grown and flourished economically—have funded their domestic and overseas programs for at least one hundred and fifty years on the basis of a widespread understanding that giving money to the local congregation was automatically equivalent to giving money to God's work. The congregation in turn gave some percentage to a judicatory organization, which in turn gave some percentage to national boards, agencies, and organizations. This system is tottering for two reasons. The laity in increasing numbers questions the old equation between giving to God and giving to their denomination through their local congregation. No number of new stewardship programs is going to change this questioning very much. It is a mark of the times to question things functionally, empirically. Laymen are quite naturally reflecting the criteria of the times when they begin to wonder how well church structures use their money. They want to know whether they cannot themselves find more effect from their giving by exercising their own judgment about that to which their money goes. One young wealthy layman said recently, "I give my parish ten thousand dollars every year, and I will not give them any more, because they do not know what to do with what they have now. But I am open to being challenged to give not only my money in larger sums, but also my power to enable major social change to take place. However, my church doesn't seem to know what I am talking about, much less to be able to help me find the leverage points for change." The system is beginning to crumble for another reason too. The layers of church structure—local congregation to judicatory to national agencies and boards—are no longer seen at any level as monolithic. The man in the pew does not identify with his denomination at the national or even at the judicatory level. Reflecting the authority crisis in nearly every segment of American society, he is no longer content to let faraway councils and boards decide to do anything they wish with his money. Thus institutional church budgets are beginning to decline because the systems are not equipped to handle questioning of this sort. And the decline is likely to continue for a number of years to come.

The other significant shift has to do with the demography of the churches' constituencies. One denomination now has two-thirds of its congregations in towns of less than fifty thousand population and two-thirds of its members in metropolitan regions. The effects of this are devastating. While it struggles to keep a salaried clergyman and a building in each of thousands of small towns serving a handful of older people in each, it has no effective strategy for building an effective base which is capable of dealing with the bewildering array of problems in the metropolitan regions. And the effect of its "let-the-people-decide" principle for its urban mission is to shift its metropolitan constituency more and more toward the lower middle class and the poor, who are not capable of supporting its inherited expensive structures.

To sum up, then, many denominations are discovering that less and less money is coming in and that their former cushion of prestige and status is disappearing.

Structures—Denominational

Within the denominations, streamlining at the national levels is taking place. One denomination with three hundred thirty-seven employed staff in its national organization in 1964 is down to two hundred seventy-three in 1969 and is contemplating further reductions. During that period it has drastically reorganized its national bureaucracy and now has no separate boards and agencies. All administrative functions for domestic and overseas operations are in one organization under one board and with its subunits designed and named functionally rather than traditionally. The entire organization operates with one budget determined through one process of planning and priority setting. Other denominations are moving in the same direction, though with varying speeds.

Ecumenically speaking, the National Council of Churches is assuming less and less prominence as *the* ecumenical agency for the denominations. Fundamental questions about the future of the conciliar movement of former years are being raised, not by the vociferous Right, but by the very church leaders who have been most active in defending it. And the questions are coming up on functional grounds. The fact is that the National Council of Churches is often prevented from moving with sufficient vigor to engage new styles of mission because of the diversity of its constituent communions.

The discovery of mass-based community organization as a tool of urban mission at the beginning of this decade by several of the major denominations is a case in point. The denominations principally involved (United Presbyterian, United Church of Christ, and Episcopal) tried until early 1965 to get the National Council of Churches to act as the coordinating agency for what those denominations were already determined to do with community organization. At first the NCC was very helpful to them through conducting such dialogical and educational operations as the Consultation on Community Organization in Philadelphia in December of 1964. But the interdenominational dialogue served only to lay bare the wide differences among the denominations on the question of whether community organization was a methodology of mission to the poor that Christian churches should employ. Since the NCC can move as a body only by majority vote of some thirty-three denominations with vote on its general board, and since a majority of those denominations were against community organization, the United Presbyterian church, the United Church of Christ, and the Episcopal church were blocked in the NCC and moved in 1965 to found the Interreligious Foundation for Community Organization as an ecumenical agency for this activity. IFCO quickly grew to include the United Methodist church, the American Baptist church, the Presbyterian church, U.S., several Roman Catholic groups, and the American Jewish Committee. It is now a major factor in the efforts of the churches and other segments of the voluntary sector to help the poor gain economic, social, and political power, and the NCC is not an important factor in this field.

Similarly, the same constellation of denominations joined with private business and labor interests in Urban America, Inc., to foster participation of the churches in providing housing for the poor after the NCC had encountered resistance from many of its member communions. A parallel process and experience led to the formation of the Joint Strategy and Action Committee (JSAC) in 1967 for the purpose of coordinating denominational funding of experimental ministries and to enable a common process of planning and strategy development. JSAC includes the Episcopal church, the United Presbyterian church, the Presbyterian church, U.S., the United Church of Christ, the United Methodist church, and the American Baptist Convention.

Finally, in 1969 "The Commons" began operation as a bold attempt to coalesce important institutions in the voluntary sector of American society for the purpose of developing a multidisciplinary staff of professionals to explore basic issues of the future and to provide member institutions with strategy alternatives for dealing with major specific issues before they become crises. The NCC was helpful in the founding of The Commons but could not contain such an operation within its own structure. In this case, the same denominations which have found themselves collaborating on urban mission through community organization, housing, experimental ministries, and action training are moving toward much broader coalition with nonchurch institutions such as the YWCA, the National Welfare Rights Organization, the Urban League, the League of Women Voters, and others.

It is likely that the National Council of Churches will be most affected by the coming organic union of the nine denominations participating in the Consultation on Church Union. These denominations (African Methodist Episcopal; African Methodist Episcopal Zion; Christian Methodist Episcopal; Christian [Disciples]; United Church of Christ; United Presbyterian; Presbyterian Church, U.S.; United Methodist; and Episcopal) constitute the overwhelming strength of the NCC member communions financially and numerically. Just how the COCU churches' union will mesh with the proliferation of task-centered coalitions such as IFCO, JSAC, and The Commons is not yet clear. But it is certain that structures at the national denominational level are developing rapidly along lines which no longer grant a copyright on ecumenicity to the NCC. And it is further clear that the crisis of the cities has accelerated the pace of ecumenical structural development drastically.

Structures—Metropolitan

Three needs became so clear to many of the denominational judicatories in the early 1960's that significant structural changes began to appear.

1. New forms of urban mission appearing demanded special skills and theological articulateness far beyond that possessed by most clergy and laity. Thus the need for ecumenical programs and centers of theological reflection and intensive training in the skills of community organization, as an example, became apparent.

2. The complexity of urban issues demanded a capacity for ecumenical planning and strategy development.

3. The speed with which crises on the urban scene arise regularly demanded fast-response facilities for accurate communication and coordination of church resources.

Riots in the cities laid bare the inability of city councils of churches to meet these needs. In some cases local councils of churches were able to begin to engage the judicatories in a process of determining what new structure was needed to supplant the council and meet the needs enumerated above. Where this has happened, important structural evolution has occurred. In Kansas City the former council of churches has been willingly supplanted by the Metropolitan Inter-Church Agency (MICA) which, though brand new, was able to swing into effective action in the riots which followed the assassination of Martin Luther King in the spring of 1968. In other cases the council has not been able to adapt and is well along in a process of being supplanted involuntarily by ecumenical action-training and strategy-development centers, and other types of task-centered coalitions of many of the larger denominations. The Interreligious Council for Urban Affairs in Chicago is one such example of a task-centered coalition growing stronger, while the Church Federation of Greater Chicago grows weaker.

Structures—Congregational

The name of the scene at the congregational level in the church in the cities is *diversity of forms*. The parish has been much maligned—and rightly so—in many types of situations. It is beginning to be seen as one form of the church, but not any longer as the only form. It is beginning to be one tool on the church strategy shelf—not the only tool for any situation. Cell congregations meeting an evening per week in apartments and served by a non-stipendiary priest; *ad hoc* congregations formed up for an issue or a task and then disbanded when their task is accomplished; small congregations formed of Christians in the same secular organization, structure, or profession; shopping-center congregations; house churches in the suburbs; ghetto block clubs; and community organizations which begin some liturgical expression presided over by their community organizer, ordained for a sacramental ministry —all these and many more are forms of congregation which exist and multiply daily. From them will emerge a new church rich in its diversity and freed of sole dependence on the parish.

Summary

The focus has been on structure, since structure is a process word. It does not mean "institution." It does not mean a static condition that can be mechanistically charted. It is a dynamic word describing the continually changing shape and form of an identity in human society. The church is such an identity. Now as never before in its history, it is dynamic and changing. God is bringing a new church to birth in these very times, and we have now laid the ground to dare to list what his church seems to be becoming in the cities. The list is presented in full recognition that to do so is like trying to describe Niagara Falls with a single snapshot.

1. A shakeout of church membership is taking place that will produce declining membership and financial statistics for several years. There are some exceptions to this generality. Predominantly black denominations, especially the ones which are most aggressive in terms of the issues that affect black people, are growing and will continue to grow. Also, the predominantly white denominations will grow in the new suburbs, but their growth in such areas will be inversely proportional to their aggressiveness on the core city issues.

2. Many new forms of congregations will develop, and the parish will subside in importance, although it will still be an important unit, where it is viable—mainly in suburbia and at strategic downtown locations.

3. Stewardship will become much more specific. The churches will learn how to serve as brokers between willing lay persons and leverage points on situations of human need. But funds will increasingly pass directly from the giver to the need rather than through formal church structures.

4. Denominational identity will become increasingly unimportant. Ecumenical structures will proliferate along lines allowing organic unity but able to contain and encourage great diversity of mission, ministry, and liturgical expression. *Ad hoc* coalitions will multiply, and many of them will accept the short-lived nature of *ad hoc* existence.

5. A revolution in what has been known as Christian education and seminary education will gain momentum, and the new forms will be along the lines of action-training and strategy centers at a metropolitan level. Nearly all Christian education and theological education will be ecumenical. Focus will be on teaching specific skills for specific mission strategies and on teaching theology as a reflective process on involvement experience rather than as the impartation of a body of lore.

6. Denominational bureaucracies will shrink and will be forced to become much more skilled at the disciplines of long-range planning and objective evaluation of programs.

7. Team ministries will become the norm and will advance in the development of complementary skills on each team, so that ministry becomes truly a corporate effort of specialists.

8. The numbers of full-time professional clergy will decrease, but the total number of ordained clergy will increase because of spectacular growth in the self-supporting ordained ministry. Training and education of such clergy will less and less be done by the seminaries and more and more by the action-training centers and other community-centered programs, permitting preparation for ordination without disturbance of community relationships and without a break in the continuity of secular careers.

In all this the driving search will be for "community," and it will be found by the churches in non-place-centered forms around

issues and secular structures. What an exciting era in which to be
alive and to be a Christian!

> . . . we must take the current when it serves,
> Or lose our ventures.

Chapter 16

Prospects
and Parables

BY F. NILE HARPER

In an oversimplified form we can say that the church has moved through three different styles of relating to the city in the last century. The first style was focused on *evangelizing* the population, bringing the people into the church, churching the city. This style characterized the Protestant churches during their period of primacy just before the turn of the century. The second style focused on the church as the *moral voice of the city* and as the provider of *philanthropic services* for individual needs. In various degrees this posture remains at the present time and provides a set of images in relation to which newer styles are being formed. The third style, the *new creation as metropolis*, focuses on the church as God's agent for humanizing life and seeking social justice in the city. This is a posture which the church is beginning to develop as it moves toward the next decade.

The Denominational Response

What are the prospects for the church in the city in the decade of the 1970's? A brief review of some of the developments of the 1960's will help to show the challenges which face the churches in the city in the next decade. During the 1960's within the major

The writer acknowledges the assistance of Tom Kilpatrick with the material in the parables.

cities the exodus of white Protestants continued at a rapid pace.
Numerically, the Protestant church has become more and more a
suburban phenomenon. Hundreds of mainline Protestant congregations have closed their doors and either moved out or died out
altogether. The remaining mainline Protestant congregations have
continued in a strategy of selective evangelism which has essentially excluded black and Spanish-speaking peoples.

Denominational and ecumenical urban-mission agencies have
been increasing in number. They have launched programs of urban
training, community organization, clusters for joint mission action,
and cooperative research and planning projects. As the 1960's
passed the midpoint, a reaction began to develop within the
denominations. Conservative elements began to organize and to
criticize urban mission programs. By the late 1960's denominational urban mission agencies were experiencing a significant cut-
back in funds. They were forced to do fewer things more carefully.
The basis of denominational financing remained largely in local
congregations through their contributions to national program
agencies, although some alternative means of funding were beginning to be developed.

Urban clergy were far out in front of church members in questioning the traditional Christian doctrines and in struggling to
formulate what they considered to be more meaningful theology.
But clergy had largely failed to involve the laity in the theological
revolution. As clergy and laity drew farther apart over differences
of belief and mission strategy, a growing struggle for power
emerged. Although laymen predominated numerically in any denomination, clergy tended to control the administrative apparatus
and to wield effective power in the decision-making processes. On
the other hand, laymen controlled the financial sources and used
this power to exert leverage on policy.

At the end of the 1960's the conflict over church renewal versus
radical reformation continued unresolved. No sophisticated theological consensus emerged which pointed beyond the conflict.
Renewal seemed to be the popular interest in local churches. On
the other hand, creating new structures for mission seemed to be
primarily the concern of certain nonparish clergy and denominational executives and agencies that were not tied to servicing local
churches. Most renewal efforts in city churches fell into one of

two styles. Either they tried to bring the world into the church through utilizing contemporary media and bringing in nonchurch people, or they tried to take the church into the world through involvement in community affairs and social issues. Neither style dealt with the fundamental urban problems at their source. The significance of the attempts was mainly in educational value for the church and very little for the cities. Many renewal programs that alerted churchmen to urban problems without creating the necessary structures for action tended to generate frustration.

Metropolitan Approach Needed

Whether the church would lose the city was not so much a question of whether individual congregations would grow and prosper. It was much more a question of whether the church at large could radically expand its vision of life and work in metropolis. In a very real sense, only if the church could conceive of its mission on a metropolitan scale could there be hope for significant progress. Clearly, local congregations were too socially homogeneous, limited in resources, and immobilized by prevailing patterns to become the base for effective metropolitan mission. Denominations might be able cooperatively to effect new structures for joint mission and action. Even at this level the picture was not one of solid accomplishment, but of hope for future fulfillment of things begun.

The prospects for the 1970's are ambiguous. It is likely that there will be a deepening of the conflict between clergy and laity. There will continue to be a decline in white church membership inside major cities. There will probably be a continuing struggle for power as the major denominations move toward organic merger (COCU) and as they continue efforts at social and economic witness in the cities. Clearly, the churches have not found viable ways of doing significant Christian education of the laity. There have been useful experiments and creative work, but implementation of new and more appropriate styles of Christian education has not taken place on a significant scale inside the cities.

On the positive side, the growth of the black and Spanish-speaking churches provides a major hope for the redevelopment of vigorous Protestant life and mission. The black experience offers the possibility of liberation and new purpose for the city churches. The COCU development of new alliances among eight or ten of the major Protestant denominations may enable metropolitan planning and mission on a scale large enough to have significance. This will be in great part determined by whether a new united Protestant church can devise creative means of decentralized administration instead of massive bureaucratic immobilization.

The prospects for the 1970's confront the churches of the city with many questions:

1. Can significant lay ministry be developed and freed from the limitations of local congregations?

2. Can adequate structures for metropolitan mission be developed?

3. Can the gap between clergy and laity be bridged?

4. Can a meaningful Christian theology adequate to the urban situation emerge soon enough to be helpful?

5. Can a pluralism of initiatives be developed that will be adequate to the pluralism of urban society?

6. Can the black and Spanish-speaking churches bring a vital force into the presently faltering situation?

7. What will be the effects of the COCU merger on urban mission?

8. What will be the effects of the developing Catholic-Protestant cooperation on urban mission?

9. What new agenda will the volatile urban crises generate?

10. What new forces will be created in the city by the technological revolution? For the churches the decade ahead will be filled with struggle, partial accomplishments, frustrations, and all the agony which the cities themselves contain.

Parables of the Church in the City

The following parables illustrate types of initiatives taken by city churches or church-related groups in attempting to address themselves to part of the urban situation. The parables are broadly stroked sketches. They are not case studies. Their main value is to stimulate imagination. They represent only a limited sampling of the types of missionary imagination necessary for the new creation in metropolis.

Certain themes occur repeatedly throughout the parables. They suggest some trends which are developing in the ministry of the church in urban society:

1. Focus on the institutions and issues of the public sector.
2. Setting Christians free from congregational maintenance.
3. Action-reflection approach to doing theology.
4. Experimentation, creation of new models that enable change.
5. Development of more broadly based structures of ecumenical coalition.
6. The importance of appropriate skills, adequate planning, and new sources of financing.

These themes provide important clues for the initiatives of the churches in the city in the coming decade.

A Congregation in Missionary Pilgrimage

The historical traditions of the Broadway United Church of Christ in New York City extend back to the pre-Civil War abolitionist movement. Between then and now, Broadway has continued to be involved in a variety of critical social issues, responding with appropriate pioneering actions. Broadway's continued willingness to experiment in the past has often enabled it to point the way to the future.

The church building, strategically located at the corner of Broadway and 56th Street in midtown Manhattan, occupied about one-fourth of a city block of extremely valuable real estate. The building was very old and needed extensive repair to make it structurally safe, as well as costly remodeling to make it more useful. The minister, Dr. Lawrence Durgin, led his congregation into a period of self-study and long-range planning. Months of research, with help from an expert urban planner and various other consultants, led the congregation to a new vision involving redevelopment of the entire city block in which the church was located. The new vision centered on meeting some of the crucial needs of the city.

In the congested midtown New York area there was a need for open space to serve the crowded theater and business community. There was a great need for apartment housing for a variety of income and racial groups. But most important was the need for a pilot commercial and housing complex that would serve as a model for building developers to apply to their own construction projects.

In response to these needs, Broadway planned to level the entire city block in which it was situated, building in the midst of the cleared area a combination office and apartment building more than forty stories tall. The actual floor space of the proposed structure would not begin until the fifth-story level. Beneath it would be a full city block of open space, allowing free movement for the people of the area. On the ground level, at opposite corners of the block, would be a bar-restaurant (many midtown New Yorkers tend to gravitate to the "local pub" as a natural meeting site) and a moderate-sized meeting facility. The building itself was to contain office facilities for large and small businesses, plus apartments for all income levels and temporary offices for the *ad hoc* action groups that abound in New York City.

The congregation came very near to succeeding with its plan. Certain problems arose which prevented the plan from being fulfilled. The complexity of the New York City construction situation made it wiser for the church to seek a different means of mission. Faced with this disheartening turn, the congregation decided to demolish the church building, lease its property (for ninety-nine years), and become a "congregation in mission." The income from leasing the property would enable the congregation to invest substantial resources in urban mission. Having been liberated from its "historic" edifice in March, 1969, the congregation triumphantly proceeded out of the church sanctuary to its new temporary place of worship, nearby St. Paul's Roman Catholic Church. The congregation has taken office space in a nearby building and rented other facilities for small group meetings. During the months in which these arrangements were being worked out, the congregation shifted its focus more and more to problems of social justice in the New York City school system, the West Side Urban Renewal area, and other pressing issues.

The Broadway Church has launched out on a pilgrimage. There is no going back to the comfort of the old sanctuary. Its missionary goals are becoming clearer. The struggle to realize them will be difficult, but the first steps have been taken.

Instant Action in Urban Crisis

Many urban crises arise so fast that only rapid, flexible responses can possibly deal with them. Yet the very city agencies we expect to resolve these troubles tend to suffer acute paralysis at times of grave crisis. A properly conditioned urban clergy, however, can band together rapidly to prod reluctant officialdom into action.

A case in point is the New York City Clergy Vigil, born during the 1968–69 schoolteacher-strike crisis and credited with a key social-action role in the school-decentralization controversy. The aftermath of the teachers' strike left the local governing board and the school administrator suspended and the black community angry. Seeds of the Clergy Vigil were planted well before the school crisis reached its peak. Some ministers—black, white, and Spanish-American; Catholic, Protestant, and Jewish—had been working as individuals in various community-oriented groups related to the school issues. Others had focused on developing black-Jewish and black-white dialogue. But a peak point of the crisis brought the ministers together in the interracial, interfaith, city-wide bond known as the Clergy Virgil. Its first move was to stand solidly in support of Rhody McCoy, Ocean Hill-Brownsville Experimental School District Administrator, who had been peremptorily suspended along with the community governing board as part of an effort to appease the Teachers Union (UFT).

The responsibility for this and other serious missteps was rapidly being passed back and forth between state and city education officials, but the Clergy Vigil was mobile enough to follow the buck wherever it went. The center of responsibility moved from the City Board of Education to the State Board of Education.

On December 13 the Clergy Vigil (numbering about twenty-five) left the following demands with state functionaries, vowing to return daily in increasing numbers until the demands were met: (1) reinstatement of McCoy as District Administrator; (2) reinstatement of the local Governing Board (also under suspension); (3) removal of the currently appointed state trustee for the area, who had caused more community bitterness than any other official except the city Superintendent of Schools; and (4) reopening of a key junior high school in the area which had been shut down without proof that it could not be safely operated.

State education officials found it embarrassing to confront a growing group of black and white clergy in the state offices each day. Unexpectedly, the State Trustee left his post for reasons of "ill health," satisfying one of the demands of the Clergy Vigil. The new state trustee met with thirty members of the Clergy Vigil. He told the clergymen that McCoy, the administrator, was reinstated (demand number one), that the junior high school would be re-opened (demand four) and that he would "start the process within three days" to have the governing board reinstated (the second demand).

During this meeting the broad concept of the Clergy Vigil's mission began to take form. The schools of the city were in the hands of a political trusteeship; the ministers would assume a "moral and spiritual trusteeship" on the school crisis. Its members would "maintain a pastoral presence at scenes where the issues of power and justice in the school situation are being played out."

Optimism over the results quickly waned, for two reasons: (1) the number of areas involved in the controversy and the number of issues in the dispute both increased sharply; and (2) the educational establishment began almost immediately to renege on certain of their proposed actions.

At this point the flexibility of the Vigil was to begin to prove itself. One wing of the group persisted with state education officials, drawing up a bill of particulars in response to community concerns, including a push to remove the city School Superintendent. Another wing moved to arrange quiet meetings with Governor Nelson Rockefeller and Attorney General Louis Lefkowitz on assuring equal justice for all parties involved in the dispute. At the same time, Vigil units were continuing their presence at both state and city education headquarters. In fact, wherever in the city critical events of the crisis occurred, clergy were present as witnesses and/or advocates.

During the entire period, from before Christmas well into the new year, educational officialdom saw fit to promise what it could not or would not deliver to the clergy and the community. It assured Vigil representatives that Ocean Hill-Brownsville board reinstatement was "imminent—a matter of three or four days" from mid-December into mid-February. And it urged clergymen to return to their communities and "keep the natives cool" in the interim. This was increasingly difficult. More militant groups, bitter and impatient, were eager to take actions that might have caused whole neighborhoods to explode over the prolonged school crisis.

Vigil members fully recognized that they were being used by the politicians, but they continued to hope that the Vigil's persistent presence and appeals would move the State at least to candor, if not to action. But an incident late in January prompted the Vigil to pursue new and stronger avenues. At the close of still another fruitless meeting at the State Education Office in Manhattan, a State functionary had declared: "Now you pray for us, fathers, and maybe you'll get results."

In response to the comment, and to the frustrations of the past weeks, Vigil members voted to pray together for New York's school system. They decided to pray *en masse* day and night in the Madison Avenue offices of the State Education Department. The Vigil's position was that the State had assumed a political trusteeship over New York's schools with no results and less integrity. In turn, the Vigil would undertake a *moral* trusteeship over the school crisis, in behalf of those most often forgotten—the community's citizens and their children. Vigil members would stay and pray until they were assured honest efforts were under way to reinstate the local governing board and restore sound education to the area.

About forty clergymen began the new presence in the State Offices. Some forty-eight hours later, they numbered more than one hundred fifty of all denominations and from all parts of the city. Laymen had gathered on the street outside in support. New promises were made: If only the Vigil would cease its presence, the local governing board would be reinstated "in a few days." Again the clergy took the word of state officials. (This time the state-appointed Trustee and the Deputy Commissioner of Education gave their word.) And again the State reneged.

Clergy Vigil members were forced to return for another day and night of prayer at the State Offices, this time accompanied by parents from the affected communities. Under a State complaint, a group of clergy and parents was arrested that night for refusing to leave the building. Seminarians, clergy, and citizens joined the arrested persons at a court session the following week. Vigil members told state personnel that they would return to the offices in large numbers unless the state took immediate action to reinstate the local governing board.

On the next day after the courtroom declaration of persistence by the Clergy Vigil, the local governing board was finally reinstated. The Clergy Virgil's determined action and continuous presence had been one key factor in bringing about this goal. The Vigil could best be described as a catalyst in the process of social justice.

Clergy Consultation Service on Abortion

In June of 1967 thirty-one New York City ministers and rabbis began the Clergy Consultation Service on Abortion in an effort to meet what they termed their "pastoral responsibility to women in trouble." Present laws throughout the nation force more than one million women annually to seek illegal abortions, often at the penalty of great mental anguish, physical suffering, and even death. Half of these are married women.

The Clergy Consultation Service has much to say about the social injustices of the existing laws on abortion: "These laws brand as criminals wives and mothers who are often driven as helpless victims to desperate acts. The largest percentage of abortion deaths are found among 35-to-39-year-old married women with five to six children. The present abortion law in New York State deeply oppresses the poor and the minorities. A 1965 report shows that 94 percent of the abortion deaths in New York City were among blacks and Puerto Ricans."

The Clergy Consultation set up a central telephone-answering service. A caller to the service hears a recording that lists ministers and rabbis in various parts of the city who are available for abortion counseling. Members of the service work certain hours and days on a rotating basis. The caller can then phone any of the listed ministers and make an appointment with complete discretion. It is unnecessary to mention pregnancy at all until the private pastoral interview. In the early interview stages, the clergyman determines the nature of the situation, advises on such alternatives as keeping the child or putting it up for adoption, and investigates with the woman the possibilities for legal, therapeutic abortion.

If legal, therapeutic abortion is not possible, yet an abortion is indicated, the service will try to get the woman "the best possible medical advice toward terminating the pregnancy," a spokesman explained. "We are mindful that there are duly licensed, reputable physicians who in their wisdom do perform therapeutic abortions which some may regard as illegal. When a doctor performing such operations is motivated by compassion and concern for the patient, and not simply for monetary gain, we . . . regard him as living by the highest standards of religion and of the Hippocratic oath."

In its first twenty months of existence, the Clergy Consultation Service has seen more than four thousand women with problem pregnancies. Its tape-message center receives an average of three hundred calls weekly. Even abortion-law *reform* at its best would leave close to ninety-five percent of those four thousand women unaffected and unhelped.

The Reverend Howard Moody, spokesman for the service, stresses that statistics "don't make a thing better. I could horrify you with the numbers of illegal abortions performed and the number of women injured or killed under present practices. But I don't believe in statistical morality. A bad law is no less bad a law for the fact that five hundred rather than five thousand deaths result from illegal abortion practices." Moody also notes that abortion-law reform would by no means resolve the true problem, which he believes is one of "social policy."

Abortion reform as now proposed offers little hope for the plight of the inner-city poor. Had it been law in 1966 it would not have noticeably affected the eighteen thousand black and the Puerto Rican out-of-wedlock births reported in New York City in that year alone.

Similar abortion-counseling services are being started in other cities. Doctors and clergy are joining to serve the needs of the women beset by "problem pregnancy." There is some legal risk in these efforts, although no clergyman has yet been prosecuted, and the participating clergy maintain that "we do not concede that this activity is illegal." Even with radical reform of the abortion law, the need for this service would continue. "There would continue to be large numbers of women, especially poor women, unaware of the opportunities open to them," Moody predicts. "They will need someone to offer them compassion, counsel, and companionship along this dark road."

Ministry of the Laity: Two Models

Enabling the body of Christ to function meaningfully in the institutional structures of urban society is the special concern of the Ecumenical Institute (EI) in Chicago and the Metropolitan Associates of Philadelphia (MAP).

The Ecumenical Institute

EI is based in the old buildings formerly used by the Bethany Theological Seminary in Chicago. The institution has been working for over a decade to develop renewal in the churches. It currently reaches over thirty thousand persons a year with its long- and short-term programs of intensive training. It is worldwide in its scope and is clearly focused on enabling the laity to develop a vision, discipline, skills, and corporate style appropriate to mission in an urban society. The institution is committed to the proposition that denominational structures are constantly changing and that this is a peculiar moment in history when a mandate for change is radically thrust upon the church. From its base in Chicago, staff members and hundreds of lay emissaries fan out to every major city in the United States to bring a vision, training in skills, and mobilization of cadres of Christians for disciplined mission.

EI has dug into its own immediate neighborhood and is vigorously enabling the citizens of the area to mobilize themselves for the renewal of their sector. This venture involves the families and staff resident at the Institute with the people of the community in redeveloping from its faith and experience the institutions that effect the quality of human life. The EI has developed what it calls the Fifth City model. The model provides a working pattern and process for the mission of the church in the world. It is a powerful tool for teaching and for training. The program of the Ecumenical Institute involves three elements:

1. A total world view; the institute has worked out a carefully integrated synthesis from the various "Neo-Orthodox" theologians. EI presents this theological base with the conviction that it is the best formulation for the church's present situation. They invite others to come up with a better formulation, but they assume that

in the meantime their position offers an adequate foundation for renewing the church and getting on with its work.

2. A disciplined community; at the very heart of the EI movement is the development of dedicated cadres, or core groups, for infiltrating the structures of society and the church to bring renewal.

3. Methodology of operation; the EI style is characterized by a powerful intensity, concern for technical competence, and a step-by-step outline of procedure.

The EI has developed what it calls "imaginal education," which stresses the use of models, visual material, diagrams, structured conversations, strenuous listening, and note taking. There is a strong sense that the patterns which have been developed out of its years of experience ought to be accepted and used with little questioning, unless a cadre can clearly develop a better model. The undeniable virtue of the EI is that it takes seriously equipping and involving the laity. The EI has undoubtedly reached more Christians in this country, perhaps even in the world, than any other contemporary agent of renewal and mission.

Metropolitan Associates of Philadelphia

MAP is a radically different kind of animal in comparison with the EI. The Metropolitan Associates of Philadelphia was launched in 1965. Today it is sponsored and partially funded by four denominations, and other bodies are interested in coming into this unique lay-oriented action-research body. The purpose of MAP is "experimental action in order to discern how persons participate in effecting change in and through the institutions and organizations that comprise the modern metropolis." The associates are concerned with the question, "How can the church enable and support the worldly ministry of its laity as they are scattered throughout the educational, political, and economic institutions that are shaping the future of our society?"

MAP operates with a professional staff of approximately eight people and ten worker-theologians who function primarily to enable the one hundred and fifty lay associates to work for change in a variety of secular and religious institutions in the Philadelphia metropolitan area. The focus is on: (1) Clarifying issues of public interest as targets for lay ministry; (2) Gathering professional and volunteer workers of competence and concern; and (3) Creating structures appropriate to action research in relation to public issues and institutions.

MAP is organized around six public sectors, including education, health, community organizations, politics and government, business and industry, physical development and planning. At present, task forces of lay associates are working on the specific problems of abortion, institutional racism, theological education for the secular lay ministry, community-based training, development of an ecumenical structure at the parish level, Philadelphia public schools, and low-income housing. The very heart of MAP is the lay men and women. These persons are gathered in groups in relation to the businesses, public institutions, and social structures in which they have their full-time employment. A recent illustration of how MAP functions can be seen in a group of business executives organized around the problem of institutional racism. Their focus is on changing the policies and practices in their companies with regard to recruitment, job training, and employment. (Such action takes certain skills, courage, and commitment to goals beyond the individual's own security.) It is for the purpose of enabling and supporting this kind of action that MAP exists.

New Centers of Training for Ministry

While traditional theological seminaries were declining, merging, and closing in increasing numbers, a new type of center for training has been emerging and rapidly multiplying. Six years ago there were none. As of 1969 there are over twenty urban ministry-training operations. Perhaps the three most widely known centers are the Urban Training Center for Christian Mission (UTC) in Chicago, the Internship for Clergymen in Urban Ministry (CIT) in Cleveland, and the Metropolitan Urban Service Training facility (MUST) in New York City.

The training centers supplement the educational work of the seminaries. They focus on the realities of urban life, the dynamics of which are relatively unknown to many city clergymen. They provide programs of exposure, engagement, and reflection on the urgent situations in urban poverty, racism, housing, public school systems, and other institutions and issues. There is strong emphasis on (1) sensitizing to the problems of metropolis; (2) the discipline of urban analysis; (3) strategy development for social change; (4) utilizing the resources of metropolis; and (5) developing skills of mobilizing communities for institutional change.

The centers help clergy to identify and develop new roles appropriate to the needs of ministry in an urban society. They are created by denominations, voluntary groups, educational institutions, and concerned individuals. Their funding comes from a variety of sources, largely from the churches, but also from foundations, federal government, and local and state church councils. Their programs train mostly clergy, but some laymen. The centers relate to numerous research and action projects in their metropolitan areas.

In New York City the Metropolitan Urban Service Training facility created:

Orientation for new pastors coming into New York City parishes for the first time.

Metropolitan Inter Year for seminary students—a year of secular work, participation in community action, and theological reflection.

Communiqué, a central telephone-message service for calling groups into action and for circulating news of events which never reach radio, TV, or press.

Joint-seminary program, bringing two Catholic and two Protestant seminaries together to provide exposure to urban structures and issues for over a hundred students every year.

Action Training Institute, enabling community leaders to mobilize people for action on welfare rights, job training, and public education.

Summer Emergency Mobilization, training for thirty metropolitan-area cluster groups of laity and clergy in sensitivity to racism, and forming a network of skills, services, personnel, and communication for "hot-summer" action.

In Chicago the Urban Training Center created:

The Plunge, a four-to-five-day experience of living on the streets of Chicago, finding food and shelter however possible, and making contact with the people of Skid Row, broadening self-understanding and human sensitivity.

Special training programs for Spanish-speaking ministries in cooperation with the major religious bodies of the Spanish-speaking communities.

Short-term training, basic introductory courses teaching use of the tools of urban analysis, strategy planning, and project development.

Longer-term training, focusing on the context of institutional white racism in collaboration with the Committee for One Society.

Training for denominational executives; twenty-six synod presidents in the Lutheran Church of America were confronted with the crisis of white racism and the meaning of black power.

Black Strategy Center, an independent body for action to design programs, set priorities, and guide the voices and forces of the black community, seeking black unity to deal with the white institutions.

In Cleveland C.I.T. created (with a federal grant from the National Institute of Mental Health):

Anchor Engagement, a thirty-two-week involvement in depth with one urban problem such as poverty, health, intergroup relations, youth, aging.

Satellite Engagement, brief two-to-eight hour exposures to persons and actual situations, which are subsequently analyzed.

Interdisciplinary Analysis Seminar, bringing the analytical tools of the social sciences to bear on urban problems.

Psychological Impacts Seminar, focusing on the relation between environmental aspects of urban problems and the individuals in the environment.

Theological Reflection Seminar, training in theological reflection on environmental change and social problems.

Personal learning groups, sensitivity-training experience for working out the dynamics of social-change experiences.

In the few years that these new centers for training have been functioning, thousands of clergy and laity have fed back into the denominations a strong impulse for action by the church in the city. The centers are developing a growing army of churchmen vigorously pressing for a militant church in the city.

Chapter 17

Focus and Future

BY KENDIG BRUBAKER CULLY

The reader of the preceding chapters of this book will have been conscious of having been taken on a sort of guided tour through the gigantic phenomenon which is the modern city. The guides have been, withal, modest about their own knowledgeability. Few have been so bold as to suggest that blueprints are at hand for the solution of urban problems of greatest magnitude. No one has ventured much farther than an educated guess at what the future might hold for man in the cities he inhabits. Yet we have amassed evidence enough concerning the problems themselves, as well as the intelligible efforts society has been making, through its more careful analysts, to confront these problems.

Not only are the urban dilemmas confusing and baffling for the urban students, but we have observed also how the theologians and practitioners of religion are bewildered, too, about the role of the church in relation to the city. What seemed abundantly clear in the 1940's and 1950's as to how the church might update itself, theoretically as well as practically, to make itself more relevant to the metropolis, now is observed as something seen only through a glass darkly. In spite of all manner of experimental efforts that have occupied the attention of church planners in recent decades —up to this very moment—it is not at all certain that the church has any clear picture of how it should relate itself to the bewildering complexities of worship, work, and witness in the contemporary urban morass.

Will the Church Lose the City?

The double confusion—within the behavioral sciences as these seek to understand and interpret man in the urban society, and within the church as its theologians and leaders attempt the task of relating people to the gospel vis-à-vis their urbanized environment —leads us to another look at the question, "Will the church lose the city?" That question has been in the background of all the writers' thinking as they have addressed themselves to particular aspects of the matter. In this concluding chapter, perhaps we can attempt a few generalizations in response to it.

Although it is abundantly clear that the Christian religion has always been identified with people in cities, from the first century on, it must be recognized that except in certain locations during a heavy ascendancy of religious leadership (one thinks of medieval Rome, or John Calvin's Geneva, or Boston during the Congregational establishment), few and far between have been the times when the urban culture has been completely saturated with Christian influence. That is to say, the question preceding the question of the book's title may in fact be, "Did the church ever *have* the city?"

A certain pessimism about the actual influence of the church in the inner realities of urban man's life is perfectly legitimate. Certainly Elizabethan London, though the capital of a Christian nation, was scarcely the sort of place a visitor would have wanted to spend much time walking about the streets at night alone. A person who had lived as a student in New York in the 1930's came back for a visit in the mid-1960's and decided to take a quiet stroll from West Side to East Side, through Central Park. Had he not done this many times before? He was quite surprised to have a police car stop him en route, the officers asking him where he was heading. When informed that he was going to his hotel on the other side of the park, he was amazed to have them insist that he get into the car and let them drive him there! Things do worsen (or change), but the Christian conscience has never completely governed the behavior of *all* the people in a city at any given time, nor have the moral exhortations from pulpits and the delicious fellowships enjoyed within the walls of churches extended into the streets necessarily. Politicians, though sometimes personally church men, have not always recognized the connection between avowals of belief in God and the ins and outs of the sanitation department. Maybe a mayor is inaugurated with pious invocations, but his reelection is often determined more by the total operation of the secular forces of his widely flung bailiwick than by the benign and holy influences which his church would like to witness as operative within the body politic.

To be sure, it is this kind of political realism constituting civic "savvy" that church men since Reinhold Niebuhr have also been learning more about. I heard a group of clergymen who had organized a sort of pray-in, preach-in, sing-in, or whatever one might care to call it, report on their experiences in trying to get through to the board of education (local and state) during the Bedford-Stuyvesant school crisis in 1968–69. Letters had failed, they said; so had resolutions and efforts to get satisfactory interviews with the educational authorities who were in decision-making seats of power. Hence the "storming" of the offices of those power figures. The power of religiously motivated presence, they figured, was the only alternative to political impotence. One distinguished old church in New York City has even gone so far as to decide to sell its aging structure, in the light of dwindling membership and community changes, rather than spend a goodly portion of its big endowment to refurbish its physical fabric. Instead, they will seek to use their financial resources, and their religious witness as a congregation, in order to try to get close to the real problems of the city.

Would it be fair to say that even though the church never really *had* the city in its control or under its influence, in any complete sense, the difference now is that the church in a fresh degree is beginning to experience a sort of despair? It is not certain as to how it can best proceed to regain a lost luster, or to make a fresh start, or to gain a tenuous foothold, even, in territory where at least in previous generations it had some pretty secure positions carved out for itself. The secularized culture does not even ask the kinds of questions, as Paul Tillich pointed out, to which the gospel can readily address itself.[1]

But if there is a note of despair in the church's attitude as it approaches the realities of today's metropolis, it cannot be said by any means that the church has given up the ghost. Such an attitude, in fact, would constitute a betrayal of the church's fundamental conviction that to it has been entrusted the gospel of reconciliation in the name and spirit of Christ. It may be that new strength of Christian witness is gathering in the very Diaspora which characterizes the seemingly enfeebled state of Christianity.

Joseph H. Fichter, S.J., has written:

> Given all of the other problems of urban adaptation, the social test for the religious group seems to rest on its ability to display disinterested, supernatural love. The freedom of the city, and the functional pluralism that it promotes, makes mandatory a social solidarity that is not merely parochial or congregational. If there is anything we have lost in the switch from ruralism to urbanism in the United States, it will not be regained by maintaining religious ghettos in the city. The city church requires a city mentality and a city type of organization.[2]

Is it possible that Father Fichter has put his pulse on the *inevitable* despair that affects many Christians as they contemplate the city today? The despair arises out of a failure to take sufficiently into account the parochial norms which still linger in the mind of church men as these have to be redefined in the light of the contemporary urban developments. The despair, ultimately, will be not over the decline or abysmal failure of many of the institutional forms to which we have given our loyalty. These are time-bound and therefore expendable. The real despair would come if Christians were so wedded to the institutional forms as to assume that those were the very norm of faith. For the *city*, in its preoccupation with ultimate struggles, is not likely to be worried over the demise of structures which—like the church buildings themselves, in many cases—have long since ceased to inform its life in any dynamic way.

Some Positive Stimuli

The church, then, as it contemplates its relation to contemporary urban society, must certainly recognize one fact, which has been suggested by a number of the writers in this book. The agenda for Christian concern and action will be set not so much by the church as by the surrounding society.

In a book entitled *The Rise of Urban America*, Constance

McLaughlin Green has outlined clearly some of the "facts of life" which the whole society—and this pertains to the church as well as to any other organized group within the society—must reckon with in the remaining years of the twentieth century. These, certainly, must be a vital part of the church's agenda if it is to witness effectively or at all: increasing automation with resultant unemployment; housing needs of the entire city population, especially of the poor, who so often are forced out of customary neighborhoods when slum clearance proceeds; the rising incidence of juvenile delinquency; the increasing rootlessness of middle- and upper-class families; the need for improved education, quantitatively as well as qualitatively; the widespread discrimination and injustice that persist in spite of court decisions and civil-rights efforts; the inability of municipalities to meet the needs of the citizenry due to inadequate command of tax income, accompanied by an unwillingness to yield authority from local to national levels which alone could command the needed moneys.[3]

The question immediately arises, of course: How can the church accept such items of agenda without running the risk that its people will be diverted from primary "spiritual" or "religious" priorities? There is reason to believe that courageous church leaders have not been running away from the challenge of the secular agenda; indeed, that they have had to work with might and main to lessen the resistance to the facing of such agenda on the part of vast numbers of Christians. Ultimately, perhaps, the willingness of the church to study and become seriously involved in exactly such urban problems will depend on the extent to which its people are led into some serious theological reflection about the nature of the faith itself. If the incarnational premise is taken seriously—that God identifies himself with man in his total situation, as illustrated and embodied in Jesus Christ's identification with the last and least of mankind—the church cannot possibly avoid getting involved with these very life-and-death issues of metropolitan existence today. "Give us this day our daily bread" is a petition that pertains not only to individuals praying for the personal sustenance they need; it is the common situation of all men, that daily bread is a necessity, and in that sense the petition at once involves us in the struggle to eliminate poverty, which is still rampant even in a society of the superabundance of things.

This insight should be the particular contribution of Christians. Often it is more apparent in sensitive humanists, who perceive such a concern as the human *sine qua non*. In the words of Michael Polanyi:

> Man is strong, noble and wonderful so long as he fears the voices of this firmament; but he dissolves their power over himself and his own powers gained through obeying them, if he turns back and examines what he respects in a detached manner. Then law is no more than what the courts will decide, art but an emollient of nerves, morality but a convention, tradition but an inertia, God but a psychological necessity. Then man dominates a world in which he himself does not exist. For with his obligations he has lost his voice and his hope, and been left behind meaningless to himself.[4]

The implications of this for the church have been set forth trenchantly by Bishop E. R. Wickham of the Church of England's diocese of Middleton in what he calls "a simple logical syllogism":

> The Christian church must be concerned with the quality of human life, both of men individually, and of their society.
> Industry, the industrial organization of society, determines to a large degree the quality of human life, both of men and of their society.
> Therefore, the church should be concerned with industry and the industrial organization of society.[5]

Bishop Wickham goes on to explain his syllogism:

> The first bold premise flows from the church's divine calling to minister to men in Christ's name, though we should hasten to repeat that the church is also a human institution, and able therefore to misuse power, even spiritual and moral power, and capable of an improper as well as a proper mode of impinging on and within secular institutions. But whatever the proper mode of influence, the concern of the church should be beyond argument when it is understood how strongly the culture-pattern determines the thinking and the freedom of men, and that the culture-pattern is itself very largely the product of the basic industrial ordering of society. All of this points to the need of understanding the structure of society, its functional mechanisms and its modes of influencing men, which can only be gathered from sociological studies.[6]

It would be equally cogent in Bishop Wickham's syllogism to substitute the words "metropolitan culture" for "the industrial organization of society," though this is scarcely necessary, since the two concepts are synchronous. Is it possible that his syllogism suggests the Christian answer to the dehumanization characteristic of contemporary urban life, as deplored by Michael Polanyi?

Perhaps the key concept of this entire book is the thought of the church as providing a central focus wherein and whereby the life of man may be completely humanized. The paradoxical situation, of course, is that the church itself can be less effective in this humanizing process than the city itself, which, despite all that is impersonal, dehumanizing, and debilitating in it, simultaneously, by reason of its very complexity, provides the possibilities for authentic humanization. It is all too easy for the church to seek to be the center through which life, soul, meaning, and purpose shall be inserted into the vast mass that the city seems to be. Actually, it is the church's interesting responsibility to accept the soul, meaning, and purpose that already exist in the city's phenomena, latching on to these, so to speak, in order to give cosmic meaning to locally manifested realities.

Monica Wilson refers to urbanization in this sense as "a universal challenge." She has said:

> The underlying challenge, which embraces all the others, is that the new mass civilization offers a potentiality for fullness of life. That is why the cities draw country folk into them: they offer opportunities of acquiring wealth, of education, of artistic creation and enjoyment which are lacking in isolation. They offer it not exclusively to a very small class as past civilizations have done, but to the people as a whole. They offer a freedom, a choice, in friends and in values, which is not there in isolated societies. The choice implies a potentiality for good or evil. The new wealth and knowledge and skills may be used to destroy, to injure oneself or others, or for more fullness of life.[7]

The church must seek ways in which to insert its concerns, believed to have a divine orientation, into the concerns that already exist, though often inarticulately, in the urban complex itself. Constantinos A. Doxiadis, an internationally prominent architect and planner of cities, has warned that in the further development of our cities, "somebody must think ahead of those who provide the technology," for "up to the end of this century . . . man is going to build on this earth as much as he has built in the six thousand years of his history." Mr. Doxiadis believes that "today, whether we want it or not, we are heading toward the universal city. The minimum of twelve billion urban dwellers to come, and the probability of tens of billions, means that within a century or two we are going to witness an evolution toward one continuous universal city. From the polis we went to the metropolis, now to the megalopolis, and in the future to the universal city or ecumenopolis."[8] Thus our question is not merely "Will the church lose the city?" but "What chance does the church have to continue to be the vibrant center of the forthcoming ecumenopolis?" In Mr. Doxiadis' words:

> The longing for an idealistic conception of one city of man, of cosmopolis, becomes now a reality, if for no other reason at least because of a complete change of the number of people, of new dimensions and the shrinking of the earth due to new technologies. Thus we witness the beginning of the birth of ecumenopolis.[9]

Elsewhere Mr. Doxiadis addresses himself to the role of the church in the developing city, which "will be a unified and universal network involving all our cities." He suggests that the ecumenical concerns of the church during the last three decades demonstrate that Christian concern does not have to be, and in fact, dare no longer be, merely parochial. He sees the role of the church as helping people "to awareness of their wide belonging." "I think now that science is one way of doing it: illuminating the issues, telling the truth. But the truth is not always enough, especially if given to men and women who lack the intellectual perception to use the truth for the benefit of man. So I have come to the conclusion that the church can be a main channel (although not the only channel) for transmitting the message that man is in danger in his cities today and will be in much greater danger there tomorrow. To be sure, the churches deal with the soul of man. But the soul is only one aspect of man. . . . Therefore the church of necessity deals with the complete man."[10]

A Laboratory of Learning

The church, like the individuals who make it up and like all other individuals and every other organized group within society, is a learning community. Sometimes it has assumed that its sole text-book was the Bible, and its only "subject matter" its own theology and existence. A new awareness has entered the mind of the church in recent decades, especially as it has been taking its perilous position more seriously. The environment in which the church lives has come to be recognized increasingly as the laboratory in which the church's "spiritual" tasks can be accomplished and tested. Thus we have witnessed the emergence of many forms of "worldly religion," the "secular gospel," etc. Robert A. Raines summarized this tendency by saying, "Contemporary theology is pointing out in a convincing way that God is at work here and now in *this* world, and that history, i.e., social change, is precisely his arena of action." Raines affirms "a secular piety" that "will affirm with the secularist the secularization of the world and the church as the work of God."[11]

There are many kinds of possibilities opening up to the church as it looks upon the secularized urban society not as its foe but as its ally. In a profound sense what happens on Broadway (and maybe, more importantly, off-Broadway), at city hall, at the often crass cinemas on 42nd Street, in Wall Street, at demonstrations in Central Park, at sit-ins in Bedford-Stuyvesant, in the alleged scandal-ridden administrative offices of municipal poverty agencies —in all these, as well as in the multitudinous other locales of activity, there are raw materials for action involvement and for reflection. Church people at least can be encouraged by their leaders to be unstintingly and unfearfully involved in these channels of human experience. Whatever else it is, the church certainly is educator of its own people. No one else, no other agency, will do for the church's people what the church alone can do for them. The structuring of educational experience, utilizing the city's re-sources, certainly might well be one of its primary concerns.

To cite only one example, the phenomenon of loneliness felt by many in our depersonalized urban culture can be portrayed more eloquently, perhaps, in an off-Broadway show than through homiletical illustration. A good example of such a portrayal is the song called "The Flowers" sung by Viola in *Your Own Thing,* which has had a long and much-acclaimed run in New York. Coming in from a much smaller place, Viola bitterly cries out against the glassy, steely, chromey, homelessness of the city. She proceeds to some adventures that might not be considered exactly "nice" by conventional church standards, but the entire piece is a social commentary pregnant with theological implications. Taking a church group to see and then to reflect together on such a play would be an example of a theological use, highly educational, of a secular medium. A class in religious education from a divinity school in a smaller city came into town to see *Hair,* whose rollicking, youthful cast do all kinds of unorthodox things on the stage, and built that exposure into their considerations of the church's ministry to adolescents.

During the summer of 1969 there is scheduled to be published a three-hundred-thousand-word "Plan for New York City" evolved by the City Planning Commission. Advance information concerning this report indicates that sweeping changes in the total life of the community are contemplated "to change the fact that, in its own words: 'For an increasingly large number of its people, New York is not working.' "[13] It is yet to be seen how seriously the churches of the city will read, mark, learn, and inwardly digest this document, which will embrace sociological, economic, political, and psychological phenomena that surely will deserve high priority as part of the church's curriculum, both for reflection and action.

Can We Be Wise Enough?

Speaking of philosophical sociology, John R. Seeley has commented: "There seems to exist neither a theory of what is to be desired, nor, in so far as that may be surmised, what is to be done to secure it."[14] Sometimes, when we attempt to take our bearings regarding the fateful question, "Will the church lose the city?" it would appear that such is also an apt description of those who bear the burden of trying to answer the question. But perhaps Mr. Seeley's further comment is even more suggestive—and for theologians and church men in general it might almost be construed as a prayer of longing: "For better or worse we are cast as Wise Men; would that we could be surer that we are, within tolerable limits, wise men."[15]

Notes

CHAPTER 2: A Sociological View

1. J. Milton Yinger, *Religion, Society and the Individual*, The Macmillan Co., 1957.

2. Harvey Cox, *The Secular City*, The Macmillan Co., 1965.

3. Nathan Glazer and Daniel Patrick Moynihan, *Beyond the Melting Pot*, M.I.T. Press, 1963.

4. Will Herberg, *Protestant-Catholic-Jew, An Essay in American Religious Sociology*, Anchor Press, 1960.

5. John K. Galbraith, *The New Industrial State*, Houghton Mifflin Co., 1967.

6. Robert Presthus, *The Organizational Society*, Alfred A. Knopf, 1962.

7. Elmo Roper Public Opinion Poll Organization, quoted in *The New York Times*, Jan. 27, 1967.

8. Emile Durkheim, *The Division of Labor in Society*, tr. by George Simpson, The Free Press, 1933.

9. Henry D. Lloyd, *Man the Social Creator*, The Doubleday Press, 1906, pp. 101 ff.

10. Friedrich Nietzsche, *The Birth of Tragedy. The Genealogy of Morals*, tr. by Francis Golfing, Oxford University Press, 1962.

11. James Baldwin, *The Fire Next Time*, The Dial Press, 1963.

12. C. Wright Mills, *The Power Elite*, Oxford University Press, 1959.

13. J. W. Fulbright, *The Arrogance of Power*, Random House, 1966.

CHAPTER 4: A Psychological View

1. Robert W. Glasgow, "The Urban Crisis," in *Psychology Today*, Vol. 2, No. 3, August 1968, pp. 18 ff.

2. A. B. Hollingshead and F. C. Redlich, *Social Class and Mental Illness*, John Wiley & Sons, 1958.

3. Erich Fromm, "Psychoanalytic Characterology and Its Application to the Understanding of Culture," in S. S. Sargent and M. W. Smith, eds., *Culture and Personality*, Wenner-Gren Foundation for Anthropological Research, 1949. See also Wilhelm Reich, *Character Analysis* (2nd ed.), Orgone Institute Press, 1945.

4. Joseph J. Michaels, "Character Structure and Character Disorders," in S. Arieti, ed., *The American Handbook of Psychiatry*, Basic Books, 1959, pp. 353–77.

5. Adorne, Frenkel-Brunswik, Levinson, and Levine, *The Authoritarian Personality*, Harper & Brothers, 1950.

6. Eric Berne, *Games People Play*, Harper & Row, 1967.

7. *Theological Education*, Vol. IV, No. 4, Summer 1968.

CHAPTER 5: An Aesthetic View

1. Whitney J. Oates, ed., *Basic Writings of St. Augustine*, Bk. I, Ch. 35, Random House, 1948.

CHAPTER 6: An Integrative View

1. These books are written respectively by Douglas Fraser, Jorge Hardoy, Paul Lampl, and Howard Saalman (Braziller, 1968).

2. Robert S. Lopez, "The Crossroads Within the Wall," in Oscar Handlin, and John Burchard, eds., *The Historian and the City*, M.I.T. and Harvard University Press, 1963, pp. 27 ff.

3. Paul Lampl, *op. cit.*, p. 120.

4. Gideon Sjoberg, *The Preindustrial City Past and Present*, The Free Press, 1960, pp. 340 ff.

5. See Carl Bridenbaugh, *Cities in the Wilderness* and *Cities in Revolt* (Alfred A. Knopf, 1955) for historical accounts of these cities, 1625–1742 and 1743–1776.

6. Lewis Mumford, *The City in History*, Harcourt, Brace & World, 1961, pp. 259, 313, 330.

7. Doubleday Anchor ed., 1965.

8. For writings of John Cotton on community, see Larzer Ziff, ed., *John Cotton on the Churches of New England*, Harvard University Press, 1968; a very important passage on covenant and grace appears in the editor's introduction, pp. 18 ff.

9. E.g., see Bernard Bailyn, *The New England Merchants in the Seventeenth Century*, Harvard University Press, 1955.

10. Richard Wade, *The Urban Frontier: The Rise of Western Cities, 1790–1830*, Harvard University Press, 1959; he concentrates on Pittsburgh, St. Louis, Cincinnati, Louisville, and Lexington.

11. See Mark Holloway, *Heavens on Earth*, Dover Publications, 1966; Holloway's bibliographical essay introduces some of the enormous literature on the subject.

12. Titles of works by Gibson Winter and Harvey Cox, neither of whom was, of course, simply Utopian.

13. See his *The Black Messiah*, Sheed and Ward, 1968.

14. *We Hold These Truths*, Sheed and Ward, 1960, p. 23.

15. Paul Tillich, *On the Boundary*, Charles Scribner's Sons, 1936, pp. 74 ff.

CHAPTER 7: The City and the Church:
Historical Interlockings

1. E.g., see the considerable attention to church life in the important work by Carl Bridenbaugh, *Cities in the Wilderness: The First Century of Urban Life in America, 1625–1742*, Alfred A. Knopf, 1938; rev. ed., G. P. Putnam's Sons, 1964.

2. Oscar Handlin and John Burchard, eds., *The Historian and the City*, M.I.T. Press, 1963.

3. "A Critical Period in American Religion, 1875–1900," in *Massachusetts Historical Society Proceedings*, LXIV, October 1930–June 1932, pp. 523–46; reprinted as a Facet Book, Fortress Press, 1967. One of Schlesinger's students, the late Aaron I. Abell, revised and published his doctoral thesis as *The Urban Impact on American Protestantism, 1865–1900*, Shoe String Press, 1943; an important work in this field.

4. See Robert D. Cross, ed., *The Church and the City, 1865–1910*, Bobbs-Merrill, 1967. The best one-volume history of American churches, Winthrop S. Hudson's *Religion in America*, Charles Scribner's Sons, 1965, pays considerable attention to the church in the city. A useful essay by Martin E. Marty calls attention to the importance of the urban scene, "Reinterpreting American Religious History in Context," in Jerald C. Brauer, ed., *Reinterpretation in American Church History*, University of Chicago Press, 1968, pp. 195–218.

5. The outstanding interpretation of these many themes is by Sidney E. Mead, *The Lively Experiment: The Shaping of Christianity in America*, Harper & Row, 1963.

6. *Journals of the General Conference of the Methodist Episcopal Church*, Vol. II, 1840, 1844 (n.d.), p. 181.

7. Cf. James F. Maclear, " 'The True American Union' of Church and State: The Reconstruction of the Theocratic Tradition," in *Church History*, XXVIII, 1959, pp. 41–62; and Robert T. Handy, "The Protestant Quest for a Christian America, 1830–1930," in *ibid.*, XXII, 1952, pp. 8–20 (reprinted under the same title as a Facet Book, Fortress Press, 1967).

8. Winthrop S. Hudson, *The Great Tradition of the American Churches*, Peter Smith, 1953, p. 108.

9. Victor Obenhaus, *The Church and Faith in Mid-America*, The Westminster Press, 1963, p. 17.

10. Josiah Strong, *Our Country: Its Possible Future and Its Present Crisis*, 1885; ed. by Jurgen Herbst, Harvard University Press, 1963.

11. David S. Monroe, ed., *Journal of the General Conference of the Methodist Episcopal Church held in Chicago . . . 1900*, 1900, pp. 63–64.

12. Joseph B. Clark, *Leavening the Nation: The Story of American Home Missions*, Baker and Taylor Co., 1903, p. 280.

13. Charles Stelzle, *Christianity's Storm Centre: A Study of the Modern City*, Fleming H. Revell, 1907, p. 173.

14. Truman B. Douglass, "The Job the Protestants Shirk," in Robert Lee, ed., *Cities and Churches: Readings on the Urban Church*, The Westminster Press, 1962, p. 90.

15. H. Paul Douglass, *1000 City Churches: Phases of Adaption to Urban Environment*, George H. Doran Company, 1926, p. 83. For a critique of this typology and others, and a presentation of a quite different one, see Frederick A. Shippey, "The Variety of City Churches," in *Review of Religious Research*, II, Summer 1960, pp. 8–19.

16. Joseph R. Gusfield, *Symbolic Crusade: Status Politics and the American Temperance Movement*, University of Illinois Press, 1966, p. 7.

17. James H. Timberlake, *Prohibition and the Progressive Movement, 1900–1920*, Harvard University Press, 1963, p. 151.

18. H. Paul Douglass, "Religion—The Protestant Faiths," in Harold E. Stearns, ed., *America Now: An Inquiry into Civilization in the United States*, Charles Scribner's Sons, 1938, p. 514.

19. I have dealt with this more fully in an article, "The Social Gospel in Historical Perspective," in *Andover Newton Quarterly*, IX, January 1969.

20. Carter G. Woodson, *The History of the Negro Church*, Associated Publishers, Inc., 1921, p. 201.

21. E. Franklin Frazier, *The Negro Church in America*, Schocken Books, 1966, p. 47.

22. Horace R. Cayton and St. Clair Drake, *Black Metropolis: A Study of Negro Life in a Northern City*, Harper & Row, 1945, p. 413.

23. Gerhard Lenski, *The Religious Factor: A Sociological Study of Religion's Impact on Politics, Economics, and Family Life*, Doubleday & Co., 1961, pp. 20, 36.

24. Frazier, *op. cit.*, pp. 51, 53.

25. For a good introduction to this complex area, see A. Leland Jamison, "Religions on the Christian Perimeter," in James Ward Smith and A. Leland Jamison, *The Shaping of American Religion* ("Religion in American Life," I), Princeton University Press, 1961, pp. 162–231. See also Arthur H. Fauset, *Black Gods of the Metropolis: Negro Cults of the Urban North*, University of Pennsylvania Press, 1944.

26. Val B. Clear, "The Urbanization of a Holiness Body," in Lee, *op. cit.*, pp. 207–17.

27. Timothy L. Smith, *Called Unto Holiness, The Story of the Nazarenes: The Formative Years*, Nazarene Publishing House, 1962, p. 28.

28. Quoted from John Lancaster Spalding, *The Religious Mission of the Irish People and Catholic Colonization*, A. C. McClurg & Co. 1880; reprinted in part in Cross, ed., *op. cit.*, pp. 11–12.

29. Quoted from Francis Clement Kelley, *The Bishop Jots It Down: An Autobiographical Strain on Memories*, Harper & Brothers, 1939, by John Tracy Ellis, ed., in *Documents of American Catholic History*, Bruce Publishing Co., 1956, p. 576.

30. Robert D. Cross, "The Changing Image of the City among American Catholics," in *The Catholic Historical Review*, XLVIII, April 1962, pp. 33–52.

31. Quoted by David J. O'Brien, *American Catholics and Social Reform: The New Deal Years*, Oxford University Press, 1968, p. 129.

32. *Ibid.*; cf. also Cross, *Catholic Historical Review*, XLVIII, pp. 40–41.

33. *Ibid.*, pp. 51–52.

34. Val B. Clear, "The Urbanization of a Holiness Body," in Lee, *op. cit.*, p. 212.

35. Robert Lee, *The Social Sources of Church Unity: An Interpretation of Unitive Movements in American Protestantism*, Abingdon Press, 1960, p. 218.

36. For details, cf. Samuel N. Cavert, *The American Churches in the Ecumenical Movement, 1900–1968*, Association Press, 1968.

CHAPTER 8: The City from a Biblical Standpoint

1. James Muilenburg, "Biblical Images of the City," in Robert Lee, ed., *The Church and the Exploding Metropolis*, John Knox Press, 1965, pp. 45–59.

2. *Ibid.*, p. 55.

3. *Ibid.*, pp. 55 ff.

4. Max Weber, *The Sociology of Religion*, tr. by E. Fischoff, Beacon Press, 1963, p. 84.

5. *Ibid.*, p. 85.

6. William Baird, *The Corinthian Church—A Biblical Approach to Urban Culture*, Abingdon Press, 1964, p. 205.

7. Cf. Juergen Moltmann, *Theology of Hope*, tr. by James W. Leitsch, Harper & Row, 1967, pp. 304–38.

8. Paul Minear, "The City Where God Dwells," in *Horizons of Christian Community*, Bethany Press, 1959, pp. 60–79.

9. As shown by Ulrich Luck, "Himmlisches und Irdisches im Hebraeerbrief," in *Charis kai Sophia, Festschrift Karl Heinrich Rengstorf*, E. J. Brill, Leiden, 1964, pp. 192–215.

10. See the illuminating article by Samuel Laeuchli, "Urban Mithraism," in *The Biblical Archaeologist*, XXXI, September 1968, pp. 73–99.

11. As indicated by Paul Minear in his essay "The Cosmology of the Apocalypse," in William Klassen and Graydon Snyder, eds., *Current Issues in New Testament Interpretation*, Harper and Row, 1962, pp. 23–37.

12. That this commitment remains constant throughout all the fireworks of the Apocalypse I have tried to demonstrate in an essay, "Vengeance in the Apocalypse," in *Catholic Biblical Quarterly*, 28, 1966, pp. 300–11.

13. The book by A. A. T. Ehrhardt, *Politische Metaphysik von Solon bis Augustin*, 2 vols., Tübingen, 1959, has material that could be discussed in this connection.

14. The criticism of H. Cox's *The Secular City* by George Peck ("The Secular City and the Bible") and by Ruel Tyson ("Urban Renewal in the Holy City"), found in Daniel Callahan, ed., *The Secular City Debate*, The Macmillan Co., 1966, is very much to the point.

CHAPTER 10: The Black Church in Search
of a New Theology

1. Joseph R. Washington, *Black Religion: The Negro and Christianity in the United States,* Beacon Press, 1964, p. 37.

2. In January, 1963, the national leadership of the Protestant, Jewish, and Roman Catholic communions came together in an unprecedented show of unity in the National Conference on Religion and Race, held in Chicago. That was also the year that the National Conference of Churches established its Commission on Religion and Race, with the largest race-relations budget in the history of the Council, under the direction of Robert Spike. Several denominations followed suit almost immediately, with special emergency programs and funds. In the late summer of 1966 Eugene Carson Blake, perhaps the most prestigious Protestant clergyman, forced the witness of white churchmen to a new level by being arrested in a demonstration at a segregated amusement park outside of Baltimore.

3. "Black Power and the American Christ," in Floyd B. Barbour, ed., *The Black Power Revolt,* F. Porter Sargent, 1968, p. 86.

4. George D. Kelsey, *Racism and the Christian Understanding of Man,* Charles Scribner's Sons, 1965, pp. 134–38.

5. Vittorio Lanternari, *The Religions of the Oppressed,* Mentor Books, 1965, p. 59.

6. "Black Religion—Past, Present and Future," position paper of the Council of Black Clergy of Philadelphia, 1968.

7. Albert B. Cieage, Jr., *The Black Messiah,* Sheed and Ward, 1968. See also Alex Poinsett, "The Quest for a Black Christ," in *Ebony,* Vol. 24, No. 5, March 1969, pp. 170–78.

8. Quoted from an unpublished paper by Lawrence Lucas submitted in a survey of black theologians and pastors.

9. Vincent Harding, "The Religion of Black Power," in Donald R. Cutler, ed., *The Religious Situation: 1968,* Beacon Press, 1968, pp. 4–6.

10. Quoted by permission of Lawrence Jones, from a sermon preached at Union Theological Seminary, 1968.

11. Lucas, *op. cit.*

12. Ruby F. Johnston, *The Religion of Negro Protestants,* Philosophical Library, 1956, p. 182.

13. See Joseph R. Washington, *The Politics of God,* Beacon Press, 1967, pp. 197, 213.

CHAPTER 12: Leadership for Change in Church
and Society

1. Erik Erikson, *Childhood and Society*, W. W. Norton & Co.,
1968.
2. Gabriel Moran, *Vision and Tactics*, Herder and Herder, 1968,
pp. 42 ff.
3. *Ibid.*, p. 56.
4. Published in the Spring 1968 issue of *Theological Education*.

CHAPTER 13: The Church in the City as a Locale
for Humanizing Life

1. Lewis Mumford, *The City in History*, Harcourt, Brace & World,
1961, p. 575.
2. T. S. Eliot, "Choruses from 'The Rock,'" in *Collected Poems
1909–1962*, Harcourt, Brace & World. Used by permission.

CHAPTER 14: What Are the Churches Actually Doing
in the City? I

1. "Structural Options for Interchurch Action in Mission Strategy,"
prepared by the Special Committee of the General Assembly on Interchurch Action in Presbytery and Parish, United Presbyterian Church
in the U.S.A., 11 pp. mimeographed, 1968.

CHAPTER 17: Focus and Future

1. Cf. Paul Tillich, *Systematic Theology*, especially Vol. III, The
University of Chicago Press and Harper & Row (3 vols. in one), 1967.
2. Joseph H. Fichter, S.J., "Church Strategy in the Metropolis:
A Roman Catholic Viewpoint," in Robert Lee, ed., *The Church and
the Exploding Metropolis*, John Knox Press, 1965, pp. 102 ff.
3. Cf. Constance McLaughlin Green, *The Rise of Urban America*,
especially Ch. VIII, "The Population Explosion and a Changing Urban
World," Harper & Row, 1965, pp. 178–195.
4. Michael Polanyi, *Personal Knowledge—Towards a Post-critical
Philosophy*, The University of Chicago Press, 1958, p. 380.

5. E. R. Wickham, *Encounter with Modern Society*, The Seabury Press, 1964, p. 77. Used by permission.

6. *Ibid.*, pp. 77 ff.

7. Monica Wilson, "Urban Revolution in South Africa," in Egbert de Vries, ed., *Man in Community: Christian Concern for the Human in Changing Society*, Association Press, 1966, p. 123. Used by permission.

8. Constantinos A. Doxiadis and Truman B. Douglass, *The New World of Urban Man*, Philadelphia: United Church Press, 1965, pp. 29–31. Used by permission.

9. *Ibid.*, p. 30.

10. Constantinos A. Doxiadis, "Life in the Cities of Tomorrow." Copyright 1968, Christian Century Foundation. Reprinted by permission from the November 6, 1968 issue of *The Christian Century*.

11. Robert A. Raines, *The Secular Congregation*, Harper & Row, 1968, p. 14.

12. Sung by Bonnie Franklin as "Viola" in the production of *Your Own Thing* at the Orpheum Theatre, New York, a "rock musical" by Hal Hester and Danny Apolinar, with book by Donald Driver.

13. *The New York Times*, Feb. 3, 1969, p. 1.

14. John R. Seeley, "Thirty-nine Articles: Toward a Theory of Social Theory," in Kurt H. Wolff and Barrington Moore, Jr., eds., *The Critical Spirit: Essays in Honor of Herbert Marcuse*, Beacon Press, 1967, p. 159.

15. *Ibid.*, p. 171.

Bibliography

PART I. Viewpoints on the City

Books

Abrams, Charles: *The City Is the Frontier.* New York: Harper & Row, 1965.

Banfield, Edward C., and James Q. Wilson: *City Politics.* New York: Vintage Books, 1963.

Blaustein, Arthur J., and Roger R. Woock, eds.: *Man Against Poverty: World War III.* New York: Vintage Books, 1968.

Bloomberg, Warner, Jr., and Henry J. Schmandt: *Power, Poverty and Urban Policy.* Beverly Hills: Sage Publications, Inc., 1968.

Cayton, Horace R., and St. Clair Drake: *Black Metropolis: A Study of Negro Life in a Northern City.* New York: Harper & Row, 1945.

Chinitz, Benjamin, ed.: *City and Suburb: The Economics of Metropolitan Growth.* Englewood Cliffs, N.J.: Prentice-Hall, 1964.

Fraser, Douglas: *Village Planning in the Primitive World.* New York: George Braziller, 1968.

Green, Constance M.: *American Cities in the Growth of the Nation.* New York: Harper & Row, 1965.

Handlin, Oscar, and John Burchard, eds.: *The Historian and the City.* Cambridge: M.I.T. and Harvard University Press, 1963.

Hardoy, Jorge: *Urban Planning in Pre-Columbian America.* New York: George Braziller, 1968.

Lampl, Paul: *Cities and Planning in the Ancient Near East.* New York: George Braziller, 1968.

Mumford, Lewis: *The City in History*. New York: Harcourt, Brace & World, 1961.
Perloff, Harvey S., and Lowdon Wingo, Jr., eds.: *Issues in Urban Economics*. Baltimore: The Johns Hopkins Press, 1968.
Saalman, Howard: *Medieval Cities*. New York: George Braziller, 1968.
Sjoberg, Gideon: *The Preindustrial City Past and Present*. Glencoe: The Free Press, 1960.
Thompson, Wilbur R.: *A Preface to Urban Economics*. Baltimore: The Johns Hopkins Press, 1965.
Wade, Richard: *The Urban Frontier: The Rise of Western Cities, 1790–1830*. Cambridge: Harvard University Press, 1959.
Weaver, Robert C.: *Dilemmas of Urban America*. Cambridge: Harvard University Press, 1965.
Weber, Max: *The City*. New York: Collier Books, 1962.
Wilson, James Q., ed.: *The Metropolitan Enigma*. Cambridge: Harvard University Press, 1968.
Wogaman, Philip: *Guaranteed Annual Income: The Moral Issues*. New York: Abingdon Press, 1968.

Articles and Journals

Bowen, Don R., and Louis H. Masotti: "Spokesmen for the Poor: An Analysis of Cleveland's Poverty Board Candidates," in *Urban Affairs Quarterly*, Vol. IV, No. 1, September 1968.
Glasgow, Robert W.: "The Urban Crisis," in *Psychology Today*, Vol. 2, No. 3, August 1968.
Commentary, Vol. 47, No. 1, January 1968; special issue on "Conflict in the Cities."
Psychology Today, Vol. II, No. 3, August 1968; special issue on the city.
Report of National Advisory Commission on Civil Disorders. New York: Bantam Books, 1968.
Scientific American. "Cities." New York: Alfred A. Knopf, September 1965; special issue on the cities.

PART II. Viewpoints on the Church in the City

Books

Abell, Aaron I.: *The Urban Impact on American Protestantism, 1865–1900*. Cambridge: Harvard University Press, 1943.
Baltzell, E. Digby: *The Protestant Establishment*. New York: Random House, 1966.

Burr, Nelson R.: *A Critical Bibliography of Religion in America.* ("Religion in American Life," IV). Princeton, N.J.: Princeton University Press, 1961.

Callahan, Daniel, ed.: *The Secular City Debate.* New York: The Macmillan Co., 1966.

Cross, Robert D., ed.: *The Church and the City, 1865–1910.* Indianapolis and New York: The Bobbs-Merrill Co., Inc., 1967.

Doxiadis, Constantinos A., and Truman B. Douglass: *The New World of Urban Man.* Philadelphia: United Church Press, 1965.

Douglass, H. Paul: *1000 City Churches: Phases of Adaption to Urban Environment.* New York: George H. Doran Co., 1926.

Fauset, Arthur H.: *Black Gods of the Metropolis: Negro Cults of the Urban North.* Philadelphia: University of Pennsylvania Press, 1944.

Fichter, Joseph H., S.J.: *Social Relations in the Urban Parish.* Chicago: The University of Chicago Press, 1954.

Fry, John R., ed.: *The Church and Community Organization.* New York: National Council of Churches, Division of *Christian Life and Mission,* 1965.

Frazier, E. Franklin: *The Negro Church in America.* New York: Schocken Books, 1964; paperback edition, 1966.

Greenwood, Elma: *How Churches Fight Poverty.* New York: Friendship Press, 1967.

Hough, Joseph C., Jr.: *Black Power and White Protestants.* New York: Oxford University Press, 1968.

Jamison, Leland: "Religions on the Christian Perimeter," in James W. Smith and A. Leland, eds.: *The Shaping of American Religion* ("Religion in American Life," I). Princeton, N.J.: Princeton University Press, 1961, pp. 162–231.

Lee, Robert, ed.: *The Church and the Exploding Metropolis.* Richmond, Va.: John Knox Press, 1965.

McNeil, Jesse Jai: *Mission in Metropolis.* Grand Rapids: Wm. B. Erdmans, 1965.

May, Henry F.: *Protestant Churches and Industrial America.* New York: Harper & Brothers, 1949.

Metz, Donald L.: *New Congregations, Security and Mission in Conflict.* Philadelphia: The Westminster Press, 1967.

Moore, Paul, Jr.: *The Church Reclaims the City.* New York: Seabury Press, 1964.

Rose, Stephen C.: *Who's Killing the Church?* Chicago: Renewal Magazine and Association Press, 1966.

Schaller, Lyle E.: *The Churches' War on Poverty.* New York: Abingdon Press, 1967.

————: *Community Organization: Conflict and Reconciliation.* New York: Abingdon Press, 1966.

Walmsley, Arthur E.: *The Church in a Society of Abundance.* New York: Seabury Press, 1963.

Washington, Joseph R.: *Black Religion: The Negro and Christianity in the United States.* Boston: Beacon Press, 1964.

Webber, George W.: "The Clergy, the Laity, and the Issues of Poverty," in Warner Bloomberg and Henry J. Schmandt, eds.: *Power, Poverty and Urban Policy.* Beverly Hills: Sage Publications, 1968, pp. 223–48.

Weisenberger, Francis P.: *Ordeal of Faith: The Crisis of Churchgoing America, 1865–1900.* New York: Philosophical Library, 1959.

Wright, Nathan, Jr.: *Black Power and Urban Unrest.* New York: Hawthorn Books, Inc., 1967.

Woodson, Carter G.: *The History of the Negro Church.* Washington, D.C.: Associated Publishers, 1921.

PART III. Actualities and Prospects

Books

Baum, Gregory: *The Credibility of the Church.* New York: Herder and Herder, 1968.

Boyd, Malcolm: *The Underground Church.* New York: Sheed and Ward, 1968.

Broholm, Richard: *Strategic Planning for Church Organizations.* Valley Forge, Pa.: The Judson Press, 1969.

Cleage, Albert B., Jr.: *The Black Messiah.* New York: Sheed and Ward, 1968.

Cleaver, Eldridge: *Soul on Ice.* New York: Dell Publishing Co., 1968.

Crowell, George: *Society Against Itself.* Philadelphia: Westminster Press, 1968.

Goodman, Grace A.: *Rocking the Ark: Nine Case Studies of Churches in Process of Change.* New York: Board of National Missions, United Presbyterian Church, 1968.

Haddon, Jeffrey: *The Gathering Storm in the Churches.* Garden City: Doubleday & Co., 1969.

Hefner, Philip J., ed.: *The Future of the American Church.* Philadelphia: Fortress Press, 1968.

Littel, Franklin H.: *The Church and the Body Politic.* New York: Seabury Press, 1968.

Lynch, William F., S.J.: *Images of Hope*. New York: New American Library, 1965.

Mano, D. Keith: *Horn*. Boston: Houghton Mifflin Co., 1969. A provocative novel on the conflict of black power and the white activist clergy.

Marty, Martin: *The Search for a Usable Future*. New York: Harper & Row, 1969.

Moran, Gabriel: *Vision and Tactics*. New York: Herder and Herder, 1968.

Neve, Herbert T.: *Sources of Change*. Geneva: World Council of Churches, 1968.

Norton, Perry: *Church and Metropolis*. New York: Seabury Press, 1964.

Raines, Robert A.: *The Secular Congregation*. New York: Harper & Row, 1968.

Ruoss, Meryl: *Citizen Power and Social Change: Challenge to Churches*. New York: Seabury Press, 1968.

Schaller, Lyle E.: *The Local Church Looks to the Future*. Nashville: Abingdon Press, 1968.

Sleeper, C. Freeman: *Black Power and Christian Responsibility*. Nashville: Abingdon Press, 1969.

Tibbetts, Orlando: *The Reconciling Community*. Philadelphia: Judson Press, 1969.

Tucker, Sterling: *Black Reflections on White Power*. Grand Rapids: Wm. B. Erdmans, 1969.

Van de Pol, William H.: *The End of Conventional Christianity*. New York: Newman, 1968.

Washington, Joseph R.: *The Politics of God*. Boston: Beacon Press, 1967.

Articles and Journals

Cross Currents, Vol. XVIII, No. 4, Fall 1968; special issue on "Perspectives on Development and Social Change in America."

Daedalus, "The Conscience of the City," Journal of American Academy of Arts and Sciences, Fall 1968; a 342-page special issue.

Hefner, Philip: "Theological Perspectives on Social Ministry," in *Context*, Vol. I, No. 2, Winter 1968, pp. 1–14.

Norton, Perry: "Patterns for Action: The Planning Process" (*The Joint Urban Program Report Series*, No. 2). New York: Executive Council of the Episcopal Church, no date.

Rehfuss, John A.: "Metropolitan Government: Four Views," in *Urban Affairs Quarterly*, Vol. III, No. 4, June 1968. pp. 91–111.

RISK, "The Negro Church in the U.S.A." Vol. IV, No. 1, 1968; special issue.

Ward, Barbara: "Action for the Future," in *The Ecumenical Review*, Vol. XX, No. 3, July 1968, pp. 255–62.

Wright, Nathan: "Black Power: Crisis or Challenge for the Churches," in *Context*, Vol. I, No. 3, Spring 1968, pp. 3–13.

Index

WILL THE CHURCH LOSE THE CITY?

Edited by
KENDIG BRUBAKER CULLY
and F. NILE HARPER

☐ "City man lives in a world of *deeds,* whereas the church man traditionally has lived in a world of *words.*"

☐ ". . . the clergy are not equipped personally and professionally for faithful and effective ministry in the contemporary world."

☐ "In the modern city, the church has been the last bastion to be overcome in the campaign to eliminate segregation. . . ."

Harsh though these words may seem, they are the considered opinions of three of the seventeen contributors to this volume . . . specialists who believe that the survival of the church in the city is dependent upon an honest and realistic appraisal of its present condition and an imaginative, dynamic revision of its role.

Structured in three units, the book looks first at the history, sociology, economy, psychology, aesthetics, and cohesiveness of the city itself. Part Two considers the urban church and how it can function in humanizing life, transferring emphasis from preaching to "doing" theology, and from doing *for* the poor to involving people in

(continued on back flap)